Alfresco CMIS

Everything you need to know to start coding
integrations with a content management server
such as Alfresco in a standard way

Martin Bergljung

[PACKT] open source *
PUBLISHING   community experience distilled

BIRMINGHAM - MUMBAI

Alfresco CMIS

Copyright © 2014 Packt Publishing

First published: March 2014

Production Reference: 1180314

Published by Packt Publishing Ltd.
Livery Place
35 Livery Street
Birmingham B3 2PB, UK.

ISBN 978-1-78216-352-7

www.packtpub.com

Cover Image by Veronika Bergljung (vbergljung@yahoo.com)

Credits

Author
Martin Bergljung

Reviewers
Robin Bramley (Ixxus)
Karol Bryd
Nicolas Raoul
Barb Mosher Zinck

Acquisition Editors
Subho Gupta

Content Development Editor
Priyanka S

Technical Editors
Pankaj Kadam
Adrian Raposo

Copy Editors
Tanvi Gaitonde
Dipti Kapadia
Kirti Pai

Project Coordinator
Akash Poojary

Proofreaders
Simran Bhogal
Maria Gould

Indexers
Mehreen Deshmukh
Tejal Soni

Graphics
Ronak Dhruv
Abhinash Sahu

Production Coordinator
Nilesh Bambardekar

Cover Work
Nilesh Bambardekar

About the Author

Martin Bergljung is a Principal ECM Architect at Ixxus, a UK Platinum Alfresco partner. He has over 25 years of experience in the IT sector, where he has worked with the Java platform since 1997.

Martin began working with Alfresco in 2007, developing an e-mail management extension for Alfresco called OpsMailmanager. In 2009, he started working on Alfresco consulting projects and has worked with customers such as Pearson, World Wildlife Fund, International Financial Data Services, NHS, VHI Healthcare, Virgin Money, Unibet, BPN Paribas, University of Westminster, Aker Oilfield Services, and Amnesty International.

He is a frequent speaker and has delivered talks at Alfresco conferences in London, Berlin, and Barcelona. He is also the author of *Alfresco 3 Business Solutions*, *Packt Publishing*.

I would like to thank Sumeet Sawant, Priyanka Shah, and Subho Gupta at Packt Publishing for suggesting the project and getting it on track.

My thanks also goes to Sherin Padayatty and Michelle Quadros, my Project Coordinators, who were always pushing me to deliver the next chapter. Thanks to the entire Packt Publishing team for working so diligently to help bring out a high-quality product.

Thanks to all the book reviewers who gave me invaluable feedback during the whole project. Specifically, I would like to thank Robin Bramely, my colleague at Ixxus, who gave me invaluable feedback, tips, and ideas throughout the book writing process, thanks!

I must also thank the talented team of developers who created the Alfresco open source product. It opens up a new way for everyone that wants to build any kind of ECM business solution.

And finally, I would like to thank Paul Samuel and Justin Haynes at Ixxus for supporting my book project.

About the Reviewers

Robin Bramley is an experienced Alfresco practitioner, having taken Version 0.6 to bits in 2005 and been using, extending, implementing, integrating, and scaling it ever since. He was the Technical Manager at the first UK Alfresco Gold partner where he built the original IMAP interface to Alfresco and is now the Chief Scientific Officer and Chief Architect at Ixxus, a global Alfresco Platinum partner.

Robin has architected many distributed systems over the past 15 years, ranging from Swaps Trading Platform to Insurance Contract Management and a global Alfresco-based DAM system. Robin has presented at various international conferences and meetups in London; he also writes for *GroovyMag*, including an article on CMIS integration with Alfresco that NASA wanted the source code for.

> I'd like to thank my wife for her patience while I've been glued to my laptop in the evenings!

Karol Bryd has been working with ECM technologies since 2005, first with Documentum and then with Alfresco since 2008. He has worked on numerous ECM-related projects mainly in the Pharmaceuticals sector, performing all manner of roles from Developer to Technical Consultant to Development Manager.

He was a technical architect at Generis (http://www.generiscorp.com) for CARA, one of the first products to fully utilize Alfresco and CMIS technologies, and subsequently, supported its deployment at major corporations. He is also the author of the Alfresco extension Stamper (http://stamper.metasys.pl) for securing and watermarking PDF content in Alfresco.

Currently, he holds the position of Documentum Expert at F. Hoffmann-La Roche, where he is working on Documentum projects that help manage large amounts of business-critical electronic documentation.

Nicolas Raoul is an ECM consultant at Aegif in Tokyo. After obtaining a Master's degree from the French Ecole Nationale d'Ingenieurs, he worked in 13 countries, successfully designing distributed architectures for the French National Library or the Schengen Information System.

Back when CMIS was still in its draft stage, he created CmisSync, a CMIS synchronization client that allows Alfresco users to work faster even when they are offline. Enjoying a strong open source community, CmisSync helps organizations combine the user friendliness and mobility of cloud storage with the security and customizability of their CMIS server, be it on-premise or in private/public clouds.

As an ECM architect, he helped Alfresco design their certification program in 2009. He has been writing open source software since the age of 16. In his free time, he created AnkiDroid, a flashcards app with a million users, and other popular programs.

Barb Mosher Zinck is a freelance writer and VP, Editorial for CMSWire (SimplerMedia Group Inc). She has over 10 years of experience as an IT solutions architect, focused on designing and supporting web-based applications.

www.PacktPub.com

Support files, eBooks, discount offers and more

You might want to visit www.PacktPub.com for support files and downloads related to your book.

Did you know that Packt offers eBook versions of every book published, with PDF and ePub files available? You can upgrade to the eBook version at www.PacktPub.com and as a print book customer, you are entitled to a discount on the eBook copy. Get in touch with us at service@packtpub.com for more details.

At www.PacktPub.com, you can also read a collection of free technical articles, sign up for a range of free newsletters and receive exclusive discounts and offers on Packt books and eBooks.

http://PacktLib.PacktPub.com

Do you need instant solutions to your IT questions? PacktLib is Packt's online digital book library. Here, you can access, read and search across Packt's entire library of books.

Why Subscribe?
- Fully searchable across every book published by Packt
- Copy and paste, print and bookmark content
- On demand and accessible via web browser

Free Access for Packt account holders

If you have an account with Packt at www.PacktPub.com, you can use this to access PacktLib today and view nine entirely free books. Simply use your login credentials for immediate access.

*This book is dedicated to my sons Bruce, Thor, and Francisco
and to my wife Veronika.*

Table of Contents

Preface   **1**

Chapter 1: Getting Started with CMIS   **7**

Understanding CMIS   **7**

Commercial products and companies supporting CMIS   **10**

The benefits of using CMIS   **11**

CMIS use cases   **12**

Repository to Repository (R2R)   12

Application to Repository (A2R)   12

Application to Multiple Repositories (A2MR)   13

An overview of the CMIS standard   **13**

The domain model (object model)   14

Services   17

Query language   18

Protocol bindings   20

RESTful AtomPub binding   20

Web Service binding   21

RESTful Browser binding (CMIS 1.1)   21

Summary   **22**

Chapter 2: Basic CMIS Operations   **23**

Setting up a CMIS server   **24**

Installing your own CMIS server   24

Using cmis.alfresco.com   24

Setting up a tool to make HTTP requests   **25**

Authenticating with the repository   **25**

Getting repository information   **26**

Repository information via the AtomPub binding   30

Repository information via the Browser binding   31

Listing the children of the root folder   **32**
Listing the children of the root folder with the AtomPub binding   36
Listing the children of the root folder with the Browser binding   39
Optional parameters when listing the children of a folder   **42**
Optional parameters when listing the children of a folder with the AtomPub binding   43
Optional parameters when listing the children of a folder with the Browser binding   45
Listing available types and subtypes   **47**
Listing the types and subtypes with the AtomPub binding   47
Listing the types and subtypes with the Browser binding   49
Getting metadata and content   **50**
Getting metadata and content with the AtomPub binding   50
Getting metadata and content with the Browser binding   53
Creating, updating, and deleting content   **57**
Creating folders   59
Creating a folder with the AtomPub binding   59
Creating a folder with the Browser binding   61
Creating documents   62
Creating a document with the AtomPub binding   63
Creating a document with the Browser binding   65
Updating folders and documents   66
Updating a document with the AtomPub binding   67
Updating a document with the Browser binding   67
Deleting a folder or a document   68
Deleting a folder or document with the AtomPub binding   68
Deleting a folder or document with the Browser binding   69
Summary   **70**
Chapter 3: Advanced CMIS Operations   **71**
Version management with check out and check in   **71**
Version management with the AtomPub binding   73
Checking out a document with the AtomPub binding   74
Cancelling the check out with the AtomPub binding   75
Updating the physical contents of the checked-out document with the AtomPub binding   75
Checking in a document with the AtomPub binding   76
Version management with the Browser binding   77
Checking out a document with the Browser binding   77
Cancelling the check out with the Browser binding   78
Updating the physical content of the checked-out document with the Browser binding   78
Checking in a document with the Browser binding   79

Managing permissions for documents and folders   80
  Access control list capabilities   80
  Access control concepts   81
  Supported permissions   82
  Allowable actions and permission mapping   83
  Managing permissions with the AtomPub binding   84
  Managing permissions with the Browser binding   87
Managing relationships between objects   90
  Creating and reading relationships with the AtomPub binding   90
  Creating and reading relationships with the Browser binding   92
Searching   93
  Searching with the AtomPub binding   95
  Searching with the Browser binding   96
  CMIS query examples   98
A word on transactions   99
Summary   100

Chapter 4: Alfresco and CMIS   101
Timeline   101
Architecture/stack   103
Alfresco content model mapping to the CMIS object model   105
  Repository capabilities   105
  Type mappings   106
  Property mappings   107
  Object paths explanation   108
  Versioning   112
  Access control   113
  Change log   115
  Renditions   116
  Search   118
Support for Alfresco-specific features   119
  Aspects   119
  Tags   123
  Categories   124
Summary   124

Chapter 5: Accessing a CMIS Server with a Java Client   127
Setting up a build environment   128
Connecting and setting up a session with the repository   129
  Connecting to a repository by ID   134
Getting repository information   134
Listing the children of the root/top folder   136

Optional parameters when listing the children of a folder	**138**
Listing available types and subtypes	**141**
Creating, updating, and deleting content	**144**
Creating folders	144
Creating documents	147
Updating folders and documents	153
Deleting a document, folder, or folder tree	156
Getting the content for a document	**160**
Copying and moving folders and documents	**162**
Working with Alfresco aspects	**165**
Using secondary types to manage aspects	166
Adding aspects when creating an object	166
Adding aspects to an existing object	167
Reading aspects	168
The Alfresco OpenCMIS extension to manage aspects	169
Adding aspects when creating an object	169
Adding aspects to an existing object	170
Reading aspects	171
Version management with check out and check in	**172**
Checking out a document	173
Updating the content of the checked-out document and then checking it in	174
Managing permissions for documents and folders	**175**
Managing relationships between objects	**178**
Searching	**181**
Summary	**182**
Chapter 6: Accessing a CMIS Server Using Scripting Languages	**183**
Using CMIS in JavaScript and web application pages	**184**
Solving the same origin policy problem	187
Using jQuery	190
Using CMIS in Groovy scripts	**196**
Using CMIS in Spring Surf Web Scripts	**200**
Setting up a build project for Spring Surf with CMIS	201
Updating the Spring Surf project so that CMIS can be used	203
Updating the home page to display repository info via CMIS	206
Updating the home page to display text from a file in the repository	208
Using CMIS calls in Alfresco Share extensions	209
Summary	**210**

Chapter 7: System Integration with CMIS	**211**
Integrating Drupal with a CMS server	**211**
The CMIS API module	212
Displaying a CMS repository file link on a Drupal page	216
The CMIS Views module	217
Displaying a CMS repository folder on a Drupal page	218
Displaying a result from a CMIS query on a Drupal page	220
Synchronizing the CMS content with Drupal content	221
Enterprise integration with CMIS	**224**
Moving a file from a folder into a CMS server using Mule	224
Getting a document from a CMS server via Mule	228
Talking to Alfresco in the Cloud via CMIS	**232**
Setting up an account	232
Registering a client application	232
Setting up a development project	235
Authorizing the client application	237
Making CMIS calls	240
Summary	**241**
Index	**243**

Preface

Content Management Servers (CMS), both proprietary and open source, have been around for a very long time, but there has not been a standard way of talking to them until recently. The Content Management Interoperability Services (CMIS) standard provides both an application programming interface and a search language (based on SQL-92). Today, most of the CMS systems out there support the CMIS standard.

Alfresco CMIS is a practical, hands-on guide that provides you with a number of clear step-by-step exercises, which will help you take advantage of the real power of CMIS and give you a good foundation in using it via HTTP/XML, Java, or scripting.

This practical companion will get you up to speed on CMIS in no time.

What this book covers

Chapter 1, Getting Started with CMIS, starts off with an introduction to the CMIS standard to quickly get you up-to-date on the service API, object model, and query language.

Chapter 2, Basic CMIS Operations, shows you how to add, update, delete, and search for content using HTTP and XML/JSON.

Chapter 3, Advanced CMIS Operations, teaches you how to version content, set permissions for content, and create relationships between content items using HTTP and XML/JSON.

Chapter 4, Alfresco and CMIS, covers specifics around the Alfresco content management server's implementation of CMIS, such as how to handle aspects, tags, and categories.

Chapter 5, Accessing a CMIS Server with a Java Client, introduces the Apache Chemistry project and the OpenCMIS Java library, which is an abstraction on top of the standard HTTP and XML/JSON protocol bindings.

Chapter 6, Accessing a CMIS Server Using Scripting Languages, shows how scripting languages such as JavaScript and Groovy can be used to talk to content management servers via the CMIS standard.

Chapter 7, System Integration with CMIS, looks at how CMIS can be used for enterprise application integration. With specific examples of how to integrate Drupal with content management servers, connect **Enterprise Service Bus** (**ESB**) with one or more content management servers, and talk to the Alfresco Cloud service.

What you need for this book

For all the chapters except the first one, you will need access to a content management server that supports CMIS, such as Alfresco. In case of Alfresco, you can use an online service available at `http://cmis.alfresco.com` or install the Alfresco community version from `http://downloads.alfresco.com` (it is recommended to have your own local server, so you have control of the content and availability).

For *Chapter 2*, Basic CMIS Operations, and *Chapter 3, Advanced CMIS Operations*, it's good to install a tool such as **curl** that can be used to make HTTP calls. *Chapter 5, Accessing a CMIS Server with a Java Client*, will require JDK and Maven installed. *Chapter 6, Accessing a CMIS Server from Scripting Languages*, requires the installation of jQuery and Groovy.

Who this book is for

This book is great for developers who want to learn how to build applications that talk to content management servers in a standard way using CMIS. It will be helpful to have a bit of programming experience, but it is not necessary for the first two chapters. The OpenCMIS chapter and Alfresco Cloud section will assume some basic knowledge of Java.

Conventions

In this book, you will find a number of styles of text that distinguish between different kinds of information. Here are some examples of these styles, and an explanation of their meaning.

Code words in text, database table names, folder names, filenames, file extensions, pathnames, dummy URLs, user input, and Twitter handles are shown as follows: "If we take Documentum as an example, its generic content type is named `dm_document` and not `cm:content`."

A block of code is set as follows:

```
<app:collection href=
    "http://localhost:8080/alfresco/cmisatom/f0ebcfb4-ca9f-4991-
    bda8-9465f4f11527/types">
    <cmisra:collectionType>types</cmisra:collectionType>
    <atom:title type="text">Types Collection</atom:title>
    <app:accept></app:accept>
</app:collection>
```

When we wish to draw your attention to a particular part of a code block, the relevant lines or items are set in bold:

```
</cmisra:template>
<cmisra:type>objectbypath</cmisra:type>
<cmisra:mediatype>application/atom+xml;type=entry
</cmisra:mediatype>
</cmisra:uritemplate>
```

Any command-line input or output is written as follows:

```
$ curl
"http://localhost:8080/alfresco/service/api/login?u=admin&pw=admin"

<?xml version="1.0" encoding="UTF-8"?>

<ticket>TICKET_39ea5e46e83a6d6e43845182f4254f9de50402fb</ticket>
```

New terms and **important words** are shown in bold. Words that you see on the screen, in menus or dialog boxes for example, appear in the text like this: "clicking the **Next** button moves you to the next screen."

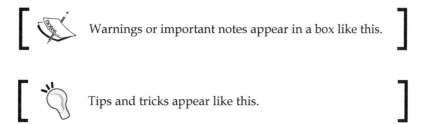

Warnings or important notes appear in a box like this.

Tips and tricks appear like this.

Reader feedback

Feedback from our readers is always welcome. Let us know what you think about this book—what you liked or may have disliked. Reader feedback is important for us to develop titles that you really get the most out of.

To send us general feedback, simply send an e-mail to feedback@packtpub.com, and mention the book title via the subject of your message.

If there is a topic that you have expertise in and you are interested in either writing or contributing to a book, see our author guide on www.packtpub.com/authors.

Customer support

Now that you are the proud owner of a Packt book, we have a number of things to help you to get the most from your purchase.

Downloading the example code

You can download the example code files for all Packt books you have purchased from your account at http://www.packtpub.com. If you purchased this book elsewhere, you can visit http://www.packtpub.com/support and register to have the files e-mailed directly to you.

Errata

Although we have taken every care to ensure the accuracy of our content, mistakes do happen. If you find a mistake in one of our books—maybe a mistake in the text or the code—we would be grateful if you would report this to us. By doing so, you can save other readers from frustration and help us improve subsequent versions of this book. If you find any errata, please report them by visiting http://www.packtpub.com/submit-errata, selecting your book, clicking on the **errata submission form** link, and entering the details of your errata. Once your errata are verified, your submission will be accepted and the errata will be uploaded on our website, or added to any list of existing errata, under the Errata section of that title. Any existing errata can be viewed by selecting your title from http://www.packtpub.com/support.

Piracy

Piracy of copyright material on the Internet is an ongoing problem across all media. At Packt, we take the protection of our copyright and licenses very seriously. If you come across any illegal copies of our works, in any form, on the Internet, please provide us with the location address or website name immediately so that we can pursue a remedy.

Please contact us at `copyright@packtpub.com` with a link to the suspected pirated material.

We appreciate your help in protecting our authors, and our ability to bring you valuable content.

Questions

You can contact us at `questions@packtpub.com` if you are having a problem with any aspect of the book, and we will do our best to address it.

1
Getting Started with CMIS

Content Management Interoperability Services (**CMIS**) is a new interface to talk to **Content Management Systems** (**CMS**) in a standard way. This chapter will introduce you to the CMIS standard, explain why it is important, and see how it came about. We will cover the different parts of the CMIS standard, the benefits of using it, and some example use cases for CMIS.

Understanding CMIS

CMIS is an effort toward standardization and is managed by the **Organization for the Advancement of Structured Information Standards** (**OASIS**) body. The latest version is 1.1 (`http://docs.oasis-open.org/cmis/CMIS/v1.1/CMIS-v1.1.html`), which was approved in May 2013. Version 1.0 specifies most of the functionalities and is quite developed being approved in May 2010. Some content servers might not yet support Version 1.1, so we will point out when a feature is only available in Version 1.1. CMIS is all about being able to access and manage content in a so-called content repository in a standard way. You can think of a content repository as something that can be used to store files in a folder hierarchy.

The CMIS interface consists of two parts: a number of repository services for things such as content navigation and content creation, and a repository query language for content search. The standard also defines what protocols can be used to communicate with a repository and what formats should be used in requests and responses via these protocols.

To really explain what CMIS is, and the background to why it came about, one has to look at how the implementation of content management systems has evolved. If we go back 15-20 years, most companies (that are large corporations) had one content management system installed for **Document Management** (**DM**) and workflow. This meant that all the content was available in one system via a single **Application Programming Interface** (**API**), making it easy for other enterprise systems to integrate with it and access content. For example, the Swedish nuclear power plant that I worked for in the mid 90s had one big installation of Documentum that everyone used.

In the last 5-10 years, there has been an explosion in the number of content management systems used by companies; most companies now have multiple content management systems in use, sometimes running into double digits.

So you are thinking that this cannot be true; companies having five content management systems? This is true alright. According to the **Association for Information and Image Management** (**AIIM**), which is the main **Enterprise Content Management** (**ECM**) industry organization, 72 percent of large organizations have three or more ECM, Document Management, or Record Management systems, while 25 percent have five or more (as mentioned in *State of the ECM Industry*, AIIM, 2011).

This is because these days we not only manage documents, but we also manage records (known as Record Management), images and media files (known as Digital Asset Management), advanced workflows, web content (known as Web Content Management), and many other types of content. It is quite often that one content management system is better than the other in handling one type of content such as records or web content, so a company ends up buying multiple content management systems to manage different types of content.

A new type of content management system has also emerged, which is open source and easily accessible for everyone to try out. Each one of these systems have different APIs and can be implemented in a different language and on a different type of platform. All this means that a lot of companies have ended up with many content silos/islands that are not communicating with each other, sometimes having duplicated content.

What this means is that when it comes to implementing the following kind of services, we might have a problem choosing what API to work with:

- Enterprise service that should aggregate content from several of these systems
- Content transfer from one system to another
- UI client that should display content from more than one of these systems

It would then be necessary to learn about a whole lot of APIs and platforms. Most of the proprietary APIs were also not based on HTTP, so if you wanted a service or client to be outside the firewall, you would have to open up new ports in the firewall to take care of security and so on.

Any company that wants to develop tools or clients to access content management systems would also have to support many different protocols and formats, making it difficult to work with more than a handful of the seasoned CMS players. This leads to people thinking about some sort of standard interface and protocol to access CMS systems.

The first established standard covering the content management area is **Web Distributed Authoring and Versioning (WebDAV)**, which was proposed in February 1999 with RFC 2518 (refer to `ftp://ftp.isi.edu/in-notes/rfc2518.txt`). It is supported by most content management systems, including Alfresco, and is usually used to map a drive to access the content management system via, for example, Windows Explorer or Mac Finder. The problem with this way of accessing content is that most of the valuable features of a content management system cannot be used, such as setting custom metadata, managing versions, setting fine grained permissions, controlling relationships, and searching for content.

So this led to more comprehensive standards such as the **Java Content Repository (JCR)** API, which is managed by the **Java Community Process** as JSR-170 (`https://www.jcp.org/en/jsr/detail?id=170`) and JSR-283 (`https://www.jcp.org/en/jsr/detail?id=283`) and was first developed in 2002. The JCR standard has been supported by Alfresco for a long time, but it has never really taken off as it is Java centric and excludes content management systems such as SharePoint and Drupal.

Something needed to be done to come up with a new standard that would be easy to learn and adopt. This is where CMIS comes into the picture. CMIS provides a standard API and query language that can be used to talk to any CMS system that implements the CMIS standard. The following figure illustrates how a client application that adheres to the CMIS standard can talk to many different content management systems through one standard service-oriented interface:

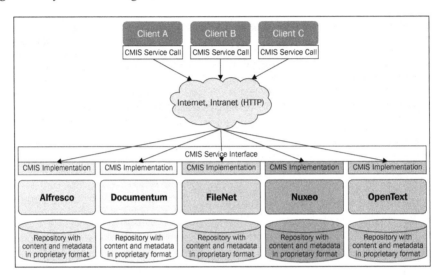

The preceding figure shows how each one of the content management systems offers access to their proprietary content and metadata via the standard CMIS service interface. The CMIS interface is web-based, which means that it can be accessed via HTTP through the Internet. Even cloud-based content management systems such as the Alfresco Cloud installation can be accessed via CMIS.

Commercial products and companies supporting CMIS

There are quite a few companies that support the CMIS standard. The participants in the standards process include Adobe Systems Incorporated, Alfresco, EMC, eXo, FatWire, HP, IBM, ISIS Papyrus, Liferay, Microsoft, Nuxeo, OpenText, Oracle, Newgen, OmniDocs, and SAP.

To get an idea of how widespread the CMIS standard is, we can have a look at the following products, clients, and libraries that support it:

- **CMS servers**: Alfresco, Documentum, HP Interwoven, IBM Content Manager and FileNet, Lotus Quickr, Microsoft SharePoint, OpenText, and SAP

- **WCM systems**: Magnolia, Liferay, Drupal, Hippo, TYPE3, and dotCMS

- **Blogging**: Wordpress

- **Clients**: Libre Office, Adobe Drive, Atlassian Confluence, SAP ECM Integration, Pentaho Data Integration, SugarCRM, Trac, Kofax, and Salesforce Files

- **SOA**: Mule ESB and Spring Integration

- **Libraries**: Apache Chemistry (which includes Java, Python, PHP, .NET, and Objective-C)

So we can see there is no doubt that the CMIS standard has been very well received and adopted.

The benefits of using CMIS

The benefits of using CMIS might be quite clear to you now, but let's walk through some of them:

- **Language neutral**: Any language can be used to access a CMS system that implements the CMIS service interface, as long as the language has the functionality for making HTTP requests and can handle XML or JSON. So you could have a C++ application accessing a content management system written in PHP.

- **Platform independence**: It doesn't matter what platform the CMS system is implemented on top of. As long as it supports the CMIS standard any client application can talk to it if it has the capability to make HTTP calls and parse XML or JSON.

- **Standard service API**: Clients need to use only one API to access content management systems and they have a much better chance of not being limited to only one vendor's API and platform. This is probably a great benefit as it means that you can work with any CMS system after you learn to work with the first one, thus saving time and money. It will also be easier to find people who can work on new CMS projects.

- **Standard and easy-to-learn query language**: The CMIS query language is easy to learn and adopt as it is based on the ANSI SQL-92 standard. So you can use SQL syntax such as `SELECT * FROM cmis:document WHERE cmis:name LIKE '*alfresco*';`.

- **One application to access them all**: End users can now use one application and user interface to access all content management systems, and do not have to learn about a new user interface for each and every CMS system that the organization has deployed.

- **Easy workflow integration**: It is now much easier for a company to deploy an enterprise workflow that interacts with content managed by multiple content management systems.

- **Repository vendors get more applications**: CMS vendors are more likely to get many more client applications using their server as any application that uses the CMIS API can access any CMIS repository.

- **Applications get a bigger customer base**: Applications that are written to support the CMIS interface are more likely to get a bigger customer base as they will work with a multitude of CMIS-compliant content management systems.

CMIS use cases

There are a number of content management use cases that can benefit from using CMIS. A couple of them are explored as follows:

Repository to Repository (R2R)

R2R is the use case when content management systems talk directly to each other. The following figure illustrates a typical scenario when content in the enterprise content management system such as Alfresco should be displayed on a website via a web content management system such as Drupal:

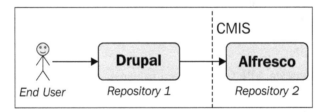

Application to Repository (A2R)

A2R is probably the most common use case. You have an application such as a collaboration application, records management application, enterprise CRM system, business process application, web application, portal, design tool, or Office package that wants to work with content in your CMS system. This is now easy with the CMIS interface. The following figure shows a mobile web application, getting its content from an Alfresco repository via CMIS:

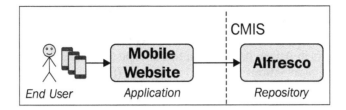

Application to Multiple Repositories (A2MR)

A2MR is quite a common use case and handles the case when you want to aggregate content from multiple repositories in an application such as a user interface, or for example a broker application. The following figure illustrates a typical scenario that represents this use case when you have an **Enterprise Service Bus** (**ESB**), fetching content from multiple repositories, processing it, and then serving it to an enterprise application:

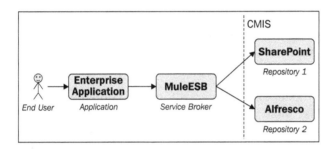

Another common scenario applicable to this use case is federated search, which is something that is really useful for end users. Instead of going into multiple applications to search for content in a disparate content management system, they can now just go into one search application that is hooked up to all the CMS systems.

An overview of the CMIS standard

This section will dig deeper into the CMIS standard and explore its domain model and the different services that it provides. It will also present the different protocol bindings that we can work with.

The domain model (object model)

All CMS vendors have their own definitions of a content model, also called an object model. For example, in Alfresco, there is a folder type (cm:folder), a generic content type (cm:content), associations described as aspects (for example, cm:contains, rn:rendition, and cm:references), and so on. These are available out of the box and are used when you create folders and upload files into the repository. In Alfresco, these types and aspects have properties and they can inherit definitions from other types and aspects. Each property has a datatype and other behavior attributes such as multi-valued and required. When you work with Alfresco in a specific domain, such as legal, it is possible to create domain-specific subtypes that extend the generic types. For example, you could create a legal case type that extends the generic folder type.

Now, as you can imagine, other vendors would not necessarily have the same definitions for their content model. If we take Documentum as an example, its generic content type is named dm_document and not cm:content. Some content management systems also do not have the concept of an aspect.

So what the CMIS Standardization group had to do was come up with an object model that was generic enough for most CMS vendors to be able to implement it. And it had to be specific enough for the implementations to be meaningful and usable. So, the group came up with something called the CMIS domain model.

The CMIS domain model defines a repository as a container and an entry point to all the content items, called objects from now on. All objects are classified by an object type, which describes a common set of properties (such as type ID, parent, and display name). There are five base types of objects: **Document**, **Folder**, **Relationship**, **Policy**, and **Item** (CMIS 1.1), and they all inherit from the **Object** type as shown in the following figure:

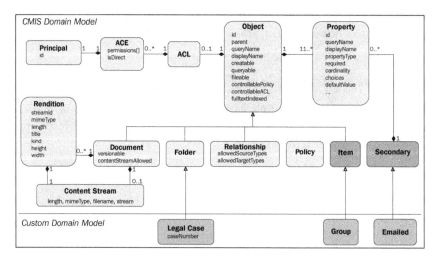

Besides these base object types, there are a number of property types that can be used when defining new properties for an object type. They are, as can be seen in the preceding figure, **String, Boolean, Decimal, Integer**, and **DateTime**. Besides these property types, there are also the URI, ID, and HTML property types, which are not shown in the preceding figure.

Let's take a closer look at each one of the following base types:

- **Document**: This base type is almost always the same as a file, although it doesn't need to have any content (when you upload a file via, for example, the AtomPub binding—explained in the *RESTful AtomPub binding* section— the metadata is created with the first request and the content for the file is posted with the second request). The base document type is automatically assigned to any file, such as an MS Office document or an image, when it is uploaded to the repository.

- **Folder**: This is self-explanatory; it is a container for fileable objects such as folders and documents. As soon as a folder or document is filed in a folder, an implicit parent-child relationship is automatically created, which is different from the relationship base object type that has to be created manually. Whether an object is fileable or not is specified in the object type definition with the `fileable` property.

- **Relationship**: This object defines a relationship between two objects (the target and source). An object can have multiple relationships with other objects. The support for relationship objects is optional.

- **Policy**: This is a way of defining administrative policies to manage objects. An object to which a policy may be applied is called a controllable object (the `controllablePolicy` property has to be set to `true`). For example, you can use a CMIS policy to define which documents are subject to retention policies. A policy is opaque and means nothing to the repository. You would have to implement and enforce the behavior for your policy in a repository-specific way. For example, in Alfresco, you could use rules to enforce the policy. The support for policy objects is optional.

- **Item** (available from CMIS v1.1): This object represents a generic type of a CMIS information asset. This could be, for example, a user or group object. Item objects are not versionable and do not have content streams like documents, but they have properties like all other CMIS objects. The support for item objects is optional.

Additional object types can be defined in a repository as custom **subtypes** of these base types, such as the **Legal Case** type in the preceding figure. CMIS services are provided for the discovery of object types that are defined in a repository. However, object type management services, such as the creation, modification, and deletion of an object type, are not covered by the CMIS standard.

An object has one primary base object type, such as document or folder, which cannot be changed. An object can also have secondary object types applied to it (CMIS 1.1). A secondary type is a named class that may add properties to an object in addition to the properties defined by the object's primary base object type (if you are familiar with Alfresco, you can think of secondary object types to be the same as aspects; for example, emailed, versionable, published, and more).

Every CMIS object has an opaque and immutable object identity (ID), which is assigned by the repository when the object is created. In the case of Alfresco, a so-called node reference is created, which becomes the object ID. An ID uniquely identifies an object within a repository regardless of the type of the object.

All CMIS objects have a set of named, but not explicitly ordered, properties. Within an object, each property is uniquely identified by its property ID. In addition, a document object can have a content stream, which is then used to hold the actual byte content for the file representing, for example, an image or a Word document. A document can also have one or more renditions associated with it. A rendition can be a thumbnail or an alternate representation of the content stream, such as a different size of an image.

Document or folder objects can have one **Access Control List** (**ACL**), which then controls the access to the document or folder. An ACL is made up of a list of ACEs. An **Access Control Entry** (**ACE**) in turn represents one or more permissions being granted to a principal, such as a user, group, role, or something similar.

Now, we may ask the questions such as, what does a document object look like?, what properties does it have?, what namespace is used?, and so on. The following figure shows you how the document object and the other objects are defined with properties:

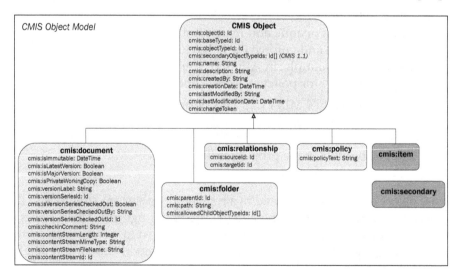

All the objects and properties are defined in the `cmis` namespace. From now on, we'll refer to the different objects and properties by their fully qualified names, for example, `cmis:document` or `cmis:name`.

Services

The CMIS specification also defines the following set of services to access and manage the CMIS objects in the content repository:

- **Repository services**: These services are used to discover information about the repository, including repository IDs (could be more than one repository managed by the endpoint), capabilities (many features are optional and this is the way to find out if they are supported or not), available object types, and descendants. If we are working with a CMIS v1.1-compliant repository, then it could also support creating new types dynamically on the fly. The repository service methods are `getRepositories`, `getRepositoryInfo`, `getTypeChildren`, `getTypeDescendants`, `getTypeDefinition`, `createType` (CMIS 1.1), `updateType` (CMIS 1.1), and `deleteType` (CMIS 1.1).

- **Navigation services**: These services are used to navigate the folder hierarchy in a CMIS repository, and to locate documents that are checked out. The navigation service methods are `getChildren`, `getDescendants`, `getFolderTree`, `getFolderParent`, `getObjectParents`, and `getCheckedOutDocs`.

- **Object services**: These services provide ID-based **CRUD (Create, Read, Update, and Delete)** operations on the objects in a repository. The object service methods are `createDocument`, `createDocumentFromSource`, `createFolder`, `createRelationship`, `createPolicy`, `createItem` (CMIS 1.1), `getAllowableActions`, `getObject`, `getProperties`, `getObjectByPath`, `getContentStream`, `getRenditions`, `updateProperties`, `bulkUpdateProperties` (CMIS 1.1), `moveObject`, `deleteObject`, `deleteTree`, `setContentStream`, `appendContentStream` (CMIS 1.1), and `deleteContentStream`.

- **Multifiling services**: These services are optional; they make it possible to put an object into several folders (multifiling) or outside the folder hierarchy (unfiling). This service is not used to create or delete objects. The multifiling service methods are `addObjectToFolder` and `removeObjectFromFolder`.

- **Discovery services**: These services are used to look for queryable objects within the repository (objects with the property `queryable` set to `true`). The discovery service methods are `query` and `getContentChanges`.

- **Versioning services**: These services are used to manage versioning of document objects, other objects not being versionable. Whether or not a document can be versioned is controlled by the `versionable` property in the object type. The versioning service methods are `checkOut`, `cancelCheckOut`, `checkIn`, `getObjectOfLatestVersion`, `getPropertiesOfLatestVersion`, and `getAllVersions`.

- **Relationship services**: These services are optional and are used to retrieve the relationships in which an object is participating. The relationship service method is `getObjectRelationships`.

- **Policy services**: These services are optional and are used to apply or remove a policy object to an object which has the property `controllablePolicy` set to `true`. The policy service methods are `applyPolicy`, `removePolicy`, and `getAppliedPolicies`.

- **ACL services**: These services are used to discover and manage the access control list (ACL) for an object, if the object has one. The ACL service methods are `applyACL` and `getACL`.

As we can see, there are quite a few services at our disposal and we will see how they are used in the upcoming chapters. Note that when working with the different types of protocols and formats that the CMIS standard supports, the preceding method names might not be used. For example, if you wanted to get the children objects for an object, you would use the `getChildren` method from the navigation service. However, if we are using the AtomPub binding, this method would be referred to as the Folder Children Collection and can be accessed via a URL that looked similar to the following: `.../children?id=...`.

Query language

The `query` method of the discovery service uses a query language that is based on a subset of the well known SQL-92 standard for database queries. It also has some ECM-specific extensions added to it. Each object type is treated as a logical relational table and joins are supported between these, creating a relational view of the CMIS model. The query language supports metadata and/or a full-text search (FTS is optional).

The CMIS object type definitions contain some properties that are related to searching, which are as follows:

- The `queryable` property should be set to `true` if the object type should be searchable. Non-queryable object types are excluded from the relational view and cannot appear in the `FROM` clause of a query statement.

- The `queryName` property of a queryable object type is used to identify the object type in the `FROM` clause of a query statement.

- The `includedInSuperType` property determines if an object subtype is included in a query for any of its supertypes. So, it may be possible that all subtypes are not included in the query for a type. If an object type is not `includedInSuperType`, a direct query for the type is still supported if it is defined as `queryable`. For example, Alfresco internally models renditions as a subtype of `cmis:document`. Renditions are not marked as `includedInSuperType` and so will not appear in queries for `cmis:document`.

The following example selects all properties for all documents but does not include thumbnails (`cm:thumbnail`):

```
SELECT * FROM cmis:document
```

On the other hand, the following example includes `cm:thumbnail` and any subtypes that are set as `includedInSuperType=true`:

```
SELECT * FROM cm:thumbnail
```

To select specific properties for all documents, use the following query:

```
SELECT cmis:name, cmis:description FROM cmis:document
```

To select all documents that have a name containing the text `alfresco`, we can use the following:

```
SELECT cmis:name FROM cmis:document WHERE cmis:name LIKE
'%alfresco%'
```

To perform a **Full-Text Search (FTS)**, we need to use the SQL-92 CMIS extension `CONTAINS()` to look for any document with the text `alfresco` in it as follows:

```
SELECT * FROM cmis:document WHERE CONTAINS('alfresco')
```

The previous query will return all properties (columns) as we have used the wildcard `*`. There are also some folder-related SQL-92 CMIS extensions to search in a folder (`IN_FOLDER`) or folder tree (`IN_TREE`):

```
SELECT cmis:name FROM cmis:document WHERE IN_FOLDER('folder id')
```

The preceding query returns all documents in the folder with the identifier `folder id`. A folder identifier would be the same as a node reference in the Alfresco world. The following query returns all objects beneath the folder with `folder id`:

```
SELECT cmis:name FROM cmis:folder WHERE IN_TREE('folder id')
```

Protocol bindings

We have covered the object model and the available repository services. We also need to have a look at how we can actually communicate with the repository from a remote client over the wire. This is where protocol bindings come into the picture. There are three of them available: RESTful AtomPub, SOAP Web Services, and RESTful Browser (CMIS 1.1). CMIS-compliant repositories must provide a service endpoint (that is, the starting URL) for each of the bindings. The service URL and an understanding of the CMIS specifications is all that a client needs to discover both the capabilities and content of a repository.

RESTful AtomPub binding

The REST binding is built on the Atom Publishing Protocol — based on XML (refer to `http://tools.ietf.org/html/rfc5023`) — with CMIS-specific extensions. In this binding, the client interacts with the repository by acquiring the **service document**. The client will request the service document using the URI provided by the vendor; in the case of Alfresco, this URL has the format `http://<hostname>:<port>/alfresco/api/-default-/public/cmis/versions/1.1/atom` (swap 1.1 with 1.0 to use that version). From the returned service document XML, the client will choose a CMIS collection, represented by a URI, and start accessing the repository by following the links in returned XML documents. There are a number of collections of objects that we can use in the service document. You can think of a collection as a URI pointing to a place in the repository. The following are the service collections:

- **Root collection**: An HTTP GET for this collection will give us information about all the objects at the top level in the repository (in Alfresco, that would be all the content under `/Company Home`). Making an HTTP POST to this collection adds objects to the top folder in the repository.

- **Query collection**: An HTTP POST to this collection executes a search.

- **Checked-Out collection**: An HTTP GET for this collection will give us a list of all checked-out documents. To check-out a document, we POST to this collection.

- **Unfiled collection**: This is a collection described in the service document to manage unfiled documents, policies, and item objects.

- **Type Children collection**: This collection can be used to GET all base types in the repository. One can then continue to navigate to the subtype hierarchy from a base type and so on.

- **Bulk Update collection** (CMIS 1.1): This collection is used to upload multiple objects to the repository at the same time.

Requests and responses made via the AtomPub binding are in the form of an Atom XML feed or an Atom XML entry. Usually, the response is extended to include CMIS-specific tags within one of the CMIS-specific namespaces.

Web Service binding

The Web Service binding uses the SOAP protocol (http://www.w3.org/TR/soap/) and maps directly to the CMIS domain model, services, and methods defined in the specification. When using Alfresco, we can access a summary page with all the services and their WSDL document links via the http://<hostname>:<port>/alfresco/cmis URL. There are two types of XSD documents that make up the WSDL for the services: one defines the data model and the other defines the message formats. For authentication, the repository should support WS-Security 1.1 for Username Token Profile 1.1 and has the option of supporting other authentication mechanisms. A CMIS-compliant repository may grant access to some or all of its services to unauthenticated clients. For content transfer, the repository should support **Message Transmission Optimization Mechanism** (**MTOM**) and must accept Base64 encoded content.

RESTful Browser binding (CMIS 1.1)

The Browser binding was introduced in Version 1.1 to make it easier to work with CMIS from HTML and JavaScript within a web browser. Content can be managed directly from HTML forms and responses from AJAX calls to CMIS services can be fed directly into JavaScript widgets.

The Browser binding also uses a REST-based approach, but instead of AtomPub feed and entry XML, it uses **JavaScript Object Notation** (**JSON**). (To learn more about JSON, refer to http://tools.ietf.org/html/rfc4627). This binding is specifically designed to support applications running in a web browser but is not restricted to them. It is based on technologies such as HTML, HTML Forms, JavaScript, and JSON. Importantly, it does not require a specific JavaScript library, but takes advantage of the existing built-in capabilities of modern browsers.

While this binding is optimized for use in browser applications, it can also serve as an easy-to-use binding in other application models. To access Alfresco repository information via the Browser binding, use the http://<hostname>:<port>/alfresco/api/-default-/public/cmis/versions/1.1/browser URL.

Summary

In this chapter, we introduced the CMIS standard and how it came about. A couple of use cases, such as one client accessing multiple repositories, were presented, which illustrated the need for the standard. Then we covered the CMIS domain model with its five base object types: document, folder, relationship, policy, and item (CMIS 1.1.). We also learned that the CMIS standard defines a number of services, such as navigation and discovery, which makes it possible to manipulate objects in a content management system repository. And finally, we looked at how we can communicate over the wire with a CMIS-compliant repository; this can be done with, for example, a REST-based approach over HTTP.

So now that we know what CMIS is, let's take it for a spin. In the next chapter, we will start using it and see how we can manipulate objects in a CMIS-compliant repository.

2
Basic CMIS Operations

In this chapter, we will dig into the CMIS API and test it by calling a CMIS server directly via HTTP, and it will respond in XML or JSON depending on whether we are using the AtomPub binding or the Browser binding. We will try out most of the common operations that would be normal to perform against a CMS system such as follows:

- Authenticating and connecting to the server
- Fetching repository information including repository ID and root-folder URL
- Listing the content of a folder
- Listing the content types that are available
- Reading content metadata and downloading content
- Creating, updating, and deleting folders and files

This chapter is particularly useful for those who cannot, for some reason, use a third-party library that abstracts the inner workings of the CMIS interface. So if you cannot use any of the libraries from the Apache Chemistry project, this chapter will be helpful as it will tell you how to interact with any CMIS-compliant server using only HTTP and XML or JSON.

This chapter will also be very useful if you are using, for example, the OpenCMIS Java library from the Apache Chemistry project as we will go through and explain a lot of the capability and object properties.

The REST-based AtomPub binding and Browser binding will be used to demonstrate how the CMIS API is used. We will not cover the Web Service binding. Each functional area will first start with a general description on the CMIS service, and then there will be one section for AtomPub followed by a section for the Browser binding.

You can choose to follow only the AtomPub examples if they are of more interest to you. Maybe you are not yet interested in the new features of CMIS 1.1 as this version was approved recently in May 2013 and your content management server might not support it yet. In that case, you can skip the Browser binding sections of this chapter.

Setting up a CMIS server

Before we start, we are going to need a CMIS server to talk to. There are a number of ways to get access to a CMIS server. You can, for example, install your own or use one that is available on the Internet. Actually, it is best to install your own so that you can have some control over it and you have the confidence that there are not loads of other users doing stuff at the same time as you.

We will focus on the Alfresco content management server in this book, but all the exercises should work with any other CMIS-compliant server too. However, if you use another CMIS server, remember that it will have a different entry point URL than Alfresco's (different from, for example, `http://localhost:8080/alfresco/cmisatom`).

Installing your own CMIS server

This book is about Alfresco and CMIS, so we will use the Alfresco CMS server when working with CMIS. The quickest way to get going with your own Alfresco installation is to download the full installation file of the Community version, which is available at `http://downloads.alfresco.com`. After you have downloaded the installation file, execute it and choose the default options for the questions you are asked during the installation process.

This will install Apache Tomcat with all the Alfresco web application files that you need. It will also install a local PostgreSQL database and a Java SDK. Also, there is a start script in the installation directory if you are on Linux; if you are on Windows or OSX, there is a special management console where you can start and stop the server and database. If you have started the server, you can check whether it is working by opening a browser and entering the `http://localhost:8080/alfresco/cmisatom` URL, which should prompt you to download the service document for the AtomPub CMIS binding.

Using cmis.alfresco.com

If you don't want to install a CMIS server on your computer, then another option is to use a freely available Alfresco server on the Internet. This server is located at the `http://cmis.alfresco.com` URL. To test whether it works, enter the `http://cmis.alfresco.com/cmisatom` or the `http://cmis.alfresco.com/cmisbrowser` URLs. When using this server, remember that there are other people using it too. So, there might be a lot more items in the responses than you expected.

Setting up a tool to make HTTP requests

So we now have an Alfresco CMIS server that we can talk to. Next, we need a tool that can be used to make HTTP requests to the server. We are going to test the AtomPub and Browser CMIS bindings, which are based on the HTTP protocol and the back and forth sending of XML and JSON.

One really good tool that can be used for this is **cURL**; it is available for most platforms. On my Ubuntu laptop, I can just use the `#sudo apt-get install curl` command to install it. On Windows, you can download cURL from `http://curl.haxx.se/download.html`. If you are on a Mac, then Apple has a different version of cURL as part of the developer tools; it's also available through Homebrew using `brew install curl`.

Later on, in this chapter, we will also look at using the Chrome browser to view XML and JSON responses and some other command-line tools to parse and display XML and JSON.

Authenticating with the repository

When using the AtomPub binding or the Browser binding, authentication is delegated to the transport protocol, which is HTTP. All CMIS-compliant servers must, at the very least, support client authentication using the HTTP Basic authentication schema. We will use this in the following examples. If the server is Alfresco, the alternative is to use the Alfresco login service. As this is not supported by other servers, we will stick to the HTTP Basic authentication, which is portable.

The `curl` tool can handle Basic Auth for us automatically; we just have to pass the username and password, as follows, with the `-u` switch when we use `curl`:

```
$ curl -u admin:admin
```

If you are going to work only with Alfresco, you can log in and get a ticket that you can use in subsequent calls as follows:

```
$ curl
"http://localhost:8080/alfresco/service/api/login?u=admin&pw=admin"
<?xml version="1.0" encoding="UTF-8"?>
<ticket>TICKET_39ea5e46e83a6d6e43845182f4254f9de50402fb</ticket>
```

You should actually never use this call in plain text; it is better to use HTTPS as follows:

```
$ curl -k
"https://localhost:8443/alfresco/service/api/login?u=admin&pw=admin"
```

The ticket that is returned from the login call can then be used in any subsequent call by specifying it as the password for the user and empty username as follows:

```
$  curl -k -u :TICKET_c49714aed211711e78ac983a11cd63f239f18223
"https://localhost:8443/alfresco/cmisatom"
```

It is also possible to set the username as ROLE_TICKET. The -k option allows curl to perform insecure SSL connections and transfers.

Getting repository information

To execute any other operation against a CMIS repository, we first need to find out its identifier, access points, and capabilities. The identifier is used when we want to connect and get a session to work within. It is also important to know the capabilities of a CMIS server, as not all requirements in the CMIS specification are mandatory, and the capabilities tell us what the repository supports and what it doesn't. The access points tell us how to, for example, get access to the top-level folders in the repository. All this information is accessible via the getRepositoryInfo service call.

Before we look at how to get repository information when using the AtomPub or the Browser binding, we will walk through the different properties that we will encounter and explain them. They are the same for all bindings, so it makes sense to describe them before looking at protocol-specific stuff.

The repository ID, identified by the repositoryId property, is usually needed to create a session when using client libraries such as the OpenCMIS Java library, which we will cover in *Chapter 5, Accessing a CMIS Server with a Java Client*. Also, there are a number of other properties that will tell you more about the product and the repository, such as repositoryName, repositoryDescription, productName, and productVersion.

The next couple of properties of interest are the rootFolderId and rootFolderUrl properties, which give us the CMIS object ID, or node reference if you speak Alfresco lingo, for the root folder in Alfresco and a URL to access it directly. The root folder in Alfresco is referred to as /Company Home, and we will see in a bit how we can fetch the child folders and files for it.

Another interesting property is the cmisVersionSupported property, which basically tells us whether we can use the Browser binding completely or not. However, the best way to find out whether a specific Version 1.1 feature is supported is to try it out with your server. The reason for this is that some earlier versions of content management servers, such as Alfresco, might say that they support only Version 1.0 even if they actually support most of the v1.1 Browser binding features.

Next, we will come to properties that indicate which functionality is supported; for example, the changesIncomplete property. If it is set to true, it means that the change log includes all the changes made since a particular point in time but not all the changes ever made. This property is only relevant if the capabilityChanges property in the capabilities section is not none (see the following table for more information on capabilities). The changesOnType property indicates which CMIS base object types will be included in the change log. Here, valid values are any combination of the five basic CMIS object types — cmis:folder, cmis:document, cmis:relationship, cmis:policy, and cmis:item (available in CMIS 1.1).

The principalAnonymous property tells us the username for the guest user in Alfresco (that is, guest), and the principalAnyone property contains what the anyone group is called within Alfresco (that is, GROUP_EVERYONE).

The repository capabilities can be found in the capabilities section, and they look something like the following code snippet when called via AtomPub:

```
<cmis:capabilities>
  <cmis:capabilityACL>manage</cmis:capabilityACL>
  <cmis:capabilityAllVersionsSearchable>false
  </cmis:capabilityAllVersionsSearchable>
    <cmis:capabilityChanges>none</cmis:capabilityChanges>
    <cmis:capabilityContentStreamUpdatability>anytime
    </cmis:capabilityContentStreamUpdatability>
<cmis:capabilityGetDescendants>true</cmis:capabilityGetDescendants>
<cmis:capabilityGetFolderTree>true</cmis:capabilityGetFolderTree>
    <cmis:capabilityMultifiling>true</cmis:capabilityMultifiling>
<cmis:capabilityPWCSearchable>false</cmis:capabilityPWCSearchable>
<cmis:capabilityPWCUpdatable>true</cmis:capabilityPWCUpdatable>
    <cmis:capabilityQuery>bothcombined</cmis:capabilityQuery>
    <cmis:capabilityRenditions>read</cmis:capabilityRenditions>
    <cmis:capabilityUnfiling>false</cmis:capabilityUnfiling>
    <cmis:capabilityVersionSpecificFiling>false
    </cmis:capabilityVersionSpecificFiling>
    <cmis:capabilityJoin>none</cmis:capabilityJoin>
</cmis:capabilities>
```

Downloading the example code

You can download the example code files for all Packt books you have purchased from your account at http://www.packtpub.com. If you purchased this book elsewhere, you can visit http://www.packtpub.com/support and register to have the files e-mailed directly to you.

We will go through these properties in more detail in their related sections. However, some of these properties of the capabilities are not related to anything we will cover in this chapter, so let's have a look at them now:

Capability	Description	Valid options
capabilityChanges	This indicates the level of changes (if any) that the repository exposes via the getContentChanges service.	• none: The repository does not support the change log feature • objectidsonly: The change log can return only the object IDs for changed objects in the repository and an indication of the type of change; not details of the actual change • properties: The change log can return the properties and object ID for the changed objects • all: The change log can return the object IDs for changed objects in the repository and more information about the actual change
capabilityRenditions	This indicates whether or not the repository exposes the renditions of the document or folder objects.	• none: The repository does not expose renditions at all • read: Renditions are provided by the repository and are readable by the client

The following capabilities' properties are also related to functionality that we do not cover in this chapter, but it is good to know about them:

Capability	Description	Valid options
capabilityMultifiling	This is the ability of an application to file a document or other fileable objects in more than one folder.	[true | false]
capabilityUnfiling	This is the ability of an application to exclude a document or other fileable objects not filed in any folder.	[true | false]

Capability	Description	Valid options
capabilityVersionSpecificFiling	This is the ability of an application to file individual versions (that is, not all versions) of a document in a folder.	[true | false]

Some CMIS 1.1-related properties are not seen in the capabilities section when you are using a CMIS 1.0 server, and we will have a look at them now. One of the major new features in Version 1.1 is the possibility to create new types via the API. Until now, you had to bootstrap new types in an XML file for Alfresco to recognize them.

The related CMIS 1.1 capabilities are as follows:

Capability	Description	Valid options
capabilityCreatable PropertyTypes (available in CMIS 1.1)	A list of all property data types that can be used by a client to create or update an object type definition	
capabilityNewTypeSettable Attributes (available in CMIS 1.1)	This capability indicates which object type attributes can be set by a client when a new object type is created.	This capability is a set of Booleans; there is one for each of the following attributes: id, localName, localNamespace, displayName, queryName, description, creatable, fileable, queryable, fulltextIndexed, includedInSupertypeQuery, controllablePolicy, and controllableACL.

Repository information via the AtomPub binding

To access repository information via the AtomPub protocol, we just need to perform an HTTP GET method on the `http://localhost:8080/alfresco/cmisatom` URL as follows:

```
$ curl -u admin:admin http://localhost:8080/alfresco/cmisatom
```

This brings back the so-called **service document**, which contains all the repository information that we have just looked at in the previous section. However, it also contains something called collections that are entry points to the repository for the root folder's children, the supported base objects types, checked out documents, and so on. The service document is an XML file that might appear a bit daunting at first, but so long as you know what you are looking for, it is not that bad.

To get the repository ID directly, you could execute the following command on a Unix system:

```
$ curl -u admin:admin http://localhost:8080/alfresco/cmisatom |
xmlstarlet sel -T -t -m '//cmis:repositoryId' -c . -n

f0ebcfb4-ca9f-4991-bda8-9465f4f11527
```

The `xmlstarlet` command-line tool (for more information, refer to `http://xmlstar.sourceforge.net/`) is great for parsing XML with **XPath** and extracting the properties that we are interested in. On a Debian-based system, it could be installed with `$ sudo apt-get install xmlstarlet`. The `sel` option tells `xmlstarlet` that we want to query the XML with XPath, the `-T` option sets the output to text instead of XML, and the `-t` option specifies a query template with the `-m` option for XPath match expression. In this case, the XPath expression is `//cmis:repositoryId`, and this means that `xmlstarlet` will search for an element with the name `repositoryId` in the `cmis` namespace anywhere (because of `//`) in the XML file. The `-c` option prints a copy of the XPath expression. The `.` operator represents the XML file piped from the `curl` execution, and `-n` puts a new line at the end.

If `xmlstarlet` is not available on your system, you could also extract the repository ID with `curl` and `grep` as follows:

```
$ curl -u admin:admin http://localhost:8080/alfresco/cmisatom | grep
-o "cmis:repositoryId.*repositoryId"

cmis:repositoryId>f0ebcfb4-ca9f-4991-bda8-
9465f4f11527</cmis:repositoryId
```

If you wanted to check what CMIS version is supported by your repository, you could use the following command:

```
$ curl -u admin:admin http://cmis.alfresco.com/cmisatom | xmlstarlet
sel -T -t -m '//cmis:cmisVersionSupported' -c . -n
1.0
```

 I am accessing the public Alfresco repository on the Internet.

You could extract most of the other properties by requesting the service document and then use XPath to extract them as specified earlier. For example, to check the searching capabilities of the repository, make the following request:

```
$ curl -u admin:admin http://localhost:8080/alfresco/cmisatom |
xmlstarlet sel -T -t -m '//cmis:capabilityQuery' -c . -n
Bothcombined
```

The meaning of Bothcombined is that both full-text search and metadata search are supported by the server.

Repository information via the Browser binding

To access the repository information via the Browser binding, we just need to do an HTTP GET on the http://localhost:8080/alfresco/cmisbrowser URL as follows:

```
$ curl -u admin:admin http://localhost:8080/alfresco/cmisbrowser
```

This brings back a JSON file with all the repository information that was described in the *Getting repository information* section.

To get the repository ID directly, you can execute the following command on a Unix system:

```
$ curl -u admin:admin http://localhost:8080/alfresco/cmisbrowser |jq
'.[] | .repositoryId'
"f0ebcfb4-ca9f-4991-bda8-9465f4f11527"
```

In the preceding command, another useful command-line tool called jq is used to extract properties from the returned JSON. In this case, we tell it to grab the first member object (the response starts with something like { "f0ebcfb4-ca9f-4991-bda8-9465f4f11527": {...) and then inside this object, we grab the repositoryId property value. As the Alfresco server contains only a single repository the response object is made up of one member named with the repository identifier, which contains information about the repository. One of the properties for the repository is repositoryId. So you can actually get to the repository identifier from two different places.

The jq tool can be installed on a Unix-based system as follows:

```
$ mkdir jq
$ cd jq/
$ wget http://stedolan.github.io/jq/download/linux64/jq
$ chmod +x jq
$ sudo ln -s /home/mbergljung/apps/jq/jq /usr/bin/jq
```

If you wanted to check the CMIS version that is supported by your repository, you could use the following command:

 I am accessing the Alfresco repository on the Internet.

```
$ curl -u admin:admin http://cmis.alfresco.com/cmisbrowser |jq '.[] |
.cmisVersionSupported'
"1.0"
```

Here is an example of an Alfresco installation that supports some of the features of Version 1.1 (that is, implementation was done before Version 1.1 was approved) but actually returns the supported version as 1.0. So it is always worth trying out the 1.1 features even if this property returns 1.0.

You could extract most of the other properties by requesting the JSON document and then the jq tool for them as mentioned previously. For example, to check the search capabilities of the repository make the following request:

```
$ curl -u admin:admin http://localhost:8080/alfresco/cmisbrowser |jq '.[]
| .capabilities.capabilityQuery'
"bothcombined"
```

 Remember to replace the f0ebcfb4-ca9f-4991-bda8-9465f4f11527 repository ID with one that matches your server in the rest of this chapter.

Listing the children of the root folder

After we have the information about the repository via the getRepositoryInfos service, we would typically want to access some folders and files in it. First, you would usually access the children of the top-level folder (also called root folder) in the repository, and this can be done via the getChildren service. This folder is called /Company Home in the Alfresco world.

The `getChildren` request returns a list of all the folders and files contained in a particular folder. This call has to be supported by the repository, but there are other navigation-related service calls too that might or might not be supported. The `getDescendants` call will return all the children of a folder to a specified depth. The `getFolderTree` call will return a complete folder tree to a specified depth (note that only folder objects are returned).

The repository information's call will return information on the navigation service calls that are supported besides the `getChildren` request:

Capability	Description	Valid options
capabilityGetDescendants	This is the ability of an application to enumerate the descendants of a folder via the `getDescendants` service call.	[true | false]
capabilityGetFolderTree	This is the ability of an application to retrieve the folder tree via the `getFolderTree` service call.	[true | false]
capabilityOrderBy (available in CMIS 1.1)	Indicates the ordering capabilities of the repository.	• none: Ordering is not supported • common: Only common CMIS properties are supported • custom: Common CMIS properties and custom object type properties are supported

All the properties of a content item are returned in the result from a navigation service call such as `getChildren`. (To return specific properties only, see the *Optional parameters when listing the children of a folder* section.) Each property is a named and typed container for zero or more values. In the AtomPub binding, a property that has no value is said to be in a *value not set* state, and it cannot have a value of `null`. This is not true for the Browser binding where the property value would be set to `null` in the JSON result.

There are a number of data types that can be used for a property in CMIS, including `string`, `boolean`, `decimal`, `integer`, `datetime`, `uri`, `id`, and `html`. All properties, like objects, must have a `queryName` attribute that can be used in queries.

The following table explains the most common CMIS properties for folders and documents:

Property	Description	Data type
cmis:allowedChildObjectTypeIds	This lists all the types of child objects that a folder can contain. For example, cmis:folder and cmis:document.	ID
	If this value is not set, then the folder can contain any content.	
cmis:objectTypeId	This is the type of the content item, for example, cmis:folder, and can also be a custom type from a custom document model such as ixxus:itDoc.	ID
	To see the base object type of the item, see cmis:baseTypeId.	
cmis:path	Path from the repository root to a folder. For example, /Data Dictionary.	String
cmis:name	The name of the content item; basically, the filename.	String
cmis:creationDate	The date and time when the content item was created.	DateTime
cmis:changeToken	Opaque token used for optimistic locking and concurrency checking.	String
	If a repository provides a value for this property for a content item, then all the invocations of the update method on that item (for example, updateProperties) will provide the value of the property as an input parameter. The repository will then throw an updateConflictException if the value specified for the change token does not match the change token value for the object being updated.	

Property	Description	Data type
`cmis:lastModifiedBy`	The username of the user who last modified the content item.	`String`
`cmis:createdBy`	The username of the user who created the content item.	`String`
`cmis:objectId`	The repository-specific unique identifier for the content item. In Alfresco, this would be a node reference. This ID will be system generated.	`ID`
`cmis:baseTypeId`	The base object type for this content item will be one of the following: `cmis:folder`, `cmis:document`, `cmis:relationship`, `cmis:policy`, and `cmis:item`.	`ID`
`alfcmis:nodeRef`	Alfresco-specific, non-CMIS standard property that contains the Alfresco node reference.	`ID`
`cmis:parentId`	This is the parent content item ID. For example, this would be the parent folder node reference in Alfresco.	`ID`
`cmis:lastModificationDate`	The date and time when the content item was last modified.	

If the content item is a document (that is, `cmis:baseTypeId` is `cmis:document`), there would be a number of additional properties that you would see in the result. These properties can be divided into two groups. The properties that have to do with versioning, only the `cmis:document` types, can be versioned. The properties that are related to streaming content, only the `cmis:document` types, can have physical content. We will look at these properties in the upcoming sections.

Listing the children of the root folder with the AtomPub binding

When using the AtomPub binding to list the folders and documents under the root folder, we have to use the root folder collection and make a GET request on its URL. The part of the service document that contains the root collection URL looks something like the following code snippet:

```
<app:collection href="http://cmis.alfresco.com/cmisatom/bb212ecb-
122d-47ea-b5c1-128affb9cd8f/children?id
=workspace%3A%2F%2FSpacesStore%2F67f87d00-a2cd-4668-9644-
d7a130435045">
   <cmisra:collectionType>root</cmisra:collectionType>
   <atom:title type="text">Root Collection</atom:title>
   <app:accept>application/atom+xml;type=entry</app:accept>
   <app:accept>application/cmisatom+xml</app:accept>
</app:collection>
```

Execute the following command to get the root folder collection URL from the service document:

```
$ curl -u admin:admin http://cmis.alfresco.com/cmisatom | xmlstarlet
sel -t -m "//app:collection[cmisra:collectionType='root']" -m "@href"
-v . -n

http://cmis.alfresco.com/cmisatom/bb212ecb-122d-47ea-b5c1-
128affb9cd8f/children?id=workspace%3A%2F%2FSpacesStore%2F67f87d00-
a2cd-4668-9644-d7a130435045
```

With this information, we can now list the root folder contents by using the preceding URL specified in the href attribute of the app:collection element as follows:

```
$ curl -u admin:admin "http://cmis.alfresco.com/cmisatom/bb212ecb-122d-
47ea-b5c1-128affb9cd8f/children?id
=workspace%3A%2F%2FSpacesStore%2F67f87d00-a2cd-4668-9644-
d7a130435045" | xmllint --format -
```

Here, another handy Unix command-line utility called xmllint is used to pretty-print the XML output (for more information, refer to http://xmlsoft.org/xmllint.html).

If you were not intimidated by the service document XML, you probably will be when you look at the result of the root collection. The XML response is massive (specifically if you are accessing cmis.alfresco.com), and you need to know where to dig in order to find the information you are looking for. The structure and content of the returned Atom feed is as follows for a standard Alfresco installation:

```
<atom:feed
    ...
    <atom:title>Company Home</atom:title>
    ...
    <cmisra:numItems>5</cmisra:numItems>
    ...
    <atom:link rel="describedby"
    <atom:link rel="http://docs.oasis-
    open.org/ns/cmis/link/200908/allowableactions" ...
    <atom:link rel="http://docs.oasis-
    open.org/ns/cmis/link/200908/foldertree" ...
    <atom:link rel="http://docs.oasis-
    open.org/ns/cmis/link/200908/acl" ...
    <atom:link rel="http://docs.oasis-
    open.org/ns/cmis/link/200908/relationships"
    ...
    <atom:entry>
        ...
            <atom:title>Data Dictionary</atom:title>
        ...
            <cmis:properties>
                <cmis:propertyId queryName="cmis:objectTypeId"
                  displayName="Object Type Id"
                  localName="objectTypeId"

propertyDefinitionId="cmis:objectTypeId">
                    <cmis:value>cmis:folder</cmis:value>
                </cmis:propertyId>
                More properties...
                <aspects:aspects ...
<appliedAspects>P:app:uifacets</appliedAspects>
                    Properties...
                <appliedAspects>P:cm:titled</appliedAspects>

<appliedAspects>P:sys:localized</appliedAspects>
                </aspects:aspects>
            </cmis:properties>
        </cmisra:object>
        <atom:link rel="up" ...
        <atom:link rel="down"  ...
        Other links...
    </atom:entry>
    <atom:entry>...<atom:title>Guest Home
    </atom:title>...</atom:entry>
    <atom:entry>...<atom:title>User Homes
```

```
        </atom:title>...</atom:entry>
        <atom:entry>...<atom:title>Imap Attachments
        </atom:title>...</atom:entry>
        <atom:entry>...<atom:title>Sites</atom:title>...</atom:entry>
    </atom:feed>
```

First, the XML document tells us that we have a listing of the Company Home folder (atom:title) that contains five items (cmisra:numItems). It then continues with a number of links that can be used to find more information about the Company Home folder. We could, for example, find the access control list by getting the /acl link URL as follows:

```
$ curl -u admin:admin
"http://localhost:8080/alfresco/cmisatom/f0ebcfb4-ca9f-4991-bda8-
9465f4f11527/acl?id=workspace%3A%2F%2FSpacesStore%2Fa5c45ceb-2603-
491f-b2c9-6ff7d6579483" | xmllint --format -
        <?xml version="1.0" encoding="UTF-8" standalone="yes"?>
<ns2:acl xmlns="http://docs.oasis-open.org/ns/cmis/messaging/200908/"
        xmlns:ns2="http://docs.oasis-open.org/ns/cmis/core/200908/"
        xmlns:ns3="http://docs.oasis-open.org/ns/cmis/restatom/200908/">
    <ns2:permission>
        <ns2:principal>
            <ns2:principalId>GROUP_EVERYONE</ns2:principalId>
        </ns2:principal>
        <ns2:permission>cmis:read</ns2:permission>
        <ns2:direct>true</ns2:direct>
    </ns2:permission>
</ns2:acl>
```

The response indicates that everyone has read access to the Company Home folder in Alfresco. This is because GROUP_EVERYONE has the cmis:read permission set. Next, there will be an atom:entry element for each child document or folder under Company Home.

Each Atom entry contains the name of the folder or document and all the properties for it. The properties section will also contain any aspects that have been set for the content item. (Aspects are specific to Alfresco and are not part of the CMIS standard; they are represented as secondary types in an Alfresco server version that supports the CMIS 1.1 specification.)

At the end of the feed entry, you will have links to navigate in different directions from the folder or document. To list the contents of the Document Library folder, you would use the down link URL. Following the up link URL will give you an Atom feed entry for just the Company Home folder.

This is basically how you navigate around in the repository when using the AtomPub binding.

Listing the children of the root folder with the Browser binding

When using the Browser binding to list the folders and documents under the root folder, we have to use the root-folder URL that can be found in the JSON document returned in response to the `http://localhost:8080/alfresco/cmisbrowser` call. You can fetch the `rootFolderUrl` property as follows:

```
$ curl -u admin:admin http://localhost:8080/alfresco/cmisbrowser |jq '.[]
| .rootFolderUrl'
```

```
"http://localhost:8080/alfresco/cmisbrowser/f0ebcfb4-ca9f-4991-bda8-
9465f4f11527/root"
```

With the root-folder URL, you can now list the root folder contents by using the URL as follows:

```
$ curl -u admin:admin "http://localhost:8080/alfresco/cmisbrowser/
f0ebcfb4-ca9f-4991-bda8-9465f4f11527/root" | jq '.'
```

The root folder (that is, `Company Home` in Alfresco) JSON response looks as follows:

```
{
    "hasMoreItems" : false,
      "objects" :
        [
          {
            "object" :
              {
                "properties" :
                  {
                    "cmis:objectTypeId" :
                      {
                        "id" : "cmis:objectTypeId",
                        "localName" : "objectTypeId",
                        "queryName" : "cmis:objectTypeId",
                        "value" : "cmis:folder",
                        "type" : "id",
                        "displayName" : "Object Type Id",
                        "cardinality" : "single"
                      },
                    "cmis:objectId" : { …
                    "value" : "workspace://SpacesStore/a89c38dd-
```

```
                              fb27-4016-a1aa-7c8e1c9e9d37", … },
                                "cmis:path" : { … "value" : "/Data
                                Dictionary", … },
                                "cmis:name" : { … "value" : "Data
                                Dictionary", … },
                                "alfcmis:nodeRef" : { … "value" :
                                "workspace://SpacesStore/a89c38dd-fb27-4016-
                                a1aa-7c8e1c9e9d37", … },
                                "aspects" : { "appliedAspects" :
                                "P:sys:localized" …
                                "cmis:allowedChildObjectTypeIds" : { …
                                "value" : null, … },
                                "cmis:creationDate" : { … "value" :
                                1352564716280, … },
                                 "cmis:changeToken" : { … "value" : null, …
                                },
                                "cmis:lastModifiedBy" : { … "value" :
                                "System", … },
                                "cmis:createdBy" : { … "value" : "System", …
                                },
                                "cmis:baseTypeId" : { … "value" :
                                "cmis:folder", … },
                                "cmis:lastModificationDate" : { … "value" :
                                1352564726570, … },
                                "cmis:parentId" : { … "value" :
                                "workspace://SpacesStore/a5c45ceb-2603-491f-
                                b2c9-6ff7d6579483", … }
                              }
                          }
                        },
                  {
                      "object" : { "properties" : { ... "Guest Home" ...
                      "object" : { "properties" : { ... "User Homes" ...
                      "object" : { "properties" : { ... "Imap Attachments" …
                      "object" : { "properties" : { ... "Sites" …
                  }
              }
          ],
        "numItems" : 5
      }
```

The JSON response that we get for the root folder listing is a lot easier to grasp than the XML returned from an AtomPub call requesting the same thing. Also, it can be easily fed into a JavaScript UI widget such as a list view or tree view.

We can see that there is one top JSON array called `objects` that contains all the returned folders and documents. Each content item is represented by a JSON property called `object` which in turn has a property called `properties` that is a list of all the properties for the content object.

You might be familiar with the CMIS properties by now, and you would be able to recognize, for example, `cmis:name`, the name of the file or folder and `cmis:objectId`, which represents the unique object/content identifier for the file or folder (node reference in Alfresco). However, there are some non-standard additions also such as `alfcmis:nodeRef` that contain the Alfresco node reference for the content item. Then, there is the `aspects` property that contains any applied Alfresco aspects to the content item.

> Note the format of the `P:sys:localized` aspect type. In Alfresco, all aspect types visible through CMIS are prefixed with `P`, document types are prefixed with `D`, and folder types are prefixed with `F`.

The `getChildren` response with the Browser binding differs from the response you get when you use the AtomPub binding. It does not contain any links to navigate up or down in the folder hierarchy. Instead, you just supply the folder path in the URL. For example, to list the `/Company Home/Data Dictionary` folder contents, use the following command:

```
$ curl -u admin:admin
"http://localhost:8080/alfresco/cmisbrowser/f0ebcfb4-ca9f-4991-bda8-
9465f4f11527/root/Data%20Dictionary" | jq '.'
```

A couple of things to be noted here; always start with `rootFolderUrl` and then add the path. Make sure that you use a valid encoded URL (for example, `%20` instead of space) for the call to work. If you want to access a document, the same technique can be used as follows:

```
$ curl -u admin:admin
http://localhost:8080/alfresco/cmisbrowser/f0ebcfb4-ca9f-4991-bda8-
9465f4f11527/root/Data%20Dictionary/Email%20Templates/invite/new-
user-email.html.ftl
```

Note that you do not get back the metadata for the document but the actual content. This is because getting a document returns the content and getting a folder returns its children by default. This can be controlled by a parameter called `cmisselector`. Setting this parameter to `properties` in the last two calls will return the metadata for the document. The same holds true for a folder; it will return the metadata instead of the children:

```
$ curl -u admin:admin
"http://localhost:8080/alfresco/cmisbrowser/f0ebcfb4-ca9f-4991-bda8-
9465f4f11527/root/Data%20Dictionary/Email%20Templates/invite/new-
user-email.html.ftl?cmisselector=properties" | jq '.'
```

We will look at the `cmisselector` parameter in more detail later in this chapter.

Optional parameters when listing the children of a folder

The `getChildren` service call allows us to specify a number of optional parameters at request time. To control the number of content items that are being returned, one can use the following parameters in the request URL:

- `maxItems`: This is the maximum number of items to return in a response. The default is repository-specific and Alfresco will, for example, return all content items if you do not specify this parameter.

- `skipCount`: This is the number of potential results that the repository will skip/page over before returning any results. This defaults to zero.

These paging input parameters work in parallel with the following output parameters in the response:

- `hasMoreItems`: This parameter will be `true` if the repository contains additional items after those contained in the response, otherwise it will be `false`. If `true`, a request with a larger `skipCount` or larger `maxItems` will return additional results (unless the contents of the repository have changed).

- `numItems`: If the repository knows the total number of items in a result set, it will include the number here.

It is also possible to specify which properties should be returned in the response by using the `filter` parameter in the request (also works for the `getDescendants` and `getFolderTree` service calls). This is very useful when you want to save the bandwidth in, for example, a mobile usage scenario. When using the `filter` parameter and specifying a filter such as `cmis:name` (that is, you want to return only the name property for each content item), more properties will be returned than just the `cm:name` property. This is because some properties such as `cmis:objectTypeId`, `cmis:objectId` and `cmis:baseTypeId` are always returned no matter what filter you specify.

If you want to see what relationships a content item has with other content items, set the `includeRelationships` parameter to one of the following values:

- `none`: No relationships are returned (default)
- `source`: Returns only relationships in which the objects returned are the source
- `target`: Returns only relationships in which the objects returned are the target
- `both`: Returns relationships in which the objects returned are the source or the target

To see what actions can be executed against returned content items, set the `includeAllowableActions` parameter to `true`.

Optional parameters when listing the children of a folder with the AtomPub binding

Here is an example of how to return a listing of the root folder with a maximum of ten items being returned, and we will only return the `cmis:name` property for each item. We will also have all the relationships for each content item in the result to be returned. Finally, allowable actions for each content item will also be returned:

```
$ curl -u admin:admin
http://localhost:8080/alfresco/cmisatom/f0ebcfb4-ca9f-4991-bda8-
9465f4f11527/children?id=workspace%3A%2F%2FSpacesStore%2Fa5c45ceb-2603-
491f-b2c9-6ff7d6579483&filter=cmis:name&includeRelationships=
both&includeAllowableActions=true&maxItems=10
```

Sometimes, it might be useful to try different combinations of parameters and be able to view the result directly, without having to save the result for each request to a file first and then open it in an editor. It is possible to do this with, for example, Google Chrome having a plugin such as XML Tree. This would give us an immediate view of the Atom feed response which is similar to the following screenshot:

Here, we can see that the result is displayed directly as soon as we enter the URL and press *Enter*. Also, the result is displayed in a nice format that is easy to view.

At the bottom of the result, we can see the values for the different allowable actions. Most of these are quite self-explanatory. There are some allowable actions that are false as `Data Dictionary object` is a folder, such as `cmis:canDeleteContentStream`, `cmis:canCheckOut`, `cmis:canCancelCheckOut`, `cmis:canCheckIn`, `cmis:canSetContentStream`, and `cmis:canGetRenditions`.

Optional parameters when listing the children of a folder with the Browser binding

Here is an example of how to return a listing of the root folder with a maximum of ten items returned, and we will only return the `cmis:name` property for each item. We will also have all the relationships for each content item in the result to be returned. Finally, allowable actions for each content item will be returned too:

```
$ curl -u admin:admin "http://cmis.alfresco.com/cmisbrowser/371554cd-
ac06-40ba-98b8-e6b60275cca7/root?includeAllowableActions=
true&includeRelationships=both&maxItems=10&filter=cmis:name"
```

Here we are accessing the public Alfresco installation on the Internet, so it is extra important to specify the maximum number of items that we want returned.

As with the AtomPub binding, it might sometimes be useful to try different combinations of parameters and view the JSON result immediately without having to save to a file and so on. It is possible to do this with, for example, Google Chrome with a plugin such as JSONView for the developer tools. This would give us an immediate view of the JSON response as shown in the following screenshot:

Again, we can see that the JSON response is more comprehensible than the corresponding Atom feed response.

Listing available types and subtypes

When we are working with a repository, it is important to be able to find out what types are available so that we can classify documents and folders properly. One of the first things to do in a CMS project is to design a domain-specific content model so that content can be classified appropriately. A proper content model improves the search capabilities and enables specific behavior to be implemented based on the type of content.

The `getTypeChildren` service is used for listing types. This service call can also use the paging parameters that the `getChildren` service call uses, such as `maxItems`. The type listing will contain a type definition with information about each type. From the type definition, we can determine whether new objects can be created from this type (`cmis:creatable`), objects of this type are fileable (`cmis:fileable`) in a folder, you can search for the objects of this type by including the type in the FROM clause (`cmis:queryable`), and whether the content of objects of this type is indexed and searchable via the CONTAINS() predicate (`cmis:fulltextIndexed`). We will cover more about searching in the next chapter.

The type definition will also have information on whether the objects of this type can have policies applied to them (`cmis:controllablePolicy`) and if the objects can be controlled by access control lists (`cmis:controllableACL`).

Listing the types and subtypes with the AtomPub binding

We can find the root types that are defined and supported by the repository by fetching the `types` collection that was returned in the service document as follows:

```
<app:collection href=
  "http://localhost:8080/alfresco/cmisatom/f0ebcfb4-ca9f-4991-
  bda8-9465f4f11527/types">
  <cmisra:collectionType>types</cmisra:collectionType>
  <atom:title type="text">Types Collection</atom:title>
  <app:accept></app:accept>
</app:collection>
```

Fetching this URL returns the base types, which would typically be `cmis:folder`, `cmis:document`, `cmis:relationship`, and `cmis:policy`:

```
$ curl -u admin:admin
"http://localhost:8080/alfresco/cmisatom/f0ebcfb4-ca9f-4991-bda8-
9465f4f11527/types" | xmllint --format -
```

Each type is returned in an Atom feed, and a type definition is available as follows:

```
<cmisra:type xsi:type="cmis:cmisTypeFolderDefinitionType"
xmlns:xsi="http://www.w3.org/2001/XMLSchema-instance"
xmlns:ns3="http://docs.oasis-open.org/ns/cmis/messaging/200908/">
  <cmis:id>cmis:folder</cmis:id>
  <cmis:localName>folder</cmis:localName>
  <cmis:localNamespace>
http://www.alfresco.org/model/cmis/1.0/cs01</cmis:localNamespace>
  <cmis:displayName>Folder</cmis:displayName>
  <cmis:queryName>cmis:folder</cmis:queryName>
  <cmis:description>Folder Type</cmis:description>
  <cmis:baseId>cmis:folder</cmis:baseId>
  <cmis:creatable>true</cmis:creatable>
  <cmis:fileable>true</cmis:fileable>
  <cmis:queryable>true</cmis:queryable>
  <cmis:fulltextIndexed>true</cmis:fulltextIndexed>
  <cmis:includedInSupertypeQuery>true
  </cmis:includedInSupertypeQuery>
  <cmis:controllablePolicy>false</cmis:controllablePolicy>
  <cmis:controllableACL>true</cmis:controllableACL>
</cmisra:type>
```

The Atom entry for a type also contains links to navigate to the subtypes. So in order to get a listing of any `cmis:folder` subtypes supported by the repository, we have to follow the `down` link:

```
<atom:link rel="down"
href="http://localhost:8080/alfresco/cmisatom/f0ebcfb4-ca9f-4991-
bda8-9465f4f11527/types?typeId=cmis%3Afolder" type=
"application/atom+xml;type=feed"/>
```

In this way, you can discover the complete type hierarchy supported by the repository. If you list the folder subtypes with the preceding URL, you will get a lot of subtypes such as `F:cm:systemfolder`, `F:pub:DeliveryChannel`, and `F:dl:dataList` back. When using Alfresco, all custom types have a prefix in front of the namespace indicator. Custom Alfresco folder types have the `F:` prefix. Any custom document subtypes would have a `D:` prefix.

Listing the types and subtypes with the Browser binding

To list the types supported by the repository, the repositoryUrl property is used with the cmisselector parameter set to typeChildren. To list all the base types, execute the following request:

```
$ curl -u admin:admin
"http://localhost:8080/alfresco/cmisbrowser/f0ebcfb4-ca9f-4991-bda8-
9465f4f11527?cmisselector=typeChildren" | jq '.'
```

This returns a JSON structure with a type definition for each type that looks similar to the following code snippet:

```
{
hasMoreItems: false,
types: [
{
  fulltextIndexed: true,
  localName: "policy",
  fileable: false,
  includedInSupertypeQuery: true,
  queryName: "cmis:policy",
  controllablePolicy: false,
  creatable: false,
  id: "cmis:policy",
  controllableACL: false,
  description: "Policy Type",
  localNamespace: "http://www.alfresco.org/model/cmis/1.0/cs01",
  displayName: "Policy",
  baseId: "cmis:policy",
  queryable: true
},
...
```

To list subtypes for one of the base types, such as cmis:folder, an extra parameter named typeId is used to specify the type we want to return subtypes for. So, to return subtypes for cmis:folder, we would use the following call:

```
$ curl -u admin:admin
"http://localhost:8080/alfresco/cmisbrowser/f0ebcfb4-ca9f-4991-bda8-
9465f4f11527?cmisselector=typeChildren&typeId=cmis:folder" | jq '.'
```

To list subtypes for an Alfresco custom type, we need to use a special prefix for folder types (F:) and documents (D:). For example, to list subtypes for myc:document, which is a custom document type in this example, we would have to use the following call:

```
$ curl -u admin:admin
"http://localhost:8080/alfresco/cmisbrowser/f0ebcfb4-ca9f-4991-bda8-
9465f4f11527?cmisselector=typeChildren&typeId=D:myc:document" | jq
'.'
```

It works in the same way to list subtypes for an Alfresco built-in subtype. For example, to list dataList subtypes, execute the following command:

```
$ curl -u admin:admin
http://localhost:8080/alfresco/cmisbrowser/f0ebcfb4-ca9f-4991-bda8-
9465f4f11527?cmisselector=typeChildren&typeId=F:dl:dataList | jq '.'
```

Getting metadata and content

We now know how to list the contents of a folder. What we would want to do next is to probably download content files and list metadata (that is, properties) for individual content items.

Getting metadata and content with the AtomPub binding

If we take a closer look at the end of the AtomPub service document (that is, the response from http://localhost:8080/alfresco/cmisatom), we will find sections with URI templates; one for getting metadata by ID, which is listed as follows:

```
<cmisra:uritemplate>
<cmisra:template>
http://localhost:8080/alfresco/cmisatom/f0ebcfb4-ca9f-4991-bda8-
9465f4f11527/id?id={id}&filter={filter}&includeAllowableActions=
{includeAllowableActions}&includeACL={includeACL}&includePolicyIds
={includePolicyIds}&includeRelationships={includeRelationships}
&renditionFilter={renditionFilter}
</cmisra:template>
<cmisra:type>objectbyid</cmisra:type>
<cmisra:mediatype>application/atom+xml;type=entry
</cmisra:mediatype>
</cmisra:uritemplate>
```

And another section for getting metadata by path, listed as follows:

```
<cmisra:uritemplate>
<cmisra:template>
http://localhost:8080/alfresco/cmisatom/f0ebcfb4-ca9f-4991-bda8-
9465f4f11527/path?path={path}&filter={filter}
```

```
&includeAllowableActions=
{includeAllowableActions}&includeACL={includeACL}&includePolicyIds={in
cludePolicyIds}&includeRelationships=
{includeRelationships}&renditionFilter={renditionFilter}
</cmisra:template>
<cmisra:type>objectbypath</cmisra:type>
<cmisra:mediatype>application/atom+xml;type=entry
</cmisra:mediatype>
</cmisra:uritemplate>
```

In these templates, the response from the URLs contains the metadata (that is, properties such as name, created date, created by, and object ID) for the objects. For example, to request the properties of an object by ID (that is, via node reference in the Alfresco world), do as follows:

```
$ curl -u admin:admin
"http://localhost:8080/alfresco/cmisatom/f0ebcfb4-ca9f-4991-bda8-
9465f4f11527/id?id=workspace%3A%2F%2FSpacesStore%2F13b534f3-374c-
4d56-a704-c0f1aec9aa06" | xmllint --format -
```

Requesting the metadata via an object path is done in a similar way as follows:

```
$ curl -u admin:admin
"http://localhost:8080/alfresco/cmisatom/f0ebcfb4-ca9f-4991-bda8-
9465f4f11527/path?path=/MyFolder/helloworld.txt" | xmllint --format -
```

 The path in this call does not include the root folder name (/Company Home in Alfresco). Requesting metadata like this works for both folders and documents.

To download content (that is, the content stream of bytes for a document) when using the AtomPub binding, you would look for the atom:content element in the Atom entry for the document (that is, in the metadata returned with either the object by ID or object by path call). If you list the children of a folder, you will also get a content element for each contained document, similar to when navigating via the up or down link to a document:

```
<atom:content src="http://localhost:8080/alfresco/cmisatom/
f0ebcfb4-ca9f-4991-bda8-9465f4f11527/content/helloworld.txt?id=
workspace%3A%2F%2FSpacesStore%2F9113eee7-5b14-4868-9117-
b584e1293ba1%3B1.1" type="text/plain"/>
```

Using this link downloads the document. Note that at the end of the link there is version information. By default, the link will represent the latest version of the document, which in this case is `1.1`. And this means, you will be downloading Version 1.1 of this document. If you wanted to download Version 1.0 of the document, just change the version number at the end of the link to `1.0`. The filename `helloworld.txt` is used by the server to set a header, indicating what the filename should be in the download dialog that will pop up if you do this from a browser. The filename has no relation to what file to download in the repo; the object ID determines this.

In the upcoming sections of this chapter, we will look at how to upload, update, and delete content in the repository. Doing these kind of operations needs more than just read permissions, so it might be useful to know how to get information about the actions that the current user is allowed to perform on an object; basically, what actions the users are allowed to do with the permissions they have in a certain folder or on a certain document.

To see allowable actions, we can use an extra parameter named `includeAllowableActions` in the object by ID or object by path call as follows:

```
$ curl -u admin:admin
"http://localhost:8080/alfresco/cmisatom/f0ebcfb4-ca9f-4991-bda8-
9465f4f11527/path?path=/MyFolder/helloworld.txt&
includeAllowableActions=true" | xmllint --format -

<cmis:allowableActions>
<cmis:canDeleteObject>true</cmis:canDeleteObject>
<cmis:canUpdateProperties>true</cmis:canUpdateProperties>
<cmis:canGetProperties>true</cmis:canGetProperties>
<cmis:canGetObjectRelationships>true
</cmis:canGetObjectRelationships>
<cmis:canGetObjectParents>true</cmis:canGetObjectParents>
<cmis:canMoveObject>true</cmis:canMoveObject>
<cmis:canDeleteContentStream>true</cmis:canDeleteContentStream>
<cmis:canCheckOut>true</cmis:canCheckOut>
<cmis:canSetContentStream>true</cmis:canSetContentStream>
<cmis:canGetAllVersions>true</cmis:canGetAllVersions>
<cmis:canAddObjectToFolder>true</cmis:canAddObjectToFolder>
<cmis:canRemoveObjectFromFolder>true
</cmis:canRemoveObjectFromFolder>
<cmis:canGetContentStream>true</cmis:canGetContentStream>
<cmis:canGetAppliedPolicies>true</cmis:canGetAppliedPolicies>
<cmis:canCreateRelationship>true</cmis:canCreateRelationship>
<cmis:canGetRenditions>true</cmis:canGetRenditions>
<cmis:canGetACL>true</cmis:canGetACL>
```

```
<cmis:canApplyACL>true</cmis:canApplyACL>
</cmis:allowableActions>
```

In this case, we used the Alfresco admin user who has full access to all operations in the repository. So, if you cannot delete a folder or a document in the coming sections, check the `canDeleteObject` and `canDeleteContentStream` properties, respectively, and make sure that they are set to `true` for the user that is used to make the call.

Getting metadata and content with the Browser binding

Getting content and metadata with the Browser binding is similar to how it's done with the AtomPub binding. Both the object by ID and object by path operations are available. When we have the root-folder URL (returned in the `http://localhost:8080/alfresco/cmisbrowser` response we discussed earlier), the template to get object metadata by ID will be similar to the following code:

```
<rootFolderUrl>?objectId=<objectId>&cmisselector=object
```

The code for getting metadata by path will be similar to the following:

```
<rootFolderUrl>/<object path>?cmisselector=object
```

The response from these URLs contains the metadata (that is, properties such as name, created date, created by, and object ID) for the objects. For example, to request the properties for an object by ID (that is, via node reference in the Alfresco world), do as follows:

```
$ curl -u admin:admin
"http://localhost:8080/alfresco/cmisbrowser/f0ebcfb4-ca9f-4991-bda8-
9465f4f11527/root?objectId=workspace%3A%2F%2FSpacesStore%2F9113eee7-
5b14-4868-9117-b584e1293ba1%3B1.1&cmisselector=object" | jq '.'
```

Requesting the metadata instead via an object path is done in a similar way as follows:

```
curl -u admin:admin
"http://localhost:8080/alfresco/cmisbrowser/f0ebcfb4-ca9f-4991-bda8-
9465f4f11527/root/MyFolder/helloworld.txt?cmisselector=object " | jq
'.'
```

 The path used in this call does not include the root folder name (`/Company Home` in Alfresco). Requesting metadata like this works for both folders and documents.

To get content for a file when using the Browser binding is easy. Just use the same URLs as used earlier without the `cmisselector` parameter. For example, in order to get content by using path, do as follows:

```
$ curl -u admin:admin
"http://localhost:8080/alfresco/cmisbrowser/f0ebcfb4-ca9f-4991-bda8-
9465f4f11527/root/MyFolder/helloworld.txt
```

In this case, I am downloading the latest version of the `/Company Home/MyFolder/helloworld.txt` file from Alfresco.

In the upcoming sections in this chapter, we will look at how to upload, update, and delete content in the repository. Doing these kind of operations needs more than just read permissions, so it might be useful to know how to get information about the actions that the current user is allowed to perform on an object; basically, what actions the users are allowed to do with the permissions they have in a certain folder or on a certain document.

To see allowable actions, we can set `cmisselector` to `allowableActions` in the object by ID or object by path call as follows:

```
curl -u admin:admin
"http://localhost:8080/alfresco/cmisbrowser/f0ebcfb4-ca9f-4991-bda8-
9465f4f11527/root/MyFolder/helloworld.txt?cmisselector=
allowableActions" | jq '.'
```

```
{
    "canApplyACL": true,
    "canGetACL": true,
    "canGetRenditions": true,
    "canDeleteTree": false,
    "canCreateItem": false,
    "canCreateRelationship": true,
    "canCreateFolder": false,
    "canCreateDocument": false,
    "canGetChildren": false,
    "canRemovePolicy": false,
    "canGetAppliedPolicies": true,
    "canApplyPolicy": false,
    "canGetContentStream": true,
    "canRemoveObjectFromFolder": true,
    "canGetDescendants": false,
    "canGetFolderParent": false,
    "canGetObjectParents": true,
    "canGetObjectRelationships": true,
```

```
    "canGetProperties": true,
    "canGetFolderTree": false,
    "canUpdateProperties": true,
    "canDeleteObject": true,
    "canMoveObject": true,
    "canDeleteContentStream": true,
    "canCheckOut": true,
    "canCancelCheckOut": false,
    "canCheckIn": false,
    "canSetContentStream": true,
    "canGetAllVersions": true,
    "canAddObjectToFolder": true
}
```

In this case, we used the Alfresco admin user that has full access to all operations in the repository. So, if you cannot delete a folder or a document in the coming sections, check the `canDeleteObject` and `canDeleteContentStream` properties, respectively, and make sure that they are set to `true` for the user that is used to make the call.

When using the Browser binding, we can also get the repository to return an even more compact JSON response of the properties by using a feature called **succinct** representation of properties (this is unique to the Browser binding):

```
curl -u admin:admin
"http://localhost:8080/alfresco/cmisbrowser/f0ebcfb4-ca9f-4991-bda8-
9465f4f11527/root?objectId=workspace%3A%2F%2FSpacesStore%2F9113eee7-
5b14-4868-9117-b584e1293ba1%3B1.1&cmisselector=object&succinct=true"
| jq '.'
```

This returns only one object named `succinctProperties` with each property represented only by name and value:

```
{
  "succinctProperties": {
    "cm:title": [
      "Hello World!"
    ],
    "cm:description": [
      "This is the usual Hello World example"
    ],
    "cm:lastThumbnailModification": [
      "doclib:1387272471009",
      "webpreview:1391759148652"
    ],
    "ixdd:md5-digest": [
      "b7ec301cd62eb7e20912a15a7df74f5f"
    ],
```

```
    "cmis:contentStreamFileName": "helloworld.txt",
    "cmis:lastModificationDate": 1391759148144,
    "cmis:description": null,
    "cmis:baseTypeId": "cmis:document",
    "cmis:isMajorVersion": false,
    "cmis:isImmutable": false,
    "cmis:objectId": "workspace://SpacesStore/9113eee7-5b14-4868-
    9117-b584e1293ba1;1.1",
    "cmis:checkinComment": null,
    "cmis:secondaryObjectTypeIds": [
      "P:ixdd:digestable",
      "P:cm:thumbnailModification",
      "P:cm:titled",
      "P:cm:copiedfrom",
      "P:rn:renditioned",
      "P:sys:localized"
    ],
    "cmis:changeToken": null,
    "cmis:creationDate": 1391758674403,
    "cmis:isLatestVersion": true,
    "cmis:versionLabel": "1.1",
    "cmis:versionSeriesId": "workspace://SpacesStore/9113eee7-
    5b14-4868-9117-b584e1293ba1",
    "cmis:isPrivateWorkingCopy": null,
    "cmis:versionSeriesCheckedOutId": null,
    "cmis:versionSeriesCheckedOutBy": null,
    "cmis:objectTypeId": "cmis:document",
    "cmis:contentStreamLength": 20,
    "cmis:isVersionSeriesCheckedOut": false,
    "cmis:lastModifiedBy": "admin",
    "cmis:createdBy": "admin",
    "alfcmis:nodeRef": "workspace://SpacesStore/9113eee7-5b14-
    4868-9117-b584e1293ba1",
    "cmis:isLatestMajorVersion": true,
    "cmis:contentStreamId": "store://2014/2/7/7/45/dfba1362-3ce4-
    4fdd-9c78-3af4abf32592.bin",
    "cmis:name": "helloworld.txt",
    "cmis:contentStreamMimeType": "text/plain"
  }
}
```

This can be particularly useful to manage HTTP forms and also if you need to minimize the payload because of a low-bandwidth scenario. The usual properties object will not be populated in this case.

The following is a list of most of the values that can be specified for the cmisselector parameter and the responses they generate:

- object: The properties (or metadata) for the object (extra parameters such as filter, includeRelationships, includePolicyIds, renditionFilter, includeACL, includeAllowableActions, and succinct)

- properties: The same as specifying object but response is not wrapped in the properties property (extra parameters are filter and succinct)

- children: The child objects such as documents and subfolders (for example, folders and documents) of a node (extra parameters are maxItems, skipCount, filter, includeAllowableActions, includeRelationships, renditionFilter, orderBy, includePathSegment, and succinct)

- allowedActions: The actions that current user is allowed to perform with permissions currently set for him or her on the object in question

- relationships: The relationships/associations with other objects (extra parameters are includeSubRelationshipTypes, relationshipDirection, typeId, maxItems, skipCount, filter, includeAllowableActions, and succinct)

- renditions: Other formats/renditions of the object such as thumbnails and web previews (extra parameters are renditionFilter, maxItems, and skipCount)

Creating, updating, and deleting content

After you have listed content (that is, CMIS objects) in the repository, you would probably want to be able to create, update, and delete content. This is handled via the CMIS object services.

The following table gives you an overview of the available object service calls that are related to creating the content of different types:

Service call name	Short description	Long description
createDocument	Creates a document	Creates a document object of the specified type (given by the cmis:objectTypeId property) in the (optionally) specified location.
createDocumentFromSource	Copies a document	Creates a document object as a copy of the given source document in the (optionally) specified location.

Service call name	Short description	Long description
createFolder	Creates a folder	Creates a folder object of the specified type in the specified location.
createRelationship	Creates a relationship	Creates a relationship object of the specified type.
createPolicy	Creates a policy	Creates a policy object of the specified type.
createItem (CMIS 1.1)	Creates an item	Creates an item object of the specified type.

The following service operations are all about getting information about different types of objects, and we have already covered some of them such as getObject and getObjectByPath:

Service call name	Short description	Long description
getAllowableActions	Get a list of actions that can be executed	Gets the list of allowable actions for an object.
getObject	Get content information by objectId	Gets the specified information for the object such as properties, relationships, permissions, and policies.
getProperties	Get metadata for content by objectId	Gets the list of properties for the object.
getObjectByPath	Get content information by object path	Gets the specified information for the object such as properties, relationships, permissions, and policies.
getContentStream	Get/download physical content	Gets the content stream for the specified document object or gets a rendition stream for a specified rendition of a document or folder object.
getRenditions	Get associated renditions	Gets the list of associated renditions for the specified object. Only rendition attributes are returned, not the rendition stream.

The last couple of object service operations, listed as follows, have to do with updating properties and deleting content items:

Service call name	Short description	Long description
updateProperties	Update metadata	Updates the properties and secondary types of the specified object.
bulkUpdateProperties (CMIS 1.1)	Bulk updates	Updates the properties and secondary types of one or more objects.
moveObject	Move content	Moves the specified fileable object from one folder to another.
deleteObject	Delete content	Deletes the specified object.
deleteTree	Delete folder tree	Deletes the specified folder object and all of its child and descendant objects.
setContentStream	Upload content	Sets the content stream for the specified document object.
appendContentStream	Add content to existing content stream	Appends to the content stream for the specified document object.
deleteContentStream	Delete content	Deletes the content stream for the specified document object.

As you can see, there are quite a few object service calls. We will cover the most used ones in the coming sections.

Creating folders

In this section, we will go through how to create folders with the AtomPub and Browser bindings. Creating a new folder involves posting the folder data to the server. To do this, we use the `createFolder` service call.

Creating a folder with the AtomPub binding

To create a new folder with the AtomPub binding, we have to create an Atom entry with the folder data and post it to the server. The Atom entry will look similar to the following code:

```
<entry xmlns="http://www.w3.org/2005/Atom"
  xmlns:app="http://www.w3.org/2007/app"
  xmlns:cmis="http://docs.oasis-open.org/ns/cmis/core/200908/"
```

```
xmlns:cmisra="http://docs.oasis-
open.org/ns/cmis/restatom/200908/">
<title>CMIS Demo</title>
<summary>Created via CMIS AtomPub</summary>
<cmisra:object>
 <cmis:properties>
    <cmis:propertyId propertyDefinitionId="cmis:objectTypeId">
      <cmis:value>cmis:folder</cmis:value>
    </cmis:propertyId>
  </cmis:properties>
</cmisra:object>
</entry>
```

In this case, we have only included the minimum number of properties necessary to create a folder, the type of the folder, and its name. Note that the `<atom:summary>` element will be set as `cmis:description` and the `<atom:title>` element, when it is specified, will override the `cmis:name` property value.

Save the following code in a file named, for example, `folder.atom.xml` and then look up the folder collection in the service document. In this case, we will create the folder under the root folder (that is, under /Company Home in Alfresco):

```
<app:collection
    href="http://localhost:8080/alfresco/cmisatom/f0ebcfb4-ca9f-
4991-bda8-9465f4f11527/children?id=
workspace%3A%2F%2FSpacesStore%2Fa5c45ceb-2603-491f-b2c9-
6ff7d6579483">
    <cmisra:collectionType>root</cmisra:collectionType>
    <atom:title type="text">Root Collection</atom:title>
    <app:accept>application/atom+xml;type=entry</app:accept>
    <app:accept>application/cmisatom+xml</app:accept>
</app:collection>
```

Execute the following `curl` command to post the XML file to the root collection and to have Alfresco create the folder under /Company Home:

```
$ curl -v -u admin:admin -d @folder.atom.xml -H "Content-
Type:application/atom+xml;type=entry"
"http://localhost:8080/alfresco/cmisatom/f0ebcfb4-ca9f-4991-bda8-
9465f4f11527/children?id=workspace%3A%2F%2FSpacesStore%2Fa5c45ceb-
2603-491f-b2c9-6ff7d6579483"
```

The `-d` cURL switch is used to specify data to POST, and the `-H` switch is used to add HTTP request headers, such as in this case, when we need to tell the server that we are POSTing an Atom entry by specifying the MIME type. If this call is successful, it will return an Atom entry with information about the newly created folder, such as its object ID (Alfresco node reference in the Alfresco world).

Creating a folder with the Browser binding

The Browser binding is specifically created to make it easy to work with CMIS from an HTML page in a browser. Creating a new folder with the Browser binding means we have to POST form data to the server. Create a file named `createFolder.html` with the following HTML Form:

```
<html>
<body>
<form
  name="createFolderForm"
  action="http://localhost:8080/alfresco/cmisbrowser/f0ebcfb4-
  ca9f-4991-bda8-9465f4f11527/root"
  method="post">
  <input name="cmisaction" type="hidden" value="createFolder" />
  <input name="propertyId[0]" type="hidden" value="cmis:name" />
  Folder name: <input name="propertyValue[0]" type="text"
  value="CMIS Demo Browser Binding" />
  <input name="propertyId[1]" type="hidden"
  value="cmis:objectTypeId" />
  <input name="propertyValue[1]" type="hidden"
  value="cmis:folder"></td>
  <input type="submit" value="Create Folder" />
</form>
</body>
</html>
```

Here, we are creating a folder named CMIS Demo Browser Binding under the root folder in the repository, which would be under /Company Home in Alfresco. Any HTML form that is used to POST CMIS content must include a control named `cmisaction`, which indicates the CMIS operation to be performed.

The way to pass properties is to create two input fields for each property as previously mentioned, one carrying the name of the property (that is, `propertyId[#]`) and the other the value (that is, `propertyValue[#]`). If you want to create the folder under a different parent folder than /Company Home, just add the subfolder name after /root, for example, .../root/Data%20Dictionary.

Not sure why the CMIS standard uses two name-value pairs to persist a single name-value property. It probably has to do with properties that can be multivalued.

You could also have POSTed the following data via `curl` in a similar way to what you did for the AtomPub binding example. Create a file named `CreateFolderPostData.txt` with the following content:

```
cmisaction=createFolder&propertyId%5B0%5D=cmis%3Aname&propertyValu
e%5B0%5D=CMIS+Demo+Browser+Binding2&propertyId%5B1%5D=cmis%3Aobjec
tTypeId&propertyValue%5B1%5D=cmis%3Afolder
```

Then, POST it to the server as follows:

```
$ curl -v -u admin:admin -d @CreateFolderPostData.txt -H
"Content-Type:text/plain"
"http://localhost:8080/alfresco/cmisbrowser/f0ebcfb4-ca9f-4991-bda8-
9465f4f11527/root"
```

Creating documents

In this section, we will go through how to create documents with the AtomPub and Browser bindings. Creating a new document involves POSTing the document metadata and the physical content bytes to the server. For this, we use the `createDocument` service call.

A document can have an associated content stream. It represents the bytes that make up the physical file. The maximum permissible file size is specific to the repository implementation. Alfresco stores the physical file in the filesystem; so, in the case of Alfresco, the maximum length is dependent on the OS. Each content stream has a MIME media type and a number of attributes. These are represented as properties on the document object..

The following are some of the content stream properties:

Property	Description	Datatype
`cmis:contentStreamLength`	The size of the document file in bytes.	`Integer`
`cmis:contentStreamMimeType`	The MIME type for the document.	`String`
`cmis:contentStreamId`	This is the identifier for accessing the content stream, representing the document. For Alfresco, this ID would look like this:	`ID`
	`store://2012/12/1/12/47/9b7d35e5-35bc-45cc-a3b9-3f170611563e.bin`.	
	And, this points to where the content file is located under `<alfrescoinstall>/alf_data/contentstore`.	

Property	Description	Datatype
cmis: contentStreamFileName	This is the filename that the content stream will be represented by during, for example, a download. In the case of Alfresco, this is the same as the cmis:name property.	String

Creating a document with the AtomPub binding

To create a new document with the AtomPub binding, we have to first create an Atom entry with the document metadata and content and post it to the server. The Atom entry will look something like the following:

```
<entry xmlns="http://www.w3.org/2005/Atom"
  xmlns:app="http://www.w3.org/2007/app"
  xmlns:cmis="http://docs.oasis-open.org/ns/cmis/core/200908/"
  xmlns:cmisra=
  "http://docs.oasis-open.org/ns/cmis/restatom/200908/">
  <title>simple.txt</title>
  <summary>A simple text file</summary>
  <cmisra:object>
    <cmis:properties>
      <cmis:propertyId propertyDefinitionId="cmis:objectTypeId">
        <cmis:value>cmis:document</cmis:value>
      </cmis:propertyId>
    </cmis:properties>
  </cmisra:object>
</entry>
```

In this case, we have only included the minimum number of properties necessary to create a document, the type of the document, and its title/name. Also note that the `<atom:summary>` element will be set as cmis:description, and the `<atom:title>` element will be set as the cmis:name property value. The cmis:objectTypeId property is currently set to the base type cmis:document. If you wanted to set it to a custom subtype defined in Alfresco, you would prefix the type with D:, for example, `<cmis:value>D:myc:itDocument</cmis:value>`.

Save the preceding Atom entry in a file named, for example, document.atom.xml and then look up the folder collection in the service document. In this case, we will create the document under the root folder (that is, under /Company Home in Alfresco).

Execute the following `curl` command to post the XML file to the root collection and to have Alfresco create the document under /Company Home:

```
$ curl -v -u admin:admin -d @document.atom.xml -H "Content-
Type:application/atom+xml;type=entry"
"http://localhost:8080/alfresco/cmisatom/f0ebcfb4-ca9f-4991-bda8-
9465f4f11527/children?id=workspace%3A%2F%2FSpacesStore%2Fa5c45ceb-
2603-491f-b2c9-6ff7d6579483"
```

If this call is successful, it will return an Atom entry with information about the newly created document node, such as its object ID (Alfresco node reference in the Alfresco world). At this point, the document object is only made up of metadata; there is no physical content. To add physical content, we have used PUT to upload a file and to associate it with the metadata.

We can use the `edit-media` link for this as it operates on the media resource, which represents the contents of the document. The `edit-media` URL can be found in the returned Atom entry, as follows, from when we created the document object:

```
<atom:link rel="edit-media"
href="http://localhost:8080/alfresco/cmisatom/f0ebcfb4-ca9f-4991-bda8-
9465f4f11527/content?id
=workspace%3A%2F%2FSpacesStore%2Ff3b354b4-5f3e-47f5-a39e-
2844496c3862%3B1.0"
type=""/>
```

Use the following link to execute an HTTP PUT method and upload the physical content for the some.txt file:

```
curl -v -u admin:admin -T some.txt
"http://localhost:8080/alfresco/cmisatom/f0ebcfb4-ca9f-4991-bda8-
9465f4f11527/content?id=workspace%3A%2F%2FSpacesStore%2Ff3b354b4-
5f3e-47f5-a39e-2844496c3862"
```

You might be wondering if you really need to make two calls to create a document. There is actually another way that requires only one operation to do it. However, you have to Base64-encode the file before you can upload it as part of the Atom feed. To do this in Linux, Mac, or Windows (via CygWin), you can use the OpenSSL library as follows:

```
$ openssl base64 -in some.txt -out some.txt.base64
```

Then, take the contents of the some.txt.base64 file and add it to the document. atom.xml file that we created earlier. The encoded content is wrapped by the cmisra:base64 element, which is contained in the cmisra:content element. The content element also includes a cmisra:mediatype element that specifies the content's MIME type. The Atom entry should now look as follows:

```
<entry xmlns="http://www.w3.org/2005/Atom"
  xmlns:app="http://www.w3.org/2007/app"
  xmlns:cmis="http://docs.oasis-open.org/ns/cmis/core/200908/"
  xmlns:cmisra="http://docs.oasis-
  open.org/ns/cmis/restatom/200908/">
  <title>simple.txt</title>
  <summary>A simple text file</summary>
  <cmisra:content>
        <cmisra:mediatype>text/plain</cmisra:mediatype>
        <cmisra:base64>VGhpcyBpcyBzb211IHR1eHQhCg==</cmisra:base64>
    </cmisra:content>
  <cmisra:object>
    <cmis:properties>
      <cmis:propertyId propertyDefinitionId="cmis:objectTypeId">
        <cmis:value>cmis:document</cmis:value>
      </cmis:propertyId>
    </cmis:properties>
  </cmisra:object>
</entry>
```

Now we can run `curl` again and POST the Atom entry to the server (remember to remove the `simple.txt` file first if it exists in the repository):

```
$ curl -v -u admin:admin -d @document.atom.xml -H "Content-
Type:application/atom+xml;type=entry"
"http://localhost:8080/alfresco/cmisatom/f0ebcfb4-ca9f-4991-bda8-
9465f4f11527/children?id=workspace%3A%2F%2FSpacesStore%2Fa5c45ceb-
2603-491f-b2c9-6ff7d6579483"
```

Creating a document with the Browser binding

Creating a new document with the Browser binding means that we have to POST form data, including both the metadata and the content for the document, to the server. Create a file named `createDocument.html` with the following HTML Form:

```
<html>
<body>
<form
  name="createDocumentForm"
  action="http://localhost:8080/alfresco/cmisbrowser/f0ebcfb4-
  ca9f-4991-bda8-9465f4f11527/root"
  method="post"
  enctype="multipart/form-data">
  <input name="cmisaction" type="hidden" value="createDocument" />
  <input name="propertyId[0]" type="hidden" value="cmis:name" />
  File name: <input name="propertyValue[0]" type="text"
  value="Simple (from Browser binding).txt" />
```

```
   File: <input name="content" type="file">
   <input name="propertyId[1]" type="hidden"
   value="cmis:objectTypeId" />
   <input name="propertyValue[1]" type="hidden"
   value="cmis:document" />
   <input type="submit" value="Create Document" />
</form>
</body>
</html>
```

Here, we are creating a document named `simple(from Browser binding).txt` under the root folder in the repository, which would be under `/Company Home` in Alfresco. We set the `cmisaction` parameter to `createDocument` as we want to perform this action with this HTML Form.

To attach content to the POST, a `file` select input control with the name `content` should be used. It should not have any value set as the control will be a normal file picker and you can select the file from any local disk location. The mandatory `cmis:name` and `cmis:objectTypeId` properties are also set. If you want to set the object type to something other than the `cmis:document` base type, then you have to use the prefix `D:` for custom Alfresco types, such as `D:myc:itDocument`. If you want to create the document under a different parent folder than `/Company Home`, then just add the subfolder name after `/root`, for example, `.../root/Data%20Dictionary`.

Updating folders and documents

Updating the properties, or metadata if you want, is done in the same way for folders and documents. We will have a look at how to do this for documents. Let's set a property value on the files that we just created. Instead of a POST, which is used to create a new resource, we will perform an HTTP PUT method, which is used to update an existing object. For this, we use the `updateProperties` service call from the object services.

The following capability from the repository information is relevant to updating a document's content stream:

Capability	Description	Valid options
`capabilityContent StreamUpdatability`	Indicates the support a repository has for updating a document's content stream (basically, the physical content for the document).	• none: The content stream may never be updated • anytime: The content stream may be updated any time • pwconly: The content stream may be updated only when checked out to a **Private Working Copy (PWC)**

Updating a document with the AtomPub binding

To update a document, or a folder for that matter, with the AtomPub binding, we have to first create an Atom entry with the document metadata, leave out the content stream, and POST it to the server. The Atom entry will look something like the following:

```
<entry xmlns="http://www.w3.org/2005/Atom"
  xmlns:app="http://www.w3.org/2007/app"
  xmlns:cmis="http://docs.oasis-open.org/ns/cmis/core/200908/"
  xmlns:cmisra="http://docs.oasis-
  open.org/ns/cmis/restatom/200908/">
  <title>simple.txt</title>
  <cmisra:object>
  <cmis:properties>
    <cmis:propertyString propertyDefinitionId="cmis:description">
      <cmis:value>A new description for this doc</cmis:value>
    </cmis:propertyString>
  </cmis:properties>
  </cmisra:object>
</entry>
```

In this case, we are updating the description of the document. Save the preceding Atom entry in a file named, for example, `document-update.atom.xml` and then look up the object ID (that is, node reference) that was returned from the earlier `createDocument` call we made.

Execute the following `curl` command to update the document:

```
$ curl -X PUT -v -u admin:admin -d @document-update.atom.xml -H
"Content-Type:application/atom+xml;type=entry"
"http://localhost:8080/alfresco/cmisatom/f0ebcfb4-ca9f-4991-bda8-
9465f4f11527?id=workspace%3A%2F%2FSpacesStore%2Fd60c6243-e96a-401b-
9537-b4917c0eb8ba"
```

Updating a document with the Browser binding

Updating a document or folder with the Browser binding means that we have to POST form data, including metadata but not content, for the document to the server. Create a file named `updateDocument.html` with the following HTML form:

```
<html>
<body>
<form
  name="updateDocumentForm"
  action="http://localhost:8080/alfresco/cmisbrowser/f0ebcfb4-
  ca9f-4991-bda8-9465f4f11527/root?objectId=
```

```
workspace%3A%2F%2FSpacesStore%2Ff574db8e-c9ac-4e5e-81b6-
c9b6bc2b9cba"
  method="post"
  enctype="multipart/form-data">
  <input name="cmisaction" type="hidden" value="update" />
  <input name="propertyId[0]" type="hidden"
  value="cmis:description" />
  Description: <input name="propertyValue[0]" type="text"
  value="A new description (from Browser binding)" />
  <input type="submit" value="Update Document" />
</form>
</body>
</html>
```

Here we are updating the description of the document. We set the cmisaction
parameter to update as that is the action that we want to perform with this HTML
form. A POST method is used to update the specified properties.

Deleting a folder or a document

Folders and documents are deleted by using the deleteObject service call that is
part of the object service. If you want to delete all the content in a folder recursively,
then the deleteTree service call should be used.

There is an extra parameter named allVersions, which is true by default and
controls whether all document versions should be deleted. If set to false, only then
the specified document object is deleted. The repository will ignore this value if
delete is invoked on a non-document object (that is, non-versionable object).

Deleting a folder or document with the AtomPub binding

To delete a document, or folder for that matter, with the AtomPub binding, we have
to perform an HTTP DELETE method on the entry.

Execute the following curl command to delete the simple.txt document we
created earlier:

```
$ curl -X DELETE -v -u admin:admin  "http://localhost:8080/alfresco/
cmisatom/f0ebcfb4-ca9f-4991-bda8-9465f4f11527/entry?id=workspace%3A%2F%2F
SpacesStore%2Fd60c6243-e96a-401b-9537-b4917c0eb8ba"
```

You will see an output similar to the following (the output is shown for completeness):

```
* About to connect() to localhost port 8080 (#0)

*    Trying 127.0.0.1... connected

* Server auth using Basic with user 'admin'

> DELETE /alfresco/cmisatom/f0ebcfb4-ca9f-4991-bda8-
9465f4f11527/entry?id=workspace%3A%2F%2FSpacesStore%2Fd60c6243-e96a-
401b-9537-b4917c0eb8ba HTTP/1.1

> Authorization: Basic YWRtaW46YWRtaW4=

> User-Agent: curl/7.22.0 (x86_64-pc-linux-gnu) libcurl/7.22.0
OpenSSL/1.0.1 zlib/1.2.3.4 libidn/1.23 librtmp/2.3

> Host: localhost:8080

> Accept: */*

>

< HTTP/1.1 204 No Content
```

After a successful deletion of the file (or any other object), an HTTP 204 is returned. If you just want to delete any object, then find out the node reference first and then change the preceding id parameter. Remember that you need appropriate permissions to delete a file, and if it is done with the Alfresco admin user as in this case, it will always work no matter where the file is located in the repository.

Deleting a folder or document with the Browser binding

Deleting a document or folder with the Browser binding means that we have to POST with the cmisaction parameter set to delete and have the object ID in the URL. Create a file named deleteDocument.html with the following HTML Form, which will delete the simple (from Browser binding).txt document we created earlier:

```html
<html>
<body>
<form
  name="deleteDocumentForm"
  action="http://localhost:8080/alfresco/cmisbrowser/f0ebcfb4-
  ca9f-4991-bda8-9465f4f11527/root?objectId=
  workspace://SpacesStore/f574db8e-c9ac-4e5e-81b6-c9b6bc2b9cba"
  method="post"
  enctype="multipart/form-data">
  <input name="cmisaction" type="hidden" value="delete" />
  <input type="submit" value="Delete Document" />
</form>
</body>
</html>
```

Summary

In this chapter, we have gone through most of the basic functionalities that are likely to be used on a day-to-day basis and learned how to use them with both the AtomPub protocol and the Browser binding protocol. We have seen how we can list the contents of a folder and navigate to the subfolders. The Browser binding has shown us that it is quite easy to work with CMIS via this binding as you can use HTML forms for almost all operations and it is easy to integrate with the UI this way.

In this chapter, we also looked into how to download the content types that the repository supports, which is important as you are likely to set custom types when uploading new content. We also covered how to create, read, update, and delete documents and folders for a specific domain. And finally, we went through how to download a document.

In the next chapter, we will look into more features supported by CMIS such as version management, access control, and searching for content.

3
Advanced CMIS Operations

This chapter explores some of the more advanced features of CMIS such as version management and access control lists. We will continue to work with both the AtomPub protocol and the Browser binding protocol just like in the previous chapter.

In this chapter, we will look at the following:

- Version management with check in and check out
- Updating the physical content of a document during check in
- Permission management with access control lists
- Managing relationships between objects
- Searching

It is highly recommended that you read the previous chapter first, as it takes you through all the basic operations and explains how to set up a server, authenticate it, and what tools to use when calling a CMIS server. Note that the tools mentioned are primarily for experimenting and familiarization with the mechanics of CMIS rather than for the actual integration work.

Version management with check out and check in

Sometimes, when you are working with documents in a team, it is useful to be able to check out and lock a document so that other people cannot update it at the same time as you. This can be accomplished by using the checkOut service call from the **versioning** services. When you have finished editing the so-called working copy, it can be checked in with the checkIn service call, which creates a new version and updates the version label.

The physical content of a document might not be updateable in the particular repository that you are using. To find out if an object's content is updateable, check the value of the `capabilityContentStreamUpdatability` property. This property is returned in the `getRepositoryInfo` service call in the capabilities sections.

Valid values for this property are the following:

- `none`: The content may never be updated
- `anytime`: The content may be updated anytime
- `pwconly`: The content may be updated only when checked out to a **Private Working Copy (PWC)**

For my Alfresco installation, this property is set to `anytime` so I am able to update content for a document in the repository at any time, even if it is not checked out. If the value was `pwconly`, I would be required to check out the document, creating a PWC before updating it.

Checking out a document turns on versioning. (In Alfresco, this means that the `cm:versionable` aspect is applied automatically if it is missing.) The following versioning capabilities are related:

Capability	Description	Valid options
`capabilityPWCUpdatable`	This is the ability of an application to update the PWC of a checked-out document.	[true | false]
`capabilityPWCSearchable`	This is the ability of the repository to include the PWC of checked-out documents in query search scope; otherwise, PWCs are not searchable.	[true | false]
`capabilityAllVersionsSearchable`	This is the ability of the repository to include all the versions of the document. If `false`, either the latest or the latest major version will be searchable.	[true | false]

If we look at the versioning properties, the following are a couple of concepts that we need to know about:

- **Version series**: A version series in CMIS is the same thing as the version history for a document. The position of a document in a version series is determined by its version label.

- **Latest version**: The document that has the most recent *last modification date* (cmis:lastModificationDate) is called the latest version of that document in a version series.

- **Major version**: This is an optional property that can be designated to a document in a version series. The CMIS standard does not define any semantic differences between the major versions and minor versions. In Alfresco, we can use major and minor versions for documents such as 2.1.

The following are the main properties related to versioning:

Property	Description	Data type
cmis:isLatestVersion	This would be set to true if this document item is the latest version (such as 3.1) in the version series, or this will be set to false if we are looking at a previous version in the version series/version history.	Boolean
cmis:isLatestMajorVersion	This would be set to true if this document item is the latest major version (such as 3.0), or this would be set to false if we are looking at a previous major version in the version series/version history.	Boolean
cmis:versionSeriesId	A unique identifier that gives access to the version series/version history. In Alfresco, this would be a node reference pointing to the version history node for this document.	ID
cmis:versionLabel	The version label, such as 1.1, for this document. Denotes the order of this document in the version series.	String

Remember to replace the f0ebcfb4-ca9f-4991-bda8-9465f4f11527 repository ID with one that matches your server in the rest of this chapter.

Version management with the AtomPub binding

This section shows you how to check out a document with the AtomPub binding, update its physical content, and finally, how to check in the updated document.

Checking out a document with the AtomPub binding

Checking out a file with the AtomPub binding involves POSTing the document's `Object Id` (the Alfresco node reference in the Alfresco world) in an Atom feed to the `checkedout` collection URL, which you can find in the Service Document, looking something like the following:

```
<app:collection
  href="http://localhost:8080/alfresco/cmisatom/f0ebcfb4-ca9f-
    4991-bda8-9465f4f11527/checkedout">
  <cmisra:collectionType>checkedout</cmisra:collectionType>
  <atom:title type="text">Checked Out Collection</atom:title>
  <app:accept>application/cmisatom+xml</app:accept>
</app:collection>
```

The `Object Id` property can be found in a folder listing response, object by path response, or an object navigation response. Make sure the object is of type `cmis:document` as you cannot check out anything else; see the `cmis:baseTypeId` property. The following is how the object ID looks:

```
<cmis:propertyId queryName="cmis:objectId" displayName="Object Id"
  localName="objectId" propertyDefinitionId="cmis:objectId">
  <cmis:value>workspace://SpacesStore/a5c45ceb-2603-491f-b2c9-
  6ff7d6579483</cmis:value>
</cmis:propertyId>
```

To have something to check out, we are going to create a file named `simple.txt` with some random text in it. (We created and deleted a file with this name in the previous chapter; if you never deleted it, then you are ready to go.) Log in to Alfresco with the `http://localhost:8080/share` URL using the `admin` username and the password given during installation. Then create the file and make a note of the `Object Id`. The `Object Id` (that is, the node reference) can be found in the **Document Details** page for the file in Alfresco Share (the main Alfresco user interface). Then, put together the checked-out Atom entry and put it in a file named, for example, `checkout.atom.xml` as follows:

```
<?xml version="1.0" encoding="utf-8"?>
<entry xmlns="http://www.w3.org/2005/Atom"
  xmlns:cmisra="http://docs.oasis-
    open.org/ns/cmis/restatom/200908/"
  xmlns:cmis="http://docs.oasis-open.org/ns/cmis/core/200908/">
  <cmisra:object>
    <cmis:properties>
      <cmis:propertyId propertyDefinitionId="cmis:objectId">
        <cmis:value>workspace://SpacesStore/d60c6243-e96a-401b-
          9537-b4917c0eb8ba</cmis:value>
      </cmis:propertyId>
```

```
      </cmis:properties>
    </cmisra:object>
  </entry>
```

Finally, we POST this check-out Atom entry to the checked-out collection by executing the following cURL command:

```
$ curl -v -u admin:admin -d @checkout.atom.xml -H "Content-
Type:application/atom+xml;type=entry" "http://localhost:8080/alfresco/
cmisatom/f0ebcfb4-ca9f-4991-bda8-9465f4f11527/checkedout"
```

This locks the simple.txt document in the repository and creates a PWC that can be edited (in Alfresco, you can log in as the admin and navigate to the working copy via the **Node Browser**).

The working copy's Object Id is returned by the check-out call.

Cancelling the check out with the AtomPub binding

If you have changed your mind and want to cancel the check out that was just done, then you can just delete the PWC that was created from the check out. This is done with an HTTP DELETE as follows:

```
$ curl -X DELETE -v -u admin:admin  "http://localhost:8080/alfresco/
cmisatom/f0ebcfb4-ca9f-4991-bda8-9465f4f11527/entry?id=workspace%3A%2F%2F
SpacesStore%2Fbb815533-1929-419f-86c5-c095b6538cf9"
```

This will delete the simple (Working Copy).txt file. The URL's id parameter is a node reference for the PWC; if you cannot find this node reference, you can log in to Alfresco as an administrator and locate the PWC via the **Node Browser**.

Updating the physical contents of the checked-out document with the AtomPub binding

What you would want to do now is to probably update the checked-out document. Doing this is very similar to creating a new document; just use PUT instead of POST.

The Atom entry for an update contains the updated Base64 content that is coded as follows (see *Chapter 2*, *Basic CMIS Operations*, for how to do Base64 encoding of text):

```
<entry xmlns="http://www.w3.org/2005/Atom"
  xmlns:app="http://www.w3.org/2007/app"
  xmlns:cmis="http://docs.oasis-open.org/ns/cmis/core/200908/"
  xmlns:cmisra="http://docs.oasis-
  open.org/ns/cmis/restatom/200908/">
  <title>simple (Working Copy).txt</title>
  <cmisra:content>
```

```
        <cmisra:mediatype>text/plain</cmisra:mediatype>
          <cmisra:base64>VGhpcyBpcasdadsyBzb2llIadsasdasdsHRleHQhCg
            ==</cmisra:base64>
      </cmisra:content>
      <cmisra:object>
        <cmis:properties>
          <cmis:propertyString propertyDefinitionId="cmis:name">
            <cmis:value>simple (Working Copy).txt</cmis:value>
          </cmis:propertyString>
        </cmis:properties>
      </cmisra:object>
    </entry>
```

Note that you have to use the working copy's filename as the title, and the name property has to be specified too. Save this Atom entry in a file named something similar to `document-content-update.atom.xml` and PUT it to the server via the working copy's URL that was in the response Atom entry from the check out.

Execute the following cURL command:

```
$ curl -X PUT -u admin:admin -d @document-content-update.atom.xml -H
"Content-Type: application/atom+xml;type=entry" "http://localhost:8080/
alfresco/cmisatom/f0ebcfb4-ca9f-4991-bda8-9465f4f11527/entry?id=workspace
%3A%2F%2FSpacesStore%2Fbb815533-1929-419f-86c5-c095b6538cf9"
```

If this did not work, make sure that the `capabilityPWCUpdatable` property is `true`. If not, then the PWC is not updateable and you will have to resort to updating the document during the check in instead.

If you prefer to do the update without having to Base64 encode the content then use the edit-media link for the PWC instead and PUT the file directly into this URL, as demonstrated in *Chapter 2, Basic CMIS Operations*.

Checking in a document with the AtomPub binding

When we have finished updating the file, it can be checked-in by POSTing the following empty Atom entry to the server:

```
<?xml version="1.0" encoding="utf-8"?>
<entry xmlns="http://www.w3.org/2005/Atom"/>
```

When calling the server, we use the Atom entry URL and a URL parameter called `checkin` that is set to `true`. Put the above Atom entry in a file called `empty.atom.xml`, and use the following cURL command:

```
$ curl -X PUT -v -u admin:admin -d @empty.atom.xml -H "Content-
Type: application/atom+xml;type=entry" "http://localhost:8080/
alfresco/cmisatom/f0ebcfb4-ca9f-4991-bda8-9465f4f11527/entry
?id=workspace%3A%2F%2FSpacesStore%2Fbb815533-1929-419f-86c5-
c095b6538cf9&checkin=true&checkinComment=some%20updates"
```

This unlocks the file and removes the working copy. It's also possible to update the content, and any properties, at the same time as when the check in is being done. Just add the content and properties to the empty Atom entry previously discussed when doing the check in. Note that this is the only way to update the content if the optional `capabilityPWCUpdatable` property is not supported.

Version management with the Browser binding

This section shows you how to check out a document with the Browser binding, update its physical content, and finally, how to check in the updated document.

Checking out a document with the Browser binding

Checking out a file with the Browser binding involves an HTTP form submission with the `cmisaction` parameter set to `checkout`.

Look up the object URL for the `Simple (from Browser binding).txt` document that we created in the last chapter (or log in to Alfresco and look up the details page for the file, and grab the node reference from there); we will use it to check out the document. Note that you might have to recreate this document if you followed *Chapter 2, Basic CMIS Operations*, and deleted it.

Now, create an HTML file named `checkoutDocument.html` with the following content:

```html
<html>
<body>
<form
  name="checkoutDocumentForm"
  action="http://localhost:8080/alfresco/cmisbrowser/f0ebcfb4
    -ca9f-4991-bda8-
    9465f4f11527/root?objectId=workspace%3A%2F%2FSpacesStore%
    2Ff574db8e-c9ac-4e5e-81b6-c9b6bc2b9cba"
  method="post"
  enctype="multipart/form-data">
  <input name="cmisaction" type="hidden" value="checkout" />
  <input type="submit" value="Check-out Document" />
</form>
</body>
</html>
```

This locks the document in the repository and creates a PWC that can be edited. (In Alfresco, you can log in as the administrator and navigate to the Working Copy via the **Node Browser**.)

The working copy's Object Id is returned by the check-out call.

Cancelling the check out with the Browser binding

If you have changed your mind and want to cancel the check out that was just done, then you can delete the PWC that was created from the check out. With the Browser binding, this means that we have to POST the cmisaction parameter set to delete and have the Object Id for the PWC in the URL.

Create a file named cancelCheckOutDocument.html with the following HTML form, which will delete the Simple (from Browser binding) (Working Copy). txt document:

```
<html>
<body>
<form
  name="cancelCheckOutDocumentForm"
  action="http://localhost:8080/alfresco/cmisbrowser/f0ebcfb4-
    ca9f-4991-bda8-
    9465f4f11527/root?objectId=workspace%3A%2F%2FSpacesStore%
    2F25cea9bf-d355-426d-b490-21c0a8e561b8"
  method="post"
  enctype="multipart/form-data">
  <input name="cmisaction" type="hidden" value="delete" />
  <input type="submit" value="Cancel Check-out" />
</form>
</body>
</html>
```

Updating the physical content of the checked-out document with the Browser binding

What you would want to do now is to probably update the checked-out document. Doing this is very similar to creating a new document; just set the cmisaction parameter to update.

The HTTP form looks as follows; put it in a file called updateDocumentContent. html:

```
<html>
<body>
<form
```

```
  name="updateDocumentForm"
    action="http://localhost:8080/alfresco/cmisbrowser/f0ebcfb4-
      ca9f-4991-bda8-
      9465f4f11527/root?objectId=workspace%3A%2F%2FSpacesStore%
      2F25cea9bf-d355-426d-b490-21c0a8e561b8"
  method="post"
  enctype="multipart/form-data">
  <input name="cmisaction" type="hidden" value="update" />
  Simple (from Browser binding).txt<br/>
  Update with file: <input name="content" type="file"><br/>
  <input name="propertyId[0]" type="hidden" value="cmis:name" />
  <input name="propertyValue[0]" type="hidden" value="Simple (from
    Browser binding) (Working Copy).txt" />
  <input type="submit" value="Update Document Content" />
</form>
</body>
</html>
```

Note that the action URL is referencing the PWC URL, which is for the `Simple`
`(from Browser binding)` `(Working Copy).txt` document. You have to use the
PWC filename as `cmis:name`, or the update will not work, and the properties section
would need to be set. The dialog will present you with a file picker, so any local file
can be used to update the PWC.

Checking in a document with the Browser binding

When we have finished updating the file, it can be checked-in by POSTing an HTML
form with `cmisaction` set to `checkin` and the `action` URL set to the PWC object
URL. A check-in comment can also be specified via a `checkinComment` control.

The following is the HTML form:

```
<html>
<body>
<form
  name="checkinDocumentForm"
  action="http://localhost:8080/alfresco/cmisbrowser/f0ebcfb4-
    ca9f-4991-bda8-
    9465f4f11527/root?objectId=workspace%3A%2F%2FSpacesStore%
    2F25cea9bf-d355-426d-b490-21c0a8e561b8"
  method="post"
  enctype="multipart/form-data">
  <input name="cmisaction" type="hidden" value="checkin" />
  <input name="checkinComment" value="some comment" />
  Simple (from Browser binding) (Working Copy).txt<br/>
  <input type="submit" value="Check-in Document" />
</form>
</body>
</html>
```

This unlocks the file and removes the working copy. It's also possible to update the content, and any properties, at the same time as when the check in is being done. Just add the contents and properties to the previously discussed form when doing the check in, as was previously demonstrated when updating content for the PWC.

Managing permissions for documents and folders

An **access control list** (**ACL**) is used to manage permissions for folders and documents. The ACL services with the getACL and applyACL calls are used to get and set permissions.

Access control list capabilities

A repository does not have to support the management of ACLs at all. To find out if it does, look at the following properties, as they explain what support is available. These properties are returned by the getRepositoryInfo service call:

Capability	Description	Valid options
capabilityACL	This indicates the level of support for the ACLs by the repository.	• none: The repository does not support ACL services. • discover: The repository supports the discovery of ACLs (getACL and other services). • manage: The repository supports the discovery of the ACLs and applying ACLs (getACL and applyACL services).
propagation	This specifies how a non-direct **access control entry** (**ACE**) can be handled by the repository.	• objectonly: This indicates that the repository is able to apply ACEs to an object without changing the ACLs of other objects. • propagate: This indicates that the ACEs might be inherited by other objects. propagate includes the support for objectonly. • repositorydetermined: This indicates that the repository has its own mechanism of computing how changing an ACL for an object influences the non-direct ACEs of other objects.

The Alfresco 4.2 server that I am using has the `capabilityACL` property set to `manage`; so, it should work to both read and write permissions to the repository.

Access control concepts

An ACL is a list of zero or more ACEs. If no ACL is assigned to the object, no permission is granted (unless specified differently by a `cmis:policy` applied to the object).

An ACE holds the following:

- A `principal` that represents a user management object, for example, a user, group, or role. It holds one string with `principalId`, such as, for example, `martin`.

- One or more strings with the names of `permissions`, such as `cmis:write`.

- A Boolean flag, `direct`, which indicates that the ACE is directly assigned to the object when `true`, and indicates that the ACE is somehow derived or inherited when `false`.

The following is an example of an ACE used for the AtomPub binding:

```
<ns2:acl xmlns="http://docs.oasis-
  open.org/ns/cmis/messaging/200908/"
  xmlns:ns2="http://docs.oasis-open.org/ns/cmis/core/200908/"
  xmlns:ns3="http://docs.oasis-open.org/ns/cmis/restatom/200908/">
  <ns2:permission>
    <ns2:principal>
      <ns2:principalId>GROUP_EVERYONE</ns2:principalId>
    </ns2:principal>
    <ns2:permission>cmis:read</ns2:permission>
    <ns2:direct>false</ns2:direct>
  </ns2:permission>
</ns2:acl>
```

In this case it tells us that the Alfresco group called EVERYONE has read access to the object that the access control list is associated with. The `direct` flag is `false` so this means that these permissions have been inherited from the parent folder.

Supported permissions

A repository can support either a base set of CMIS defined permissions and/or its own set of repository specific permissions. The supportedPermissions property tells us whether the repository supports both the CMIS permissions and its own custom permissions. It is returned by the getRepositoryInfo service called together with the propagation property, as shown in the following table:

Capability	Description	Valid options
supportedPermissions	This indicates if the repository supports both the CMIS permissions and its own custom permissions.	• basic: This indicates that the CMIS basic permissions are supported. • repository: This indicates that repository-specific permissions are supported. • both: This indicates that both CMIS basic permissions and repository-specific permissions are supported.
propagation	This specifies how non-direct ACEs can be handled by the repository.	• objectonly: This indicates that the repository is able to apply ACEs to an object without changing the ACLs of other objects. • propagate: This indicates that the ACEs might be inherited by other objects. propagate includes the support for objectonly. • repositorydetermined: This indicates that the repository has its own mechanism of computing how changing an ACL for an object will influence the non-direct ACEs of other objects.

The Alfresco 4.2 version I am running has the supportedPermissions property set to both, so it should be possible to manage both CMIS permissions and Alfresco-specific permissions. Also, the propagation property is set to propagate, indicating that the access control entries (that is, permissions) might be inherited by other objects.

Looking at the result from the `getRepositoryInfo` service call, I can see that the Alfresco-specific permissions are returned as shown in the following example:

```
<cmis:aclCapability>
...
  <cmis:permissions>
    <cmis:permission>
    {http://www.alfresco.org/model/content/1.0}
      cmobject.Coordinator</cmis:permission>
    <cmis:description>
    {http://www.alfresco.org/model/content/1.0}
        cmobject.Coordinator</cmis:description>
  </cmis:permissions>
```

The `getACL` service allows the caller to specify that the result should be expressed using only the CMIS-defined permissions. The `applyACL` service permits either CMIS permissions or repository-specific permissions, or a combination of both to be used.

The following are the three basic permissions predefined by CMIS:

- `cmis:read`: This means that you have the permission to read the properties and content of an object.

- `cmis:write`: This means that you have the permission to write the properties and content of an object. It may also include the `cmis:read` permission.

- `cmis:all`: This means that you have all the permissions of a repository. It should also include all other basic CMIS permissions.

How these basic permissions are mapped to the allowable actions is repository specific.

Allowable actions and permission mapping

CMIS provides a mechanism called **allowable actions** that permits an application to discover the set of service operations that can be currently performed on a particular object by the current user without having to actually invoke the service.

If a repository supports ACLs, then the repository will provide a mapping table that defines how the permissions supported by the repository interact with the CMIS allowable actions, that is, which permissions are necessary for a principal to have on one or more objects in order to potentially perform each action, subject to the other constraints on allowable actions mentioned.

The actual repository semantics for basic permissions with regard to allowable actions can be discovered by the `mapping` properties returned by the `getRepositoryInfo` service. These properties can be seen in the following example:

```
<cmis:aclCapability>
...
  <cmis:mapping>
    <cmis:key>canCreateFolder.Folder</cmis:key>
      <cmis:permission>cmis:all</cmis:permission>
      <cmis:permission>
      {http://www.alfresco.org/model/system/1.0}
        base.CreateChildren
      </cmis:permission>
  </cmis:mapping>
</cmis:mapping>
```

Here, we can see that for the user to be able to execute the `canCreateFolder` operation, he or she needs to have the `cmis:all` CMIS permission on the parent folder and the `CreateChildren` proprietary Alfresco permission.

Since several allowable actions require permissions on more than one object, the mapping table is defined in terms of permission `keys`. For example, moving a document from one folder to another may require permissions on the document and on each of the folders.

Each permission key combines the name of the allowable action (for example, `canCreateFolder`) and the object for which the principal needs the required permission (for example, `Folder`).

Managing permissions with the AtomPub binding

To get permissions for an object in the repository, we use the `getACL` service call. The URL for this call can be found by looking at the links for the object and finding the Atom link that has a relationship URL ending in `/acl`, as in the following code:

```
<atom:link rel="http://docs.oasis-open.org/ns/cmis/link/200908/acl"
href="http://localhost:8080/alfresco/cmisatom/f0ebcfb4-ca9f-4991-bda8-
9465f4f11527/acl?id=workspace%3A%2F%2FSpacesStore%2Fd60c6243-e96a-
401b-9537-b4917c0eb8ba"
```

When we have `href` for this link, we can use it to get the ACL for the file as follows:

```
$ curl -v -u admin:admin "http://localhost:8080/alfresco/cmisatom/
f0ebcfb4-ca9f-4991-bda8-9465f4f11527/acl?id=workspace%3A%2F%2FSpacesStore
%2Fd60c6243-e96a-401b-9537-b4917c0eb8ba" | xmllint --format -
```

```
<?xml version="1.0" encoding="UTF-8" standalone="yes"?>
<ns2:acl xmlns="http://docs.oasis-
   open.org/ns/cmis/messaging/200908/"
   xmlns:ns2="http://docs.oasis-open.org/ns/cmis/core/200908/"
   xmlns:ns3="http://docs.oasis-open.org/ns/cmis/restatom/200908/">
   <ns2:permission>
     <ns2:principal>
       <ns2:principalId>GROUP_EVERYONE</ns2:principalId>
     </ns2:principal>
   <ns2:permission>cmis:read</ns2:permission>
     <ns2:direct>false</ns2:direct>
   </ns2:permission>
</ns2:acl>
```

Here, we can see that everyone has read access (`cmis:read`) to the `simple.txt` file. And the permission is inherited from the parent `/Company Home` folder (`ns2:direct` set to `false`). By default, only the basic CMIS permissions are returned. We can also add the parameter `&onlyBasicPermissions=false` to the URL, and we will then get the following proprietary permissions returned:

```
...
<ns2:permission>{http://www.alfresco.org/model/content/1.0}cmobjec
   t.Consumer</ns2:permission>
...
```

So, in Alfresco, everyone has a consumer access to the file, meaning a read-only access.

To add a permission for the `simple.txt` file, we need to use the `applyACL` service call. This involves doing an HTTP PUT on a CMIS ACL XML file containing the authority (group or user) and the actual permission to set. Create a file named `applyacl.xml` and add the following to it:

```
<?xml version="1.0" encoding="UTF-8" standalone="yes"?>
<ns2:acl xmlns="http://docs.oasis-
   open.org/ns/cmis/messaging/200908/"
   xmlns:ns2="http://docs.oasis-open.org/ns/cmis/core/200908/"
   xmlns:ns3="http://docs.oasis-open.org/ns/cmis/restatom/200908/">
   <ns2:permission>
     <ns2:principal>
       <ns2:principalId>GROUP_MARKETING</ns2:principalId>
     </ns2:principal>
   <ns2:permission>cmis:write</ns2:permission>
     <ns2:direct>true</ns2:direct>
   </ns2:permission>
</ns2:acl>
```

In this case, we have given the `cmis:write` permission to the marketing group, which needs to exist in Alfresco for this to work (for information on how to create a group in Alfresco, see `http://docs.alfresco.com/4.2/index.jsp`). The permission is only valid for this file as we have set the `direct` parameter to `true`.

To apply the permission, execute the following PUT command:

```
$ curl -X PUT -u admin:admin -d @applyacl.xml -H "Content-Type:
application/cmisacl+xml" "http://localhost:8080/alfresco/cmisatom/
f0ebcfb4-ca9f-4991-bda8-9465f4f11527/acl?id=workspace%3A%2F%2FSpacesStore
%2F0be16ca8-3562-47c1-8a81-3be52a725d56" | xmllint --format -


<?xml version="1.0" encoding="UTF-8" standalone="yes"?>
<acl xmlns="http://docs.oasis-open.org/ns/cmis/core/200908/"
    xmlns:ns2="http://docs.oasis-open.org/ns/cmis/messaging/200908/"
    xmlns:ns3="http://docs.oasis-open.org/ns/cmis/restatom/200908/">
    <permission>
        <principal>
            <principalId>GROUP_MARKETING</principalId>
        </principal>
        <permission>cmis:write</permission>
<permission>{http://www.alfresco.org/model/system/1.0}base.Write</
permission>
        <direct>true</direct>
    </permission>
    <permission>
        <principal>
            <principalId>GROUP_EVERYONE</principalId>
        </principal>
        <permission>cmis:read</permission>
<permission>{http://www.alfresco.org/model/content/1.0}cmobject.
Consumer</permission>
        <direct>false</direct>
    </permission>
</acl>
```

The CMIS server responds with the new permission settings for the object.

Managing permissions with the Browser binding

To get permissions for an object with the Browser binding, we use the getACL service call and set the cmisselector parameter to acl. We can also specify if we just want the basic permissions returned with the onlyBasicPermissions parameter.

The URL is a normal get-object-by-ID URL with the following parameters (look up the node reference / Object Id for the Simple (from Browser binding).txt file):

```
$ curl -v -u admin:admin "http://localhost:8080/alfresco/cmisbrowser/
f0ebcfb4-ca9f-4991-bda8-9465f4f11527/root?objectId=workspace%3A%2F%2FSpac
esStore%2Ff574db8e-c9ac-4e5e-81b6-c9b6bc2b9cba&cmisselector=acl&onlyBasic
Permissions=false"" | jq '.'


{
  aces: [
    {
      isDirect: false,
      principal: {
        principalId: "GROUP_EVERYONE"
      },
      permissions: [
        "cmis:read",
        "{http://www.alfresco.org/model/content/1.0}cmobject.Consumer"
      ]
    }
  ],
  isExact: true
}
```

Here, we can see that everyone has read access (cmis:read) to the simple (from Browser binding).txt file. The permission is inherited from the parent / company home folder (isDirect set to false). In Alfresco, everyone has a consumer access to the file, meaning a read-only access.

To add a permission for the simple (from Browser binding).txt file, we need to use the applyACL service call. This involves POSTing an HTTP form with cmisaction set to applyAcl, the authority (group or user), and the actual permission to be set.

Create a file named `applyAcl.html` and add the following to it (I looked up the node reference / `Object Id` for the file via its Document Details page in Alfresco):

```
<html>
<body>
<form
  name="applyAclForm"
  action="http://localhost:8080/alfresco/cmisbrowser/f0ebcfb4-
    ca9f-4991-bda8-
    9465f4f11527/root?objectId=workspace%3A%2F%2FSpacesStore%
    2Ff574db8e-c9ac-4e5e-81b6-c9b6bc2b9cba"
  method="post"
  enctype="multipart/form-data">
  <input name="cmisaction" type="hidden" value="applyAcl" />
  <input name="addACEPrincipal[0]" type="hidden"
    value="GROUP_MARKETING" />
  <input name="addACEPermission[0][0]" type="hidden"
    value="cmis:write" />
  Set permission for "Simple (from Browser binding) (Working
    Copy).txt"<br/>
  <input type="submit" value="Set Permission" />
</form>
</body>
</html>
```

In this case, we have given the `cmis:write` permission to the MARKETING group, which needs to exist in Alfresco for this to work. The permission is only valid for this file as we have set the direct parameter to `true`.

When we submit the form the CMIS server responds with the new permission settings for the object as follows in a JSON structure:

```
{
    "aces" :
        [
            {
                "isDirect" : true,
                "principal" :
                    {
                        "principalId" : "GROUP_MARKETING"
                    },
                "permissions" :
                    [
                        "cmis:write",
                        "{http://www.alfresco.org/model/system/1.0}base.
Write"
                    ]
```

```
            },
            {
                "isDirect" : false,
                "principal" :
                    {
                        "principalId" : "GROUP_EVERYONE"
                    },
                "permissions" :
                    [
                        "cmis:read",
                        "{http://www.alfresco.org/model/content/1.0}
cmobject.Consumer"
                    ]
            }
        ],
    "isExact" : true
}
```

In order to add an ACE to a CMIS object, a client passes a control named
addACEPrincipal along with a set of corresponding addACEPermission controls.
An index value <addACEIndex> links the principal with its permissions (note that
the index does not imply any order), and a second index <permIndex> differentiates
the permissions.

To set permissions for several principals, you would do something like the following:

```
...
    <input name="addACEPrincipal[0]" type="hidden" value="martin" />
    <input name="addACEPermission[0][0]" type="hidden"
      value="cmis:read" />
    <input name="addACEPermission[0][1]" type="hidden"
      value="{http://www.alfresco.org/model/system/1.0}
      base.LinkChildren}" />
<input name="addACEPrincipal[1]" type="hidden" value="veronika" />
<input name="addACEPermission[1][0]" type="hidden"
  value="cmis:all" />
...
```

Here, we intend to give a user with the username martin read access to an object
and the possibility to link to this object. We are also giving the user veronika full
access to an object (that is, no need to give any other permission). To find out all the
available Alfresco-specific permissions, fetch the information page for the Browser
binding with the http://localhost:8080/alfresco/cmisbrowser URL and look
at the permissions array.

Managing relationships between objects

CMIS supports relationships (the same thing as an association in Alfresco), and it's possible to set up a relationship via the `createRelationship` service call and remove a relationship via the `deleteObject` service call in the **object service**. The `getObjectRelationships` service call that is part of the **relationship service** is used to get relationships where an object is either a source or a target.

The source object in the relationship needs to have the allowable action `canCreateRelationship` set to `true` for it to be possible to set up the relationship.

Alfresco comes with a number of out of the box association/relationship types. One of them is `cm:replaces`. We will use this relationship type for the examples that follow, where we set up a relationship between two documents and one of them replaces the other. For example, let's say we have a folder with company policy documents and they can be changed on a yearly basis. The folder contains the following subfolders: `approved`, `drafts`, and `archived`. We can then use the `cm:replaces` relationship whenever a policy is updated, and it should replace an older version that is to be archived.

Creating and reading relationships with the AtomPub binding

Creating a new relationship between two objects/documents with the AtomPub binding involves POSTing an Atom entry with the source Object ID, target Object ID, and the type of relationship to be set up between the objects.

Create a file named `create-relationship.atom.xml` with the following contents:

```xml
<?xml version="1.0" encoding="utf-8"?>
<entry xmlns="http://www.w3.org/2005/Atom"
  xmlns:cmisra="http://docs.oasis-
  open.org/ns/cmis/restatom/200908/"
  xmlns:cmis="http://docs.oasis-open.org/ns/cmis/core/200908/">
<cmisra:object>
  <cmis:properties>
    <cmis:propertyId propertyDefinitionId="cmis:targetId">
      <cmis:value>workspace://SpacesStore/0be16ca8-3562-47c1
        -8a81-3be52a725d56</cmis:value>
    </cmis:propertyId>
    <cmis:propertyId propertyDefinitionId="cmis:objectTypeId">
      <cmis:value>R:cm:replaces</cmis:value>
    </cmis:propertyId>
    <cmis:propertyId propertyDefinitionId="cmis:sourceId">
```

```
      <cmis:value>workspace://SpacesStore/90d8fd59-7467-488f
        -87c3-35db4d94899d</cmis:value>
    </cmis:propertyId>
  </cmis:properties>
</cmisra:object>
</entry>
```

Here, we are setting up a `cm:replaces` relationship between a new file `simple2.txt` (source) that replaces the old `simple.txt` file (target). Because this relationship type is a subtype of `cmis:relationship` and is Alfresco specific, we need to prefix it with `R:`. The Atom entry needs to be POSTed to the relationship link's `href` for the source object; this link can be found for each object as follows:

```
<atom:link rel="http://docs.oasis-
  open.org/ns/cmis/link/200908/relationships"
   href=http://localhost:8080/alfresco/cmisatom/f0ebcfb4
  -ca9f-4991-bda8-
  9465f4f11527/relationships?id=workspace%3A%2F%2FSpacesStore%
  2F90d8fd59-7467-488f-87c3-35db4d94899d...
```

Execute the following cURL command to set up the relationship:

```
$ curl -v -u admin:admin -d @create-relationship.atom.xml -H "Content-
Type: application/atom+xml;type=entry" "http://localhost:8080/alfresco/
cmisatom/f0ebcfb4-ca9f-4991-bda8-9465f4f11527/relationships?id=workspace%
3A%2F%2FSpacesStore%2F90d8fd59-7467-488f-87c3-35db4d94899d"
```

This returns the newly created `cm:replaces` relationship object as an Atom entry. To verify that the relationship was really set up, we can list the relationships for the `simple2.txt` file as follows:

```
$ curl -v -u admin:admin "http://localhost:8080/alfresco/cmisatom/
f0ebcfb4-ca9f-4991-bda8-9465f4f11527/relationships?id=workspace%3A%2F%2FS
pacesStore%2F90d8fd59-7467-488f-87c3-35db4d94899d&includeSubRelationshipT
ypes=true"
```

This will return `atom feed`, where one of the Atom entries should be the newly set up relationship with the `simple.txt` file.

It's important to set `includeSubRelationshipTypes` to `true`; otherwise, only the `cmis:relationship` types will be returned.

Creating and reading relationships with the Browser binding

Creating a new relationship between two objects/documents with the Browser binding involves POSTing an HTTP form with the `cmisaction` set to `createRelationship`. Controls also need to be set up for the source Object ID, target Object ID, and the type of relationship to set up between the objects.

Create a file named `createRelationship.html` with the following contents:

```
<html>
<body>
<form
  name="createRelationshipForm"
  action="http://localhost:8080/alfresco/cmisbrowser/f0ebcfb4-
    ca9f-4991-bda8-
    9465f4f11527/root?objectId=workspace%3A%2F%2FSpacesStore%
    2F5a21591a-f354-4581-8972-49b3991a96f1"
  method="post"
  enctype="multipart/form-data">
  <input name="cmisaction" type="hidden"
    value="createRelationship" />
  <input name="sourceId" type="hidden"
    value="workspace://SpacesStore/5a21591a-f354-4581-8972-
    49b3991a96f1" />
  <input name="typeId" type="hidden" value="R:cm:replaces" />
  <input name="targetId" type="hidden"
    value="workspace://SpacesStore/a14f75b1-4e5a-4448-8037-
    b2185add3893" />
  Setup relationship between simpleBrowser2.txt and
    simpleBrowser.txt<br/>
  <input type="submit" value="Create Relationship" />
</form>
</body>
</html>
```

Here, we are setting up a `cm:replaces` relationship between a new file `simpleBrowser2.txt` (source) that replaces the old `simpleBrowser.txt` file (target). I created these files in Alfresco before doing this and then used their node references as source and target. Because this relationship type is a subtype of `cmis:relationship` and is Alfresco specific, we need to prefix it with `R:`.

This returns the newly created `cm:replaces` relationship object as a JSON structure. To verify that the relationship was really set up, we can list the relationships for the `simpleBrowser2.txt` file as follows:

```
$ curl -v -u admin:admin "http://localhost:8080/alfresco/cmisbrowser/
f0ebcfb4-ca9f-4991-bda8-9465f4f11527/root?objectId=workspace%3A%2F%2FSpac
esStore%2F5a21591a-f354-4581-8972-49b3991a96f1&includeSubRelationshipType
s=true"
```

This will return a JSON structure where one of the entries should be the newly set up relationship with the `simpleBrowser.txt` file. Note that it's important to set `includeSubRelationshipTypes` to `true`; otherwise, only `cmis:relationship` types will be returned.

Searching

To be able to search for content is one of the main requirements you would have on an interface like CMIS. It actually provides great functionality for **Full-Text Search** (**FTS**) and metadata search. When the CMIS specification was developed, a lot of thought was given to which query language should be used for searching that would not require everyone to start over and learn a new syntax. So they decided to use the ANSI SQL-92 standard as the base for the CMIS **Query Language** (QL), and the CMIS QL is implemented as a subset of ANSI-SQL with some extensions. What this means is that you can search using a normal SQL query like the following:

```
SELECT * FROM cmis:document WHERE cmis:name LIKE '%alfresco%';
```

This is pretty cool. We know what this means; search for all documents (that is, all content with base type set to `cmis:document`) in the repository that have the value of the meta-data property `cmis:name` containing the string `alfresco`. We can actually think of all the types in the repository as virtual tables.

To do a FTS of the content in the repository, we use a CMIS extension to SQL-92 called `CONTAINS`. This new keyword can be used in the `WHERE` clause as follows:

```
SELECT cmis:name FROM myc:itDoc WHERE CONTAINS('alfresco');
```

Here, we are searching among all the documents that have the `myc:itDoc` type set and that have the text `alfresco` somewhere in the content. The result set will only include the name of the documents as we have only selected `cmis:name`. The custom type `myc:itDoc` is from a content model that you can install, which comes with the code for this chapter (`content-model.xml`); it works only with Alfresco CMS servers. Drop it into the `Models` folder under `Data Dictionary` and make sure the `enable` property is set to `true` for the file (for more information on how to do this, go to `http://docs.alfresco.com/4.2/index.jsp` and search for `deploy content model - dynamic`).

If you are working with Alfresco, you can also try these queries out directly from the so-called **Node Browser** (for more information, go to Alfresco's online documents and search for Node Browser); just make sure to select `cmis-strict` as the query language, as shown in the following screenshot:

While searching, there are certain things we can do, and not do, depending on the CMIS capabilities of the repository.

Following are the related capabilities:

Capability	Description	Valid options
`capabilityQuery`	Indicates the types of queries that the repository has the ability to fulfill.	• `none`: Using this, no queries of any kind can be fulfilled. • `metadataonly`: On using this, only queries that filter based on object properties can be fulfilled. Specifically, the `CONTAINS()` predicate function is not supported. • `fulltextonly`: On using this, only queries that filter based on the full-text content of documents can be fulfilled. Specifically, only the `CONTAINS()` predicate function can be included in the `WHERE` clause. • `bothseparate`: On using this, the repository can fulfill queries that filter either on the full-text content of documents or on their properties, but not if both the types of filters are included in the same query. • `bothcombined`: On using this, the repository can fulfill queries that filter on both the full-text content of documents and their properties in the same query.

Capability	Description	Valid options
`capabilityJoin`	Indicates the types of `JOIN` keywords that the repository can fulfill in queries.	• none: On using this, the repository cannot fulfill any queries that include any `JOIN` clauses on two primary types. If the repository supports secondary types (CMIS 1.1), `JOIN` keywords on the secondary types might be supported even if the support level is none. • inneronly: On using this, the repository can fulfill queries that include an `INNER` `JOIN` clause but cannot fulfill queries that include the other types of `JOIN` clauses. • innerandouter: On using this, the repository can fulfill queries that include any type of `JOIN` clause defined by the CMIS query grammar.

Let's now see how you can execute these kind of SQL searches via the AtomPub binding and the Browser binding.

Searching with the AtomPub binding

Executing a CMIS query with the AtomPub binding involves sending a special CMIS query XML to the server, which looks like the following:

```
<cmis:query xmlns:cmis="http://docs.oasis-
  open.org/ns/cmis/core/200908/">
  <cmis:statement>
    <![CDATA[SELECT * FROM cmis:folder WHERE cmis:name IN ('Email
      Templates','Presentation Templates')]]>
  </cmis:statement>
</cmis:query>
```

The CMIS query file is sent with an HTTP POST to the query collection URL that you can find in the Service Document as follows:

```
<app:collection
  href="http://localhost:8080/alfresco/cmisatom/f0ebcfb4
  -ca9f-4991-bda8-9465f4f11527/query">
  <cmisra:collectionType>query</cmisra:collectionType>
  <atom:title type="text">Query Collection</atom:title>
  <app:accept>application/cmisquery+xml</app:accept>
</app:collection>
```

So, put the above Query XML in a file named, for example, `query.atom.xml` and then POST it to Alfresco as follows:

```
$ curl -v -u admin:admin -d @query.atom.xml -H "Content-Type:
application/cmisquery+xml" "http://localhost:8080/alfresco/cmisatom/
f0ebcfb4-ca9f-4991-bda8-9465f4f11527/query"
```

Note that `Content-Type` is set to `application/cmisquery+xml`. The server will respond with a search result that is formatted as an `atom:feed` with one `atom:entry` for each content item that matched the query.

It is also possible to restrict the number of items returned by the server or paginate the result set by using the `maxItems` and `skipCount` parameters that we used before while using the `getChildren` service. The parameters that control whether allowable actions and relationships should be returned also work as follows:

```
<cmis:query xmlns:cmis="http://docs.oasis-
  open.org/ns/cmis/core/200908/">
  <cmis:statement>
    <![CDATA[SELECT * FROM cmis:folder WHERE cmis:name IN
      ('Scripts')]]>
  </cmis:statement>
  <cmis:skipCount>0</cmis:skipCount>
  <cmis:maxItems>10</cmis:maxItems>
  <searchAllVersions>false</searchAllVersions>
    <includeAllowableActions>false</includeAllowableActions>
    <includeRelationships>none</includeRelationships>
</cmis:query>
```

Searching with the Browser binding

Executing a CMIS query with the Browser binding involves creating an HTTP form with `cmisaction` set to `query`, a statement field with the SQL, and any extra parameters as follows:

```
<html>
<body>
<form name="queryForm"
  action="http://localhost:8080/alfresco/cmisbrowser/f0ebcfb4
  -ca9f-4991-bda8-9465f4f11527" method="post"
  enctype="multipart/form-data">
```

```
    <input name="cmisaction" type="hidden" value="query" />
    input name="statement" type="text" value="SELECT cmis:name FROM
      cmis:document WHERE cmis:name like '%alfresco%'" />
    <input name="searchAllVersions" type="hidden" value="false" />
    <input name="includeRelationships" type="hidden" value="none" />
    <input name="renditionFilter" type="hidden" value="cmis:none" />
    <input name="includeAllowableActions" type="hidden"
      value="false" />
    <input name="maxItems" type="hidden" value="10" />
    <input name="skipCount" type="hidden" value="0" />
    <input type="submit" value="Search" />
  </form>
  </body>
  </html>
```

As you can see, it is also possible to restrict the number of items returned by the server or paginate the result set by using the `maxItems` and `skipCount` parameters that we used before when using the `getChildren` service. The parameters that control whether allowable actions and relationships should be returned can also be used.

When we submit the above form the server will respond with a JSON search result that looks like the following:

```
{
    "results":[
        {
            "allowableActions":{ ... },
            "properties":{
                "cmis:name":{... "value":"alfresco docs.js.sample",
...

        {
            "allowableActions":{ … },
            "properties":{
                "cmis:name":{... "value":"emailbody_textplain_
alfresco.ftl", ...
...
```

So, for each document, there are the `allowableactions` and the `properties` returned.

CMIS query examples

The following table contains a number of examples of CMIS queries that demonstrate the capabilities of the CMIS search functionality:

CMIS query	Explanation
`SELECT * FROM cmis:document`	This returns all the properties for all the documents in the repository, including any documents that have a type applied which is a subtype of `cmis:document`. Thumbnails are not returned.
`SELECT * FROM cmis:folder`	This returns all the properties for all the folders in the repository, including any folders that have a type applied which is a subtype of `cmis:folder`.
`SELECT cmis:name, cmis:objectId FROM cmis:document`	This returns specific properties, such as the name and Object ID (node reference) for all the documents.
`SELECT * FROM cmis:document WHERE cmis:creationDate >= TIMESTAMP '2012-12-05T00:00:00.000+00:00'`	This returns all the documents created on December 5, 2012 or after. Date collation ignores time by default.
`SELECT * from cmis:document WHERE cmis:objectId = 'workspace:// SpacesStore/4412f304-df9d-4c94-bdeb-6b90bf83b774'`	This returns documents with matching Object IDs (that is, node references).
`SELECT cmis:name FROM cmis:folder WHERE cmis:name IN ('test', 'Company Home')`	This returns any folder with the name test or Company Home. The IN predicate is supported for single-valued properties of the type: String, Integer, Decimal, DateTime, and ID.
`SELECT * FROM cmis:document WHERE cmis:name LIKE '%alfresco%'`	This returns all the documents that have the word alfresco in their name.
`SELECT cmis:name FROM myc:itDoc WHERE CONTAINS('CIFS')`	This returns the name of all My Company IT documents that have the word CIFS somewhere in the text. CONTAINS does a full text search.

CMIS query	Explanation

`SELECT SCORE() docscore`
`FROM cmis:document WHERE`
`CONTAINS('\'test\'') ORDER BY`
`docscore`
	This returns the relevance that a document has to the `CONTAINS` text.
	
	The `SCORE()` function returns a decimal value between 0.0 (no relevance) and 1.0 (complete relevance) with respect to the `CONTAINS()` function specified in the query.

`SELECT cmis:name FROM`
`cmis:document WHERE IN_`
`FOLDER('workspace://SpacesStore/`
`a89c38dd-fb27-4016-a1aa-`
`7c8e1c9e9d37')`
	This returns the name of all the immediate documents to the passed-in folder node reference for `IN_FOLDER`. If you want to search for all the documents in all subfolders for the passed-in node reference, use the `IN_TREE` predicate instead.

`SELECT d.cmis:name,d.`
`cmis:objectTypeId  FROM`
`cmis:document as d`
`JOIN cm:emailed as e`
`ON d.cmis:objectId =`
`e.cmis:objected`
	This returns all the documents that have the `cm:emailed` aspect applied (aspects are specific to Alfresco).
	
	Aspects are not supported by CMIS 1.0. To do searches that involve Aspects, you must use a `JOIN` clause.

A word on transactions

Since the CMIS protocol is a stateless protocol, each request creates its own transaction. Therefore, it is up to the developer to manage rollbacks when several operations should be part of one logical transaction. So, for example, if you create three folders and one file, and want all of these calls to be part of one logical transaction and succeed or be rolled backed so that the system is consistent, then the rolling back logic has to be written by the developer. Therefore, for example, if creating the third folder fails, the first two folders that were already created must be removed automatically.

Summary

In this chapter, we have gone through some of the more advanced features. We have looked at how version management works by doing a check out and then a check in, which creates a new version. Then we looked at how to set permissions for a node by setting up a group with write permissions for a specific document. We also looked at how to set up a relationship between two nodes. And finally, the search features were explored, which are based on the SQL 92 standard and are easy to learn.

In the next chapter, we will look into how the Alfresco platform implements the CMIS standard and how Alfresco uses CMIS between different clients and the server, including how Alfresco in the cloud supports CMIS.

4
Alfresco and CMIS

This chapter will look at how Alfresco has implemented support for the CMIS standard over the last couple of years. We will investigate how the different parts of CMIS, such as the object model and services, are supported and mapped into Alfresco's corresponding entities. This chapter also covers Alfresco-specific features, such as tags, categories, and aspects, and how to access them via CMIS.

Timeline

The support for CMIS in Alfresco has evolved over a number of years. The following diagram shows the timeline:

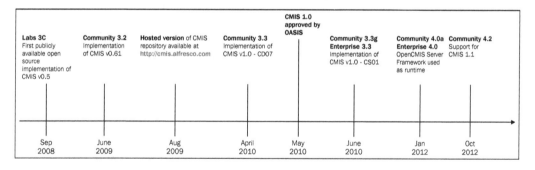

Alfresco was one of the first companies to support CMIS, making a CMIS v0.5 implementation available in 2008. In 2009, Alfresco started to host an online server where people could try out the CMIS standard. This server, which is accessible via the http://cmis.alfresco.com URL, supports the CMIS 1.0 standard and the Browser binding, which is based on the CMIS 1.1 draft.

In mid 2010, Alfresco released both a Community version and an Enterprise version that supported the recently-approved CMIS 1.0 standard.

With Version 4.0 of the server, Alfresco switched from using a home-grown CMIS runtime based on Apache Abdera libraries to handle AtomPub protocol implementation, to using the OpenCMIS Server Framework. This was done to be able to benefit the users from the development of this framework that is used by many CMIS servers. It also made the OpenCMIS Java API available for developers performing customizations for Alfresco. Developers can also use a new root object called `cmis` in the Web Script controllers implemented in JavaScript.

Note that with the release of Alfresco 4 and the move to OpenCMIS, the URLs that are used to access the CMIS services in an Alfresco server have changed. Alfresco 4.0 uses the `http://localhost:8080/alfresco/cmisatom` URL instead of the depreciated `http://localhost:8080/alfresco/service/cmis` URL that was used in Version 3.2r2 to 3.4. To confuse everyone a bit more, the Alfresco CMIS URL has changed again in Version 4.2.d Community and 4.2.0 Enterprise to `http://localhost:8080/alfresco/api/-default-/cmis/versions/1.1/atom` (you can switch version in the URL to `1.0` if Version `1.1` is not of interest). The Browser binding URL in 4.2 is the same as that for Atom except it ends in `/1.1/browser` instead of `/1.1/atom`. The repository ID also changed from being a UUID to `-default-`.

> In the two preceding chapters, we have used the Version 4.0 URLs (that is, `http://localhost:8080/alfresco/cmisatom` and `http://localhost:8080/alfresco/cmisbrowser`) when working with the 4.2 version; this also works. These were used because this book was started before the 4.2.d and 4.2.0 versions were released.

In the latest Alfresco Community and Enterprise releases of Version 4.2, there is support for parts of the new CMIS Version 1.1 standard that was released in May 2013, which are as follows:

- **The Browser binding**: As seen in the previous two chapters, the Browser binding makes it easy to work with CMIS via JSON and HTML Forms.

- **Secondary types**: Alfresco aspects are exposed as secondary types in CMIS 1.1. You can dynamically add aspects to an Alfresco object using the CMIS API.

- **Appending content**: If you have an application that uses very large files, such as a media publishing solution, you may want to upload a file in chunks. You may have large files that timeout during an upload or fail because of a bad connection. You can use the CMIS 1.1 `append` parameter in these situations.

The following features from the CMIS 1.1 standard are not supported in Alfresco Version 4.2:

- **Type mutability**: This provides the possibility to add, update, and delete content types via the CMIS API. So when this is supported in the future, you could have an application inject a domain-specific content model on the fly when it is installed. When the application is uninstalled, it could remove the content model. This could also be used by design tools and so on.

- **Retention and Hold support**: This provides a bit of records management support without having to install and use the **Alfresco Records Management** module. It defines secondary types to formally represent Retentions and Holds on CMIS objects. These, in turn, can be used by the repository to protect objects from being deleted or modified. Retention describes a period of time during which a document must not be deleted, whereas Hold marks the document as protected as long as the Hold is applied.

- **The New cmis:item Object Type**: This is a new top-level data model type that is an extension point for repositories that need to expose any other object types via CMIS that do not fit the model's definition of a document, folder, relationship, or policy. This could be used, for example, to model users and groups in Alfresco.

- **The bulkUpdateProperties service**: This is a method that supports bulk property updates on a set of objects within a single service call.

- **Extended features discovery**: This is an optional new element called `extendedFeatures`, which can be part of the `repositoryInfo` service call response.

Architecture/stack

The Alfresco implementation of the CMIS standard changed in Version 4.0 when the OpenCMIS client and server library was adopted as the CMIS server framework for the Alfresco server.

The following diagram shows the current Alfresco CMIS stack:

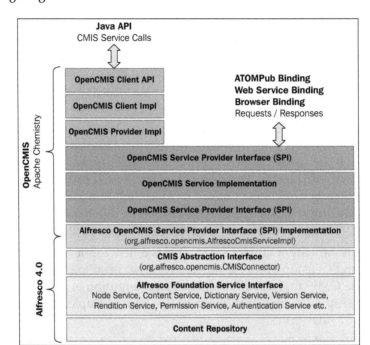

Right on top of the Alfresco Service interface is a CMIS abstraction layer called CMISConnector that works as a façade between the Alfresco system and the OpenCMIS server framework. The **OpenCMIS Service Provider Interface (SPI)** is implemented with the **AlfrescoCmisServiceImpl** component that ties together Alfresco's repository with the OpenCMIS server framework. Alfresco then just takes advantage of the OpenCMIS protocol binding implementations.

Adopting the OpenCMIS library had several benefits for Alfresco, some of which are as follows:

- The OpenCMIS server framework is used by several CMS servers and not just Alfresco; so Alfresco automatically benefits from all the bug fixes and improvements.

- Alfresco will have one code base for all CMIS protocol bindings, AtomPub, Web Services, and Browser.

- Access to the OpenCMIS client API within the repository is provided, making it easy to use it from in-process/embedded extensions.

- It provides Spring Surf OpenCMIS integration so you can use the OpenCMIS client library from Surf Web Scripts. A new cmis JavaScript root object is also available.

- Single-Sign-On support with CMIS.
- Better CMIS specification compliance.
- Better performance with less memory consumption.
- Handling big documents.

OpenCMIS does not support working with aspects prior to Version 4.2.e Community and 4.2.0 Enterprise when they are handled as secondary types. So, Alfresco has developed an extension to OpenCMIS that makes it possible to work with aspects in older Alfresco versions. This project is available at `http://apache-extras.org/p/alfresco-opencmis-extension` and we will cover that in the next chapter.

Alfresco content model mapping to the CMIS object model

This section will walk you through the CMIS object model and have a look at how Alfresco implements it.

Repository capabilities

The information in this section holds true for my Alfresco Community 4.2.e installation and 4.2.0 Enterprise installation.

Alfresco supports adding and removing ACL as the `capabilityACL` property is set to `manage`. The `capabilityAllVersionsSearchable` property is set to `false`, so Alfresco does not support searching in all the previous versions of a document when version management has been turned on.

Alfresco does not log anything when users execute operations such as creating, reading, updating, or deleting a document as the `capabilityChanges` value is `none`. By default, the change log is turned off to save space; it can be turned on by updating the `tomcat/shared/classes/alfresco-global.properties` file and setting `audit.cmischangelog.enabled` to `true`. Once set, the value of `capabilityChanges` becomes `objectidsonly`. This means that the Alfresco change log provides access to a list of the objects that have changed (those that have been created, updated, deleted, and for which permissions have been modified) but does not provide a list of the properties, or the content, that have changed.

The content of a document can be updated as the capabilityContentStreamUpdatability property is set to anytime, which means that updates are allowed both when checked out to a working copy, or just direct updates without a check-out. When a document is checked out, Alfresco also supports updating of the working copy as the capabilityPWCUpdatable property is set to true.

It is also possible to get all the descendant content items for a folder as the capabilityGetDescendants property is set to true; the same concept applies to capabilityGetFolderTree, which allows you to fetch all its subfolders recursively. The ability to file a document in multiple folders is also supported as the capabilityMultifiling property to is set true.

It is possible to search in both metadata and content because the capabilityQuery property is set to bothcombined. Searching in checked-out PWCs is not supported as the capabilityPWCSearchable property is set to false.

We can read renditions such as thumbnails as the capabilityRenditions property is set to read. Then, there a number of features that are not supported in this Alfresco version, which are as follows: capabilityUnfiling, capabilityVersionSpecificFiling, and capabilityJoin.

Type mappings

The Alfresco type cm:content is mapped to the CMIS type cmis:document. The query name is also cmis:document. All Alfresco types that extend cm:content are mapped to the CMIS type ID D:<alfresco type>, for example, D:dl:dataListItem. The CMIS query name for these Alfresco types is <alfresco type>.

The mapping for the Alfresco folder types is similar to that for documents. The Alfresco type cm:folder is mapped to the CMIS type cmis:folder. All Alfresco types that extend cm:folder are mapped to the CMIS type ID F:<alfresco type>, for example, F:dl:dataList. The CMIS query name for these Alfresco types is <alfresco type>.

All Alfresco peer-to-peer associations are mapped to the CMIS type ID R:<association type>. However, both the source and target types in the association have to be a cm:folder or cm:content derived type. If that is not the case, the association is not mapped. The CMIS query name is not relevant as relationships are not searchable. The CMIS base type cmis:relationship has no equivalent Alfresco type.

Any Alfresco type outside the cm:content and cm:folder hierarchies is not exposed via the CMIS interface.

The `cmis:policy` CMIS type has no equivalent Alfresco type. However, it is used to map aspects so that they are accessible via CMIS if you are using an Alfresco version prior to 4.2.e Community or 4.2.0 Enterprise.

Property mappings

The `cmis:objectId` property is mapped into an Alfresco node reference along with the possible version label as a serializable string such as `workspace://SpacesStore/{uuid};{versionLabel}`. An example object ID could be `workspace://SpacesStore/89f42a5a-2a82-4449-bbe3-8e17fc8bd153;1.0`, which includes the version label too. The version label is not included if it is a PWC or versioning is not enabled for a document (versioning is not applicable to folders).

> Note that in the Alfresco 4.2.d and 4.2.0 versions, the repository ID and object ID formats have changed. So if you are using the new URLs for these versions, such as `http://localhost:8080/alfresco/api/-default-/cmis/versions/1.1/browser`, the repository ID is going to be `-default-` and the object IDs are going to look like `89f42a5a-2a82-4449-bbe3-8e17fc8bd153`. However, you can still use the new URL with the old object ID format such as `workspace://SpacesStore/89f42a5a-2a82-4449-bbe3-8e17fc8bd153`. If you use the old object IDs with the new URLs, Alfresco will respond with old object IDs.

The `cmis:objectTypeId` is mapped into a `"[D|F|R|P]:{prefix}:{localName}"` serializable string; for example, `D:dl:dataListItem`.

Other common properties are mapped as follows:

CMIS property	Alfresco property
cmis:name	cm:name
cmis:createdBy	cm:creator (cm:auditable)
cmis:createdBy	cm:created (cm:auditable)
cmis:lastModifiedBy	cm:modifier (cm:auditable)
cmis:lastModificationDate	cm:modifiedDate (cm:auditable)
cmis:isLatestVersion	(document only) This defaults to `true`; set to `false` if it is a PWC.
cmis:isMajorVersion	(document only) This is set to `true` if the version type is `VersionType.Major`; otherwise, it is set to `false`. If it is a PWC, always set to `false`.
cmis:versionLabel	(document only) cm:versionLabel
cmis:contentStreamLength	(document only) cm:content.size

CMIS property	Alfresco property
`cmis:name`	`cm:name`
`cmis:contentStreamMimeType`	(document only) `cm:content.mimetype`
`cmis:contentStreamFileName`	(document only) `cm:name`
`cmis:path`	(folder only) This is the path to the folder excluding `/Company Home`. So the path to `/Company Home/Data Dictionary/ Scripts`, for example, would be `/Data Dictionary/Scripts`.
	To get the path for an object, refer to the next section.

Note that some Alfresco property types are not mapped, such as `d:any`, `d:content`, `d:childassocref`, `d:assocref`, `d:path`, `d:locale`, and `d:version`. Any property that has a type from one of these is not going to be mapped into a CMIS property.

Object path's explanation

Getting the path for an object requires a bit more explanation as it is not always straightforward. Each object in CMIS has a unique, immutable, and opaque object ID. As discussed earlier, an object ID is mapped into an Alfresco node reference. We can use the `getObject` call in the object services and pass in the object ID to get a folder, document, document version, relationship, policy, and also the new CMIS 1.1 item object.

If we now look at the object paths, things get complicated. So, a path is another mechanism to access an object in addition to the object ID. CMIS supports retrieving objects by their path via the `getObjectByPath` call in the object service. However, the path to a document does not have to be unique. If the multifiling feature is used, an object can be contained in multiple folders and have more than one path, or it can be an orphaned object that has not yet been filed in any folder. Because of this, there is no object method such as `getPath` that returns the path to the object.

The following diagram shows an example of different files (that is, document objects) that have been filed under different folders in an Alfresco repository:

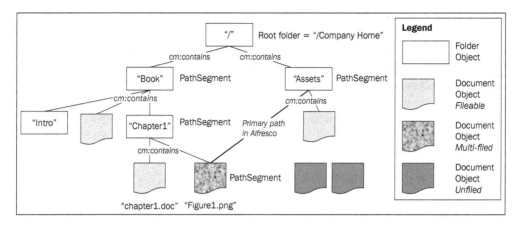

The root folder node is always at the top; it should be accessible via the / path according to the CMIS specification. This is the same folder as /Company Home in Alfresco, so when referring to the folder paths in Alfresco, the /Company Home folder is implied and should not be specified in the path, and will not be returned in the value of the cmis:path property for a folder object.

In CMIS, a path is made up of so-called **PathSegments** that are folder names and file names. In Alfresco, a PathSegement is the cm:name of the folder or file node. Path segments are connected in Alfresco with the cm:contains parent-child association. The preceding diagram shows a file **Figure1.png** that has been filed in two different folders: the /Assets folder and the /Chapter1 folder. This was done by first uploading the image file via the Alfresco Share UI to the /Assets folder, which effectively sets what's called the **primary path** for this file in Alfresco to /Company Home/Assets/Figure1.png. The primary path is not a concept that exists in CMIS. To file the image into the **Chapter1** folder, a file called MultiFileObjectPostData. txt was created with the following content:

```
cmisaction=addObjectToFolder&folderId=aa779fa8-fa01-4ee2-9938-
    def82c48a8d6
```

In the previous code, folderId is the UUID part of the Alfresco node reference for the /Chapter1 folder and addObjectToFolder is the CMIS service operation for multifiling an object. This data is then POSTed to the server using the following command:

```
$ curl -v -u admin:admin -d @MultiFileObjectPostData.txt -H "Content-
Type:text/plain" http://localhost:8080/alfresco/api/-default-/public/
cmis/versions/1.1/browser/root?objectId=83c39879-a1e8-493a-9f3f-
cea111a1668f
```

In the previous snippet, the `objectId` parameter is the UUID part of the Alfresco node reference for the **Figure1.png** file. The result of this is that Alfresco will set up a new `cm:contains` association/relationship between the **/Chapter1** folder node and the **Figure1.png** file. The only thing that is actually created in this multifiling scenario is this association. If you use Node Browser to navigate to the image file via the `/Book/Chapter1` path, the primary Alfresco path will still be `/Company Home/Assets/Figure1.png` when you get to the file. If you change any of the files' properties, such as the name, it will change in both the locations where it is filed as there is only one image-file node in the repository.

Now moving on to the paths. Getting the path for a folder is easy; just use the `getObjectById` service operation and the response will contain the `cm:path` property as follows:

```
$ curl -u admin:admin "http://localhost:8080/alfresco/api/-default-/
public/cmis/versions/1.1/browser/root?objectId=aa779fa8-fa01-4ee2-9938-de
f82c48a8d6&cmisselector=object&filter=*&succinct=true" | jq .
{
  "succinctProperties": {
...

    "cmis:name": "Chapter1",
    "cmis:path": "/Book/Chapter1",...
```

For a file such as **Figure1.png**, getting the path for a folder is not that easy as it can be multifiled as we have seen earlier. We need to use the `getObjectParents` service operation to get to all the paths leading to this file. The following command does that for the image file:

```
$ curl -u admin:admin "http://localhost:8080/alfresco/api/-default-/
public/cmis/versions/1.1/browser/root?objectId=83c39879-a1e8-493a-9f3f-ce
a111a1668f%3B1.0&cmisselector=parents&filter=*&includeRelativePathSegment
=true&succinct=true" | jq .
  [
  {
    "relativePathSegment": "Figure1.png",
    "object": {
      "succinctProperties": {...
        "cmis:name": "Assets",
        "cmis:path": "/Assets",...
  },
  {
    "relativePathSegment": "Figure1.png",
    "object": {
```

```
"succinctProperties": { …
  "cmis:name": "Chapter1",
  "cmis:path": "/Book/Chapter1",…
```

We can see in the previous code that the image file has been filed in two different folders. It is not possible via CMIS to find out which one is the primary path to the image file. If we want to get the parent folders for an object via the AtomPub binding, it is done in a similar way.

For example, let's say we have a `cmis:document` that we got via the AtomPub navigation (that is, get the root folder collection, navigate via the `down` link to the folder, and then navigate via the `down` link to the doc). The Atom entry for the document will contain an `up` link, which corresponds to the `getObjectParents` method call, as shown in the following code:

```
<atom:link rel="up" href="http://localhost:8080/alfresco/api/-
    default-/public/cmis/versions/1.1/atom/parents?id=83c39879-a1e8-
    493a-9f3f-cea111a1668f%3B1.0"
    type="application/atom+xml;type=feed"/>
```

When we have this `up` link, we can invoke it with the filter parameter set to `cmis:path` to return only the relevant properties and set the `includeRelativePathSegment` parameter to `true` (to get the related file name, which is always going to be the same), as follows:

```
$ curl -u admin:admin http://localhost:8080/alfresco/api/-default-/
public/cmis/versions/1.1/atom/parents?id=83c39879-a1e8-493a-9f3f-cea111a1
668f%3B1.0&filter=cmis%3Apath&includeRelativePathSegment=true | xmllingt
--format -
```

What we will get in return is an Atom feed of the parent folder Atom entries, even if the object has only a single parent folder. Each parent folder Atom entry will contain a path and a relative path segment, which can be concatenated to form the path:

```
    ...
    <atom:entry>...
      <cmisra:object>
        <cmis:properties>
          <cmis:propertyString propertyDefinitionId="cmis:path"
            displayName="Path" localName="path"
            queryName="cmis:path">
            <cmis:value>/Assets</cmis:value>
          </cmis:propertyString>...
      </cmisra:object>
      <cmisra:relativePathSegment>Figure1.png<
        /cmisra:relativePathSegment>
    ...
    <atom:entry>...
```

```
<cmisra:object>
  <cmis:properties>
    <cmis:propertyString propertyDefinitionId="cmis:path"
      displayName="Path" localName="path"
      queryName="cmis:path">
      <cmis:value>/Book/Chapter1</cmis:value>
    </cmis:propertyString>...
</cmisra:object>
<cmisra:relativePathSegment>Figure1.png<
  /cmisra:relativePathSegment>
```

It is not generally good practice to rely on paths when accessing objects or even object IDs for that matter if you are working with multiple CMIS-compatible servers. It is particularly bad to have an application rely on object IDs and store them locally or in a database as they can change between Alfresco versions, as we have seen, and are most likely going to have a unique format per content manager server vendor.

A better way is to use metadata to uniquely identify an object in the repository. For example, let's say we are working with legal cases and want to be able to identify them across repositories and in a repository-independent way. Then, we could add a custom metadata type such as `myc:legalCase` with a property such as `myc:legalCaseNumber` and use them to fetch the object as in the following example CMIS Query:

```
SELECT cmis:name, cmis:objectId FROM myc:legalCase WHERE
  myc:legalCaseNumber = "LC1015";
```

Versioning

CMIS supports a simple version model where each of the previous versions is stored in its entirety. Only documents are versionable and the following diagram illustrates the versioning model:

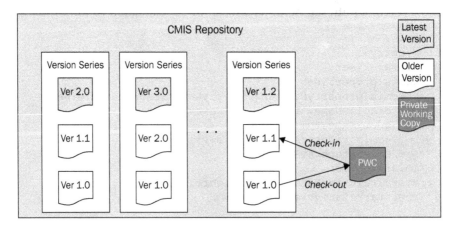

A CMIS version series contains all the versions that belong to a specific document. In Alfresco, this is implemented with the standard Version History model. This is shown in the following diagram:

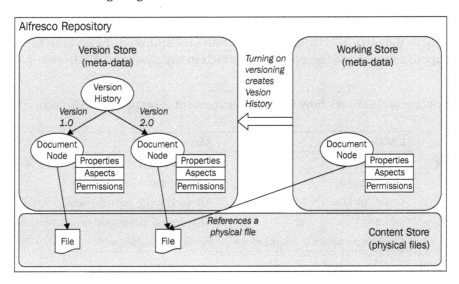

CMIS has some version management features that are not mandatory to implement. One of them is the ability to search through previous versions. Whether or not the repository supports this is indicated in the repository information's `capabilities` section with the `cmis:capabilityAllVersionsSearchable` property. In Version 4.2, which I am currently using, this property is set to `false`, so running a full-text search through all the previous versions is not supported.

Another version-related feature is the possibility to file different versions of a document in different folders. Support for this CMIS feature is indicated via the `cmis:capabilityVersionSpecificFiling` property. It is set to `false` for my Alfresco installation, so this is not supported either and all the versions are stored in the same folder.

Access control

An **Access Control List (ACL)** is used to specify what principals, such as users or groups, can do with an object in the repository. This is configured in an **Access Control Entry (ACE)**. CMIS defines three permissions: `cmis:read`, `cmis:write`, and `cmis:all`. An ACE can also contain an indication of whether or not access control definitions from parent folders should be inherited; this parameter is called `direct`.

The Alfresco repository has full support for managing ACLs for objects in the repository, which means that you can both apply and read permissions. This is indicated in the repository information's `capabilities` section with the `cmis:capabilityACL` property set to `manage`. The Alfresco repository also supports both CMIS permissions and repository-specific permissions. This can be found out by looking in the `cmis:aclCapability` section and finding out the value set for the `cmis:supportedPermissions` property, which in my case is with Alfresco 4.2, is set to `both`.

The following table shows how CMIS access control is mapped to Alfresco:

CMIS	Alfresco
`direct`	Inherited permissions
`cmis:read`	Alfresco read permissions
`cmis:write`	Alfresco write permissions
`cmis:all`	Alfresco all permissions
Repository-specific permissions	Projected as they are

The underlying permissions for an object are mapped to a set of **allowable actions**. These actions represent the operations that the current user is allowed to perform on a given object. The set of allowable actions is defined by CMIS and we can fetch them by passing the `includeAllowableActions` parameter set to `true` in a `getChildren` call, for example.

The mapping of a CMIS service call to the required Alfresco permission is as follows for document objects:

CMIS call	Alfresco permission that the user must have
`deleteObject`	DeleteNode
`updateProperties`	WriteProperties
`checkOut`	CheckOut
`cancelCheckout`	CancelCheckout
`checkIn`	CheckIn
`deleteAllVersions`	Always possible if user can delete the latest version
`addDocumentToFolder`	LinkChildren
`setContentStream`	WriteContent
`deleteContentStream`	WriteProperties
`getAllVersions`	This is always set to `true` if the user can read latest version
`getDocumentParents`	Always possible if user has read access

CMIS call	Alfresco permission that the user must have
getRelationships	Always possible if user has read access
getProperties	ReadProperties
getContentStream	ReadContent

Alfresco permissions are defined in the `permissionDefinitions.xml` file that can be found in the `model` directory under `tomcat/webapps/alfresco/WEB-INF/classes/alfresco`.

For folder objects, the permission mappings are as follows:

CMIS call	Alfresco permission that the user must have
deleteObject	DeleteNode
deleteTree	DeleteNode
updateProperties	WriteProperties
getChildren	ReadChildren
getDescendants	ReadChildren
getFolderParent	This is always set to `true` if user has read access
getProperties	ReadProperties
getRelationships	Always possible if user has read access

Change log

CMIS supports a change log that records all create, read, update, and delete operations that have been performed by different users on objects in the repository. The following diagram illustrates the CMIS change log feature:

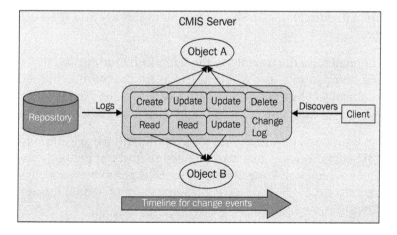

The repository logs the object ID, time, and change type when an event occurs. These logs can be read by CMIS clients. Alfresco implements the change log feature with a specific audit log application called `CMISChangeLog` that is defined in the `alfresco-audit-cmis.xml` file located in the `audit` directory under `tomcat/webapps/alfresco/WEB-INF/classes/alfresco`. The change log feature is not enabled by default in Alfresco as described previously in this chapter.

Renditions

Alfresco has had rendition support since the beginning. However, it is only since Version 3.3 that they have actually been called renditions. If you have ever used the Alfresco Share user interface, you have seen examples of content renditions, such as document thumbnails and document previews. Thumbnails are generated asynchronously after an upload. Web previews are generated on demand in Alfresco when you click on the document to see its details and preview.

The CMIS standard only supports retrieving renditions, but this is sufficient to support most use cases, such as the preview of reduced representations of a content item, fetching processed images and videos from a **Digital Asset Management (DAM)** system, and the publishing of web content from a **Web Content Management (WCM)** system.

Alfresco implements full support for CMIS renditions. Renditions created by Alfresco are accessible via the different CMIS protocol bindings in a standard way. In CMIS, renditions are categorized via its `kind` property. There is a CMIS rendition `kind` specified in the standard called `cmis:thumbnail`, the purpose of which is to provide an image preview of the document without requiring that the client download the full document content stream.

A common task that you would most likely want to do, for example, is to retrieve a thumbnail for a document in the Share Document Library and then display it in a custom client.

To fetch a thumbnail for a document via the AtomPub binding, we first need to fetch the document's Atom entry to see what the link is for the thumbnail rendition. We can do this via the object by either ID or path URI template. For more information about these operations and templates see *Chapter 2, Basic CMIS Operations*.

So to retrieve a thumbnail rendition link for a document, we are going to use the GET by object ID operation; for this, we first need to find out the node reference for the document, which will be set as the `Object id` parameter, and then specify `rendtionFilter` to `cmis:thumbnail` to get some extra metadata for the rendition using the following command:

```
$ curl -u admin:admin " http://localhost:8080/alfresco/cmisatom/f0ebcfb4-
ca9f-4991-bda8-9465f4f11527/id?id=workspace%3A%2F%2FSpacesStore%2F1f5f99
ac-a74a-4606-9fe7-85d011d13bc1&renditionFilter=cmis:thumbnail"
```

The response to the previously mentioned HTTP GET request will include additional metadata describing the cmis:thumbnail rendition and links to any renditions, as shown in the following code:

```
<atom:entry ...
  <cmisra:object ...
    <cmis:properties>
      ...
    </cmis:properties>
    <cmis:rendition>
      <cmis:streamId>workspace://SpacesStore/8b49dd01-56bb-4980-
        b161-1249ac93eb73</cmis:streamId>
      <cmis:mimetype>image/png</cmis:mimetype>
      <cmis:length>539</cmis:length>
      <cmis:kind>cmis:thumbnail</cmis:kind>
      <cmis:title>doclib</cmis:title>
      <cmis:height>100</cmis:height>
      <cmis:width>100</cmis:width>
      <cmis:renditionDocumentId>workspace:
        //SpacesStore/8b49dd01-56bb-4980-b161-1249ac93eb73
        </cmis:renditionDocumentId>
    </cmis:rendition>
  </cmisra:object>
  ...
    <atom:link rel="alternate"
      href="http://localhost:8080/alfresco/cmisatom/f0ebcfb4-ca9f-
        4991-bda8-9465f4f11527/content?id=
        workspace%3A%2F%2FSpacesStore%2F1f5f99ac-a74a-4606-9fe7-
        85d011d13bc1%3B1.0&amp;streamId=
        workspace%3A%2F%2FSpacesStore%2F8b49dd01-56bb-4980-b161-
        1249ac93eb73"
      type="image/png" cmisra:renditionKind="cmis:thumbnail"
        title="doclib" length="539"/>
    <atom:link rel="alternate"
      href="http://localhost:8080/alfresco/cmisatom/f0ebcfb4-ca9f-
        4991-bda8-9465f4f11527/content?id=
        workspace%3A%2F%2FSpacesStore%2F1f5f99ac-a74a-4606-9fe7-
        85d011d13bc1%3B1.0&amp;streamId=
        workspace%3A%2F%2FSpacesStore%2F5a401703-8b0d-4d83-845a-
        edc664c48ccb"
      type="application/x-shockwave-flash"
        cmisra:renditionKind="alf:webpreview" title="webpreview"
        length="4238"/>
  ...
</atom:entry>
```

To get to the thumbnail rendition, we can just do an HTTP GET on the `cmis:thumbnail` rendition link previously mentioned. A repository may provide any number of other rendition kinds. In this case, the document also has a web preview rendition with a repository-specific rendition kind that is `alf:webpreview`.

Search

All capabilities of the CMIS **Query Language** (**QL**) are supported by Alfresco, except `JOIN` operations between types. This means that we can search within both content and metadata. The Alfresco **full-text search** (**FTS**) language can be embedded in the `CONTAINS` predicate of the CMIS QL. See the following sections for examples of how to use the `TAG` and `PATH` keywords from the Alfresco FTS language.

 The FTS special fields, such as PATH, ASPECT, ID, QNAME, and TYPE, are available for use in the CMIS CONTAINS predicate from Alfresco Version 3.4.3.

When Alfresco FTS is embedded in the `CONTAINS` function, only the following methods can be used to identify fields:

- CMIS QL style property identifiers, such as `cmis:name`
- CMIS QL column aliases, such as `SELECT cmis:name docName ...`
- An Alfresco namespace prefix style, such as `cm:name`
- Special fields, such as `PATH` and `TAG`

Searching under a specific path is a common requirement; let's look at the following example:

```
SELECT * FROM cmis:folder WHERE
    CONTAINS('PATH:"/app:company_home/cm:Book/*"')
```

In the previous code, we are searching for all the folders in the `/Book` folder. It is important to note that display paths cannot be used as a value for the `PATH` predicate. For example, `/Company Home/Book/*` will not work. To find the correct path expression, the Alfresco Node Browser tool can be used.

 The `cmis:path` property on CMIS folder objects is not searchable. So using the PATH predicate in CONTAINS is pretty useful. The only disadvantage is that the queries will not be portable to other content manager servers.

The SQL query defines tables and table aliases after the FROM and JOIN clauses. If the SQL query references more than one table, the CONTAINS function must specify a single table for use by its alias. All properties in the embedded FTS query are added to this table and all column aliases used in the FTS query must refer to the same table. For a single table, the table alias is not required as part of the CONTAINS function.

We are going to need another example to get on top of that, which is as follows:

```
SELECT d.*, t.*, a.* FROM cmis:document AS d
  JOIN cm:titled AS t ON d.cmis:objectId = t.cmis:objectId
  JOIN cm:author AS a ON d.cmis:objectId = a.cmis:objectId
  WHERE CONTAINS(d,'Authentication')
  ORDER BY d.cmis:name
```

We have not talked about aspects yet, but to get to them, we can use JOIN as in the previous example in which we wanted to get the title (from the cm:titled aspect) and author (from the cm:author aspect) for all documents that contain the text Authentication. So, when we are bringing in more than one table with the FROM and JOIN clauses, we need to specify an alias for the table in which we want to perform an FTS operation. In the previous example, we want to perform an FTS in cmis:document, so we set up an alias called d for this table and then use it in the CONTAINS clause. You can learn more about aspects in the following section.

Support for Alfresco-specific features

Some Alfresco features, such as aspects, have no corresponding CMIS definition but are supported in different ways.

Aspects

In the Alfresco 4.2 Community and Enterprise installations that I have, the getTypeChildren call (that is, http://localhost:8080/alfresco/api/-default-/public/cmis/versions/1.1/atom/types) returns the cmis:secondary type, which means that Alfresco supports this CMIS 1.1 base type. Secondary types are used to apply extra properties to a CMIS object. More than one secondary type can be applied to an object. Alfresco exposes any aspects (basically a group of properties) that have been applied to a node using this type.

To find out what aspects have been applied to an object, we can request the properties for the object and look at the cmis:secondaryObjectTypeIds property. In the following command, we are getting the properties for the /Figure1.png file previously uploaded:

```
$ curl -u admin:admin "http://localhost:8080/alfresco/api/-default-/
public/cmis/versions/1.1/browser/root?objectId=83c39879-a1e8-493a-9f3f-ce
a111a1668f%3B1.0&cmisselector=object&filter=*&succinct=true" | jq '.'
{
  "succinctProperties": {
...
    "cmis:secondaryObjectTypeIds": [
      "P:cm:thumbnailModification",
      "P:exif:exif",
      "P:cm:titled",
      "P:cm:author",
      "P:rn:renditioned",
      "P:sys:localized"
    ],
  ...
  }
}
```

We can see that the image file already has a number of aspects applied, such as the exif metadata from the JPEG image. If we want to add a new aspect (that is, another secondary type) to this object, we would have to include the already applied secondary types too. Let's say we want to apply the cm:effectivity aspects that come out of the box with Alfresco. To do this, we have to update the cmis:secondaryObjectTypeIds property with an extra value along with whatever properties are associated with that secondary type. This is done via the updateProperties operation as usual.

When using the Browser binding and JSON, we start by creating a test file with the data we are going to perform a POST operation; let's call it AddSecondaryTypePostData.txt and have it contain the following content:

```
cmisaction=update&propertyId[0]=cmis%3AsecondaryObjectTypeIds&prop
  ertyValue[0][0]=P%3Acm%3Aeffectivity&propertyValue[0][1]=
  P%3Acm%3AthumbnailModification&propertyValue[0][2]=
  P%3Aexif%3Aexif&propertyValue[0][3]=
  P%3Acm%3Atitled&propertyValue[0][4]=
  P%3Acm%3Aauthor&propertyValue[0][5]=
  P%3Arn%3Arenditioned&propertyValue[0][6]=
  P%3Asys%3Alocalized&propertyId[1]=cm%3Afrom&propertyValue[1]=
  1387130400000&propertyId[2]=cm%3Ato&propertyValue[2]=
  1393610400000
```

The POST data will contain all the existing secondary types plus the new one and the two properties for the cm:effectivity aspect called cm:from and cm:to, which are dates. When specifying dates in JSON and the Browser binding, they have to be coded in milliseconds since 1970/01/01 00:00:00 UTC (you can visit http://currentmillis.com/ to do the encoding).

Now that we have the data to add an aspect to an object, we can do that with the following command:

```
$ curl -v -u admin:admin -d @AddSecondaryTypePostData.txt -H "Content-
Type:text/plain" "http://localhost:8080/alfresco/api/-default-/public/
cmis/versions/1.1/browser/root?objectId=83c39879-a1e8-493a-9f3f-
cea111a1668f"
{
"properties": {
"cmis:secondaryObjectTypeIds": [
"P:cm:thumbnailModification",
"P:exif:exif",
"P:cm:titled",
"P:cm:author",
"P:rn:renditioned",
"P:sys:localized",
"P:cm:effectivity"]
},
```

The call will return the new values for the secondary types that should now include the one we just added.

> The Alfresco aspects cm:referenceable, cm:auditable, and cm:versionable are not mapped to secondary types as they are already mapped to the native document/folder properties defined in the CMIS domain model.

Now, if the Alfresco server that you are using does not support secondary types, you will have to use an Alfresco-specific way of adding them. To do this with the AtomPub binding, we specify the aspect information in a section named `<alf:setAspects>` when updating the properties for an object or when creating a document object. The following example shows this when creating a document; put the following Atom entry in a file named `createDocumentAndSetAspect.atom.xml`:

```
<entry xmlns="http://www.w3.org/2005/Atom"
  xmlns:app="http://www.w3.org/2007/app"
  xmlns:cmis="http://docs.oasis-open.org/ns/cmis/core/200908/"
  xmlns:cmisra="http://docs.oasis-
  open.org/ns/cmis/restatom/200908/">
  <title>simpleWithAspect.txt</title>
  <summary>A simple text file with aspect</summary>
  <cmisra:object>
    <cmis:properties>
      <cmis:propertyId propertyDefinitionId="cmis:objectTypeId">
        <cmis:value>cmis:document</cmis:value>
      </cmis:propertyId>
      <alf:setAspects xmlns:alf="http://www.alfresco.org">
        <alf:aspectsToAdd>P:cm:effectivity</alf:aspectsToAdd>
          <alf:properties>
            <cmis:propertyDateTime propertyDefinitionId="cm:from"
              displayName="From Date" queryName="cm:from">
              <cmis:value>2012-12-26T18:00:00.000Z</cmis:value>
            </cmis:propertyDateTime>
            <cmis:propertyDateTime propertyDefinitionId="cm:to"
              displayName="To Date" queryName="cm:to">
              <cmis:value>2012-12-29T18:00:00.000Z</cmis:value>
            </cmis:propertyDateTime>
          </alf:properties>
      </alf:setAspects>
    </cmis:properties>
  </cmisra:object>
</entry>
```

Then perform a POST operation on this file to create this document with the aspect applied as follows:

```
$ curl -u admin:admin -d @createDocumentAndSetAspect.atom.xml -H
"Content-Type:application/atom+xml;type=entry" "http://localhost:8080/
alfresco/cmisatom/f0ebcfb4-ca9f-4991-bda8-9465f4f11527/children?id=worksp
ace%3A%2F%2FSpacesStore%2F5d0a13ed-d337-4e0d-a93a-05c71ab3e51e"
```

When, for example, a getObject request or a getChildren request is executed, the result will contain an Alfresco-specific section named `<aspects:aspects>` with all applied aspects as follows:

```
<cmisra:object xmlns:ns3="http://docs.oasis-
   open.org/ns/cmis/messaging/200908/">
   <cmis:properties>
 ...
   <aspects:aspects xmlns="http://www.alfresco.org"
     xmlns:aspects="http://www.alfresco.org">
     <appliedAspects>P:cm:titled</appliedAspects>
       <properties>
         <cmis:propertyString xmlns="http://docs.oasis-
            open.org/ns/cmis/core/200908/"
            propertyDefinitionId="cm:description"/>
         <cmis:propertyString xmlns="http://docs.oasis-
            open.org/ns/cmis/core/200908/"
            propertyDefinitionId="cm:title"/>
       </properties>
            <appliedAspects>P:rn:renditioned</appliedAspects>
            <appliedAspects>P:sys:localized</appliedAspects>
     ...
   </aspects:aspects>
   </cmis:properties>
</cmisra:object>
```

Alfresco aspects are queried as if they are tables and joined to types by the `Object Id`, as in the following code:

```
select d.*, e.* from cmis:document as d join cm:effectivity as e
   on d.cmis:objectId = e.cmis:objected
```

For another example, see the *Search* section in this chapter.

Tags

In Alfresco, content can be tagged to improve its filtering and narrow down the number of searches. The CMIS query language can be used to fetch documents with a certain tag and fetch all the tags for a document.

To fetch documents that have been tagged with a certain word, such as `training`, use the **CONTAINS** keyword and execute the following type of CMIS query:

```
SELECT * FROM cmis:document WHERE CONTAINS ('TAG:training')
```

To fetch all the tags for a document, perform a `JOIN` operation with the `cm:taggable` aspect as follows:

```
SELECT d.*, t.* FROM cmis:document AS d JOIN cm:taggable AS t ON
   d.cmis:objectId = t.cmis:objectId WHERE d.cmis:name='Test word
   doc.docx'
```

The response will contain the `cm:taggable` property, which is a collection of node references to tags.

Categories

To search for documents that have been categorized, we can use a similar technique as that for tags as they are actually implemented as categories under the hood. Instead of joining with `cm:taggable`, we need to use the category aspect, which is called `cm:generalclassifiable`.

Execute the following CMIS query to get all the documents that have been categorized:

```
SELECT d.*, c.* FROM cmis:document AS d JOIN
    cm:generalclassifiable AS c ON d.cmis:objectId = c.cmis:objectId
```

The response will contain the `cm:categories` property, which is a collection of node references to categories. To categorize a document, you first have to apply the `cm:classifiable` aspect to it and then select categories for it.

Categories are treated as special paths to nodes in Alfresco. To select all documents that have been categorized with the `Languages / English` category, execute the following CMIS query:

```
SELECT * FROM cmis:document WHERE CONTAINS
    ('PATH:"/cm:generalclassifiable/cm:Languages/
    cm:English/member"')
```

To find out the paths to different categories, use the Alfresco Node Browser.

Summary

In this chapter, we looked into the Alfresco platform to see how it implements support for CMIS. We have looked at the timeline and seen that Alfresco was one of the first companies to be CMIS 1.0 compliant in June 2010. The Alfresco platform uses the Apache Chemistry OpenCMIS Java library to implement support for all protocol bindings in CMIS, which makes it possible for Alfresco to benefit from all the testing and advances in that project.

Alfresco supports all content types defined by CMIS and Alfresco aspects are also handled via the CMIS 1.1 secondary type. When searching, Alfresco supports both metadata searches and FTS in content. If we would like to use the special Alfresco FTS language, it is possible to do so by including it in the CMIS QL `CONTAINS` function.

So far in the book, we have worked with the bare-bones protocol bindings without an abstraction layer between the protocols and us. This can be a bit too much sometimes and you are probably wondering whether or not there is an easier way to use CMIS from Java. This is what we will have a look at in the next chapter when we enter the world of Apache Chemistry and OpenCMIS.

5
Accessing a CMIS Server with a Java Client

Up until now, we have accessed the CMIS server via the low-level AtomPub protocol binding and the Browser protocol binding. This has required a lot of coding, which could be error prone. However, it is always good to know how low-level APIs work before going on to higher-level abstraction APIs. In this chapter, we will look at how the Apache Chemistry project (http://chemistry.apache.org/) offers a high-level API for CMIS.

In this chapter, we will see how we can perform the following tasks from a CMIS Java client:

- Authenticating and connecting to the server
- Fetching repository information including the repository ID and top folder URL
- Listing the content of a folder
- Listing the content types that are available
- Creating, updating, and deleting folders and files
- Downloading the content
- Content versioning
- Managing permissions
- Relationship management
- Searching

Apache Chemistry contains a number of libraries that abstract the CMIS low-level protocol bindings. OpenCMIS is the library used by Java developers. It provides an abstraction layer on top of all the CMIS protocol bindings, the AtomPub binding, the Web Service binding, and the Browser binding. We will be using the AtomPub binding as the transport protocol for OpenCMIS.

Setting up a build environment

We are going to use Apache Maven (`http://maven.apache.org/`) when building the examples in this chapter. Create a basic Java client project as follows by using the Maven Quick Start artifact:

```
$ mvn archetype:generate -DgroupId=com.mycompany.app -DartifactId=my-
app -DarchetypeArtifactId=maven-archetype-quickstart -
DinteractiveMode=false
```

The preceding command gives us a build project, a directory structure, and a Java file (`com.mycompany.app.App.java`) to put some code in. To use the OpenCMIS library, we need to first configure it in the Maven POM file's dependency section, open the generated `pom.xml` file, and add the following:

```
<project ...
    <dependencies>
        <!-- Bring in the OpenCMIS library for talking to CMIS
        servers -->
        <dependency>
            <groupId>org.apache.chemistry.opencmis</groupId>
            <artifactId>chemistry-opencmis-client-impl
            </artifactId>
            <version>0.10.0</version>
        </dependency>
        <dependency>
            <groupId>commons-logging</groupId>
            <artifactId>commons-logging</artifactId>
            <version>1.1.1</version>
        </dependency>
        <dependency>
            <groupId>junit</groupId>
            <artifactId>junit</artifactId>
            <version>3.8.1</version>
            <scope>test</scope>
        </dependency>
    </dependencies>
</project>
```

Version 0.10.0 of OpenCMIS is the latest version available at the moment. There might be newer versions available when you read this (see `http://chemistry.apache.org/java/opencmis.html`). I added the Apache Commons Logging library too in the preceding code, so we can do some logging from our examples. We are also going to add another Java class named `CmisClient` in the same package as the autogenerated `App` class. Let's create it with your favorite editor so that it looks as follows:

```
public class CmisClient {
    private static Log logger =
    LogFactory.getLog(CmisClient.class);
    public CmisClient() {     }
}
```

This is all that is needed; we can now start using the OpenCMIS Java library.

Connecting and setting up a session with the repository

Before we start working with the repository, we must first create a session and connect to it. In the `CmisClient` class, add the following Hash map that will contain active sessions:

```
public class CmisClient {
  private static Log logger = LogFactory.getLog(CmisClient.class);
  private static Map<String, Session> connections = new
    ConcurrentHashMap<String, Session>();
  public CmisClient() {     }
}
```

The `Session` interface is from the `org.apache.chemistry.opencmis.client.api` package in the OpenCMIS library. It represents a session/connection for a specific user with the CMIS repository. A session holds the configuration settings and cache settings to use across multiple calls to the repository. The session is also the entry point to perform all operations on the repository, such as listing folders, creating documents and folders, finding out the capabilities of the repository, and searching.

To create a new connection with the repository, use the **Session Factory** interface and query it for all the available repositories, and then create a new session for one of them. We will create a new `getSession` method in the `CmisClient` class to do the job as follows:

```
public Session getSession(
  String connectionName, String username, String pwd) {
  Session session = connections.get(connectionName);
```

```java
if (session == null) {
  logger.info("Not connected, creating new connection to" +
    " Alfresco with the connection id (" + connectionName +
    ")");

  // No connection to Alfresco available, create a new one
  SessionFactory sessionFactory =
    SessionFactoryImpl.newInstance();
  Map<String, String> parameters = new HashMap<String,
  String>();
  parameters.put(SessionParameter.USER, username);
  parameters.put(SessionParameter.PASSWORD, pwd);
  parameters.put(SessionParameter.ATOMPUB_URL,
    "http://localhost:8080/alfresco/api/-default-
    /cmis/versions/1.1/atom");
  parameters.put(SessionParameter.BINDING_TYPE,
    BindingType.ATOMPUB.value());
  parameters.put(SessionParameter.COMPRESSION, "true");
  parameters.put(SessionParameter.CACHE_TTL_OBJECTS, "0");

  // If there is only one repository exposed (e.g. Alfresco),
  // these lines will help detect it and its ID
  List<Repository> repositories =
    sessionFactory.getRepositories(parameters);
  Repository alfrescoRepository = null;
  if (repositories != null && repositories.size() > 0) {
    logger.info("Found (" + repositories.size() +
    ") Alfresco repositories");
    alfrescoRepository = repositories.get(0);
    logger.info("Info about the first Alfresco repo [ID=" +
      alfrescoRepository.getId() + "][name=" +
      alfrescoRepository.getName() + "][CMIS ver supported=" +
      alfrescoRepository.getCmisVersionSupported() + "]");
  } else {
    throw new CmisConnectionException(
      "Could not connect to the Alfresco Server, " +
      "no repository found!");
  }

  // Create a new session with the Alfresco repository
  session = alfrescoRepository.createSession();

  // Save connection for reuse
  connections.put(connectionName, session);
```

```
    } else {
      logger.info("Already connected to Alfresco with the " +
      "connection id (" + connectionName + ")");
    }

  return session;
}
```

This method starts off by checking if the Hash map already has a connection available for the connection identifier passed in. We don't want to create a new connection for every call that we do to the repository. If there is no connection, we will use the `SessionFactoryImpl` class to create a new `SessionFactory` interface, which we can use to get a list of repositories for the CMIS server.

A CMIS server can provide more than one repository, so we need to tell the server about which one we want to talk to; this is usually done by passing in a repository ID. All OpenCMIS operations require a repository ID parameter; however, there is one operation named `getRepositories` that does not, so it is used to get a list of the available repositories. When the repository information is fetched from the server, we pass in a map of configuration parameters that tells OpenCMIS what username and password to use to connect to the CMIS server, what protocol binding to use underneath OpenCMIS, and so on.

We are connecting to Alfresco and it only provides one repository, so we can grab the first `Repository` object in the `repositories` list and use it to create a session/connection.

The `Repository` object provides information about the repository, such as its ID, name, and the version of CMIS it supports. In case of Alfresco, the ID is `-default-`, and if running with the older AtomPub URL (see the following explanation), it will be a **universally unique identifier** (**UUID**) that looks something like `f0ebcfb4-ca9f-4991-bda8-9465f4f11527`.

The following table explains each configuration parameter:

Parameter names	Parameter values	Description
USER	admin	This is the repository username to use when connecting to the server.
		In case of Alfresco, this must be a username that exists in the repository database. The OpenCMIS operations that can be executed are dependent on the permissions assigned to this user.
PASSWORD	admin	This is the password for the username.
BINDING_TYPE	ATOMPUB	This is the low-level protocol binding to use when talking to the repository via OpenCMIS. The other available values are WEBSERVICES and BROWSER, which represent the other two CMIS protocol bindings.
		There is also a LOCAL binding type that is used specifically when the repository runs in the same **Java Virtual Machine (JVM)** as the client.
ATOMPUB_URL	http:// localhost:8080/ alfresco/api/- default-/cmis/ versions/1.1/atom	This is the repository-specific URL to use the AtomPub low-level binding when talking to the repository. This is only relevant when BINDING_TYPE is set to ATOMPUB. If you are using Alfresco Community version older than 4.2.e or an Alfresco Enterprise version 4.2.0, use the http://localhost:8080/alfresco/ cmisatom URL instead.
COMPRESSION	true	This is a switch to turn HTTP response compression on or off. This gives you less transport payload when set to true.

Parameter names	Parameter values	Description
CACHE_TTL_OBJECTS	0	Setting the cache **Time To Live (TTL)** to 0 means that the caching is turned off. By default, if this parameter is not specified, the cache TTL is set to 7200000, which means that all objects will be cached for 2 hours before the repository is checked for updates. This can be a bit of a problem during development as it can confuse developers and testers because not all might be aware of the cache settings. It might also be that the content is updated very frequently, so it does not make sense to have a cache. The best is to wait and set the cache when you have performance problems within an environment that is mostly read-only or where objects are not updated very frequently.

Now add the following code in the autogenerated App class:

```
public static void main(String[] args) {
    CmisClient cmisClient = new CmisClient();
    String connectionName = "martinAlf01";
    Session session = cmisClient.getSession(
      connectionName, "admin", "admin");
}
```

To run the code, go to the directory where the Maven POM resides (that is, the pom.xml file) and execute the following command:

```
my-app$ mvn compile exec:java
-Dexec.mainClass="com.mycompany.app.App"
```

Running the preceding code should produce a log that looks something like the following:

```
Feb 19, 2014 7:05:22 AM com.mycompany.app.CmisClient getSession

INFO: Not connected, creating new connection to Alfresco with the
connection id (martinAlf01)

Feb 19, 2014 7:05:22 AM com.mycompany.app.CmisClient getSession

INFO: Found (1) Alfresco repositories

Feb 19, 2014 7:05:22 AM com.mycompany.app.CmisClient getSession

INFO: Info about the first Alfresco repo [ID=-default-] [name=] [CMIS
ver supported=1.1]
```

If you are running the code with an earlier version of Alfresco using the `http://localhost:8080/alfresco/cmisatom` URL, the output should look something like the following:

```
INFO: Not connected, creating new connection to Alfresco with the
connection id (martinAlf01)

INFO: Found (1) Alfresco repositories

INFO: Info about the first Alfresco repo [ID=f0ebcfb4-ca9f-4991-bda8-
9465f4f11527] [name=Main Repository] [CMIS ver supported=1.0]
```

Connecting to a repository by ID

In a production environment, the client code will probably know the ID of the repository that it wants to connect to. The following code snippet shows how to connect to a repository using its ID:

```
parameters.put(SessionParameter.REPOSITORY_ID, "-default-");
// For older AtomPub URL
// parameters.put(SessionParameter.REPOSITORY_ID,
//    "f0ebcfb4-ca9f-4991-bda8-9465f4f11527");
Session session = sessionFactory.createSession(parameters);
```

We use the preceding code instead of using the `getRepositories` method.

Getting repository information

Now when we get a connection to the repository, we can take a look at its capabilities. The `session` object that we got a reference to has a method named `getRepositoryInfo`, which returns a `RepositoryInfo` object that can be used to get to the repository capabilities.

In the `CmisClient` class, add a new method named `listRepoCapabilities` as follows:

```
public void listRepoCapabilities(RepositoryInfo repositoryInfo) {
  RepositoryCapabilities repoCapabilities =
    repositoryInfo.getCapabilities();
  logger.info("aclCapability = " +
    repoCapabilities.getAclCapability().name());
  logger.info("changesCapability = " +
    repoCapabilities.getChangesCapability().name());
  logger.info("contentStreamUpdatable = " +
    repoCapabilities.getContentStreamUpdatesCapability().name());
  logger.info("joinCapability = " +
```

```
        repoCapabilities.getJoinCapability().name());
      logger.info("queryCapability = " +
        repoCapabilities.getQueryCapability().name());
      logger.info("renditionCapability = " +
        repoCapabilities.getRenditionsCapability().name());
      logger.info("allVersionsSearchable? = " +
        repoCapabilities.isAllVersionsSearchableSupported());
      logger.info("getDescendantSupported? = " +
        repoCapabilities.isGetDescendantsSupported());
      logger.info("getFolderTreeSupported? = " +
        repoCapabilities.isGetFolderTreeSupported());
      logger.info("multiFilingSupported? = " +
        repoCapabilities.isMultifilingSupported());
      logger.info("privateWorkingCopySearchable? = " +
        repoCapabilities.isPwcSearchableSupported());
      logger.info("pwcUpdateable? = " +
        repoCapabilities.isPwcUpdatableSupported());
      logger.info("unfilingSupported? = " +
        repoCapabilities.isUnfilingSupported());
      logger.info("versionSpecificFilingSupported? = " +
        repoCapabilities.isVersionSpecificFilingSupported());
    }
```

Here we are listing the basic capabilities of the Alfresco repository. Call this method from the App class as follows:

```
    public static void main(String[] args) {
      CmisClient cmisClient = new CmisClient();
      String connectionName = "martinAlf01";
      Session session = cmisClient.getSession(
        connectionName, "admin", "admin");
      cmisClient.listRepoCapabilities(session.getRepositoryInfo());
    }
```

Running the preceding code prints the following log:

```
INFO: aclCapability = MANAGE

INFO: changesCapability = NONE

INFO: contentStreamUpdatable = ANYTIME

INFO: joinCapability = NONE

INFO: queryCapability = BOTHCOMBINED

INFO: renditionCapability = READ

INFO: allVersionsSearchable? = false

INFO: getDescendantSupported? = true
```

```
INFO: getFolderTreeSupported? = true

INFO: multiFilingSupported? = true

INFO: privateWorkingCopySearchable? = false

INFO: pwcUpdateable? = true

INFO: unfilingSupported? = false

INFO: versionSpecificFilingSupported? = false
```

Here we can see how easy it is to get to the capabilities of the Alfresco repository with OpenCMIS instead of, for example, using the AtomPub binding directly. There is also the possibility to get to the **Access Control List** (**ACL**) capabilities of the repository by calling the `getAclCapabilities` method. It will return an `AclCapabilities` object from which we can get to supported permissions, and CMIS to Alfresco permission mappings.

For an explanation of the different capabilities, refer to *Chapter 2, Basic CMIS Operations*, which covers them in detail.

Listing the children of the root/top folder

To get a list of all the content in the top folder in the repository, we first have to get to the top folder, referred to as the root folder. The root folder can be accessed via the session. The top folder in Alfresco is named `/Company Home`.

To get the root folder and then a listing of its content, add the following code in a new method named `listTopFolder`:

```
public void listTopFolder(Session session) {
  Folder root = session.getRootFolder();
  ItemIterable<CmisObject> contentItems= root.getChildren();
  for (CmisObject contentItem : contentItems) {
    if (contentItem instanceof Document) {
      Document docMetadata = (Document)contentItem;
        ContentStream docContent = docMetadata.getContentStream();
        logger.info(docMetadata.getName() + " [size=" +
        docContent.getLength()+"] [Mimetype=" +
        docContent.getMimeType()+"] [type=" +
        docMetadata.getType().getDisplayName()+"] ");
    } else {
      logger.info(contentItem.getName() + "
        [type="+contentItem.getType().getDisplayName()+"] ");
    }
  }
}
```

The `getChildren` call returns a list of `CmisObjects` that can either be cast to `Document`, `Folder`, `Policy`, or `Relationship`. If it is a `Document` class, we can get to the information about the content via the `getContentStream` method. The `Document` class as well as the `Folder` class contains extra methods only related to these types.

Now, call this new method from the `App` class as follows:

```
public static void main(String[] args) {
  CmisClient cmisClient = new CmisClient();
  String connectionName = "martinAlf01";
  Session session = cmisClient.getSession(
    connectionName, "admin", "admin");
  cmisClient.listRepoCapabilities(session.getRepositoryInfo());
  cmisClient.listTopFolder(session);
}
```

Running the preceding code will print logs that look something like the following:

```
INFO: Data Dictionary [type=Folder]

INFO: Guest Home [type=Folder]

INFO: User Homes [type=Folder]

INFO: Imap Attachments [type=Folder]

INFO: Sites [type=Sites]

INFO: CMIS Demo [type=Folder]

INFO: CMIS Demo Browser Binding [type=Folder]

INFO: Simple (from Browser binding).txt [size=-
1] [Mimetype=text/plain] [type=Document]

INFO: simple.txt [size=-1] [Mimetype=text/plain] [type=Document]

INFO: simple2.txt [size=-1] [Mimetype=text/plain] [type=Document]

INFO: SimpleBrowser.txt [size=-1] [Mimetype=text/plain] [type=Document]

INFO: SimpleBrowser2.txt [size=-
1] [Mimetype=text/plain] [type=Document]

INFO: Some it doc.txt [size=-1] [Mimetype=text/plain] [type=My Company
IT Doc]
```

Here we are logging the name of the file and the type. The last file has a custom document type applied as we can see in the preceding log.

Optional parameters when listing the children of a folder

Listing a folder can return a lot of content items, so it might be a good idea to be able to do some form of paging of the result. It is also beneficial to be able to only fetch those properties that we are interested in, so we can minimize the payload and speed up the application response time.

For this we can use the OperationContext class. The OperationContext class allows you to tune the amount of information returned for each content item by setting property filters and renditions filters, or by setting flags to include path segments, ACLs, allowable actions, policies, and relationships. The OperationContext class is also used to control paging and caching during an operation.

Once paging is set up, OpenCMIS fetches each page asynchronously when it is requested. To set up paging, create a new method as follows:

```java
public void listTopFolderWithPagingAndPropFilter(Session session) {
  Folder root = session.getRootFolder();
  OperationContext operationContext = new OperationContextImpl();
  int maxItemsPerPage = 5;
  operationContext.setMaxItemsPerPage(maxItemsPerPage);
  ItemIterable<CmisObject> contentItems =
  root.getChildren(operationContext);
  long numerOfPages = Math.abs(contentItems.getTotalNumItems() /
  maxItemsPerPage);
  int pageNumber = 1;
  boolean finishedPaging = false;
  int count = 0;

  while (!finishedPaging) {
    logger.info("Page "+ pageNumber + " (" + numerOfPages + ")");
    ItemIterable<CmisObject> currentPage =
      contentItems.skipTo(count).getPage();
    for (CmisObject contentItem : currentPage) {
      logger.info(contentItem.getName() + " [type=" +
        contentItem.getType().getDisplayName() + "]");
        count++;
    }
    pageNumber++;
    if (!currentPage.getHasMoreItems()) {
      finishedPaging = true;
    }
  }
}
```

We start off by fetching the root folder for which we are going to get the children. Then we set up the maximum items per page to 5 and create an operational context with this configuration. The operational context is then passed in to the `getChildren` method, setting it up for asynchronous paging.

The content items for each page are then listed. We get to each new page by using the `skipTo` method on the complete resultset that is contained in the `contentItems` variable.

Running the preceding code produces a log that looks something as follows:

```
INFO: Page 1 (3)
INFO: Data Dictionary [type=Folder]
INFO: Guest Home [type=Folder]
INFO: User Homes [type=Folder]
INFO: Imap Attachments [type=Folder]
INFO: Sites [type=Sites]
INFO: Page 2 (3)
INFO: Training [type=Folder]
INFO: Test [type=Folder]
INFO: CMIS Demo [type=Folder]
INFO: CMIS Demo Browser Binding [type=Folder]
INFO: Simple (from Browser binding).txt [type=Document]
INFO: Page 3 (3)
INFO: simple.txt [type=Document]
INFO: simple2.txt [type=Document]
INFO: SimpleBrowser.txt [type=Document]
INFO: SimpleBrowser2.txt [type=Document]
INFO: Some it doc.txt [type=My Company IT Doc]
```

To set up a properties filter, use the `setFilter` method on the operational context. In the following example, only the `Created_By` and `Name` properties are returned. However, this is not strictly true; some properties such as object type ID are always returned, as we saw in *Chapter 2, Basic CMIS Operations*.

```
Set<String> propertyFilter = new HashSet<String>();
propertyFilter.add(PropertyIds.CREATED_BY);
propertyFilter.add(PropertyIds.NAME);
operationContext.setFilter(propertyFilter);
```

If you want to list the properties for each content item returned in a `getChildren` listing, the following code can be used:

```
private void listProperties(CmisObject cmisObject) {
  for (Property<?> p : cmisObject.getProperties()) {
    if (PropertyType.DATETIME == p.getType()) {
      Calendar calValue = (Calendar) p.getValue();
      logger.info("  - " +p.getId()+ " = "+ (calValue != null ?
        new SimpleDateFormat("yyyy-MM-dd HH:mm:ss z").
          format(calValue.getTime()) : ""));
    } else {
      logger.info("  - " + p.getId() + " = " + p.getValue());
    }
  }
}
```

If we now run this with the properties filter set in the operational context, we would see the following properties listed for each content item:

```
...
INFO:    - cmis:name = simple.txt
INFO:    - cmis:createdBy = admin
INFO:    - cmis:objectId = 0be16ca8-3562-47c1-8a81-3be52a725d56;1.0
INFO:    - cmis:baseTypeId = cmis:document
...
```

To see all the properties, we would have to remove the properties filter.

If we have custom types and we want to check if they are of a particular base type, we can use the `getBaseType` method on the content item as shown in the following code example:

```
if (ObjectType.FOLDER_BASETYPE_ID.equals(
  contentItem.getBaseType().getId())) {
    // We got a folder, do something...
} else if (ObjectType.DOCUMENT_BASETYPE_ID.equals(
  contentItem.getBaseType().getId())) {
    // We got a document, do something...
}
```

Listing available types and subtypes

Getting to know the content model that the CMS server supports is important so that we can classify objects according to the specific domain we are in. The OpenCMIS API provides methods to list types and their subtypes.

Add the following code to the `CmisClient` class:

```
public void listTypesAndSubtypes(Session session) {
  boolean includePropertyDefinitions = false;
  List<Tree<ObjectType>> typeTrees =
    session.getTypeDescendants(
    null, -1, includePropertyDefinitions);
  for (Tree<ObjectType> typeTree : typeTrees) {
    logTypes(typeTree, "");
  }
}
```

The preceding `listTypesAndSubtypes` method uses the `getTypeDescendants` method on the `session` object to get the type hierarchy that has been deployed to the server. The `getTypeDescendants` method takes three parameters: the first one specifies if we should start at the top of the tree or not; `null` indicates that we should start from the top. On the other hand, if we wanted to only list the type tree for the base type `Document`, we would specify the first parameter as `cmis:document`.

The second parameter specifies how deep we should search in the type hierarchy; `-1` means infinite depth. If you just want the first base type level and one more subtype level, then specify `1`, which means searching one level under the base types. The last parameter indicates if all the property type definitions should be returned for all types; we don't list the property type definitions, so it is set to `false`.

The `getTypeDescendants` method returns a list of type trees, basically one list for each one of the base types document, folder, policy, and relationship. For each base type tree, we call the `logTypes` method that looks like the following:

```
private void logTypes(Tree<ObjectType> typeTree, String tab) {
    ObjectType objType = typeTree.getItem();
    String docInfo = "";
    if (objType instanceof DocumentType) {
      DocumentType docType = (DocumentType)objType;
      docInfo = "[versionable=" + docType.isVersionable() +
      "] [content="+docType.getContentStreamAllowed()+"]";
```

```
      }
      logger.info(tab + objType.getDisplayName() + " [id=" +
      objType.getId() + "] [fileable=" + objType.isFileable() +
      "] [queryable=" + objType.isQueryable() + "]" + docInfo);

      for (Tree<ObjectType> subTypeTree : typeTree.getChildren()) {
        logTypes(subTypeTree, tab + " ");
      }
    }
  }
```

This method first checks if the object type is a document type, in which case we fetch some extra properties and store them in a string that we can add to the log message. Then we log a number of the most common properties for the type. And finally, we recursively call ourselves if there are more subtypes to log, which we find out by calling getChildren on the current type tree.

Running the preceding code produces a log with a type hierarchy that looks something like the following for Alfresco 4.2 with the custom content model that accompanies this book applied:

```
INFO: Policy [id=cmis:policy] [fileable=false] [queryable=true]


INFO: Relationship [id=cmis:relationship] [fileable=false]
[queryable=false]

INFO:   Attachment [id=R:imap:attachment] [fileable=false]
[queryable=false]

INFO:   Replaces [id=R:cm:replaces] [fileable=false]
[queryable=false]

INFO:   References [id=R:cm:references] [fileable=false]
[queryable=false]

INFO:   Attachments [id=R:dl:attachments] [fileable=false]
[queryable=false]

...

INFO: Folder [id=cmis:folder] [fileable=true] [queryable=true]

INFO:   System Folder [id=F:cm:systemfolder] [fileable=true]
[queryable=true]

INFO:   Saved Action Folder [id=F:act:savedactionfolder]
[fileable=true] [queryable=true]

INFO:   Delivery Channel [id=F:pub:DeliveryChannel] [fileable=true]
[queryable=true]

INFO:   Twitter Delivery Channel [id=F:twitter:DeliveryChannel]
[fileable=true] [queryable=true]

INFO:   Data List folder type [id=F:dl:dataList] [fileable=true]
```

```
[queryable=true]

INFO:   MyCompany Project [id=F:myc:project] [fileable=true]
[queryable=true]

...

INFO: Secondary Type [id=cmis:secondary] [fileable=false]
[queryable=true]

INFO:   Renditioned [id=P:rn:renditioned] [fileable=false]
[queryable=true]

INFO:   Restrictable [id=P:dp:restrictable] [fileable=false]
[queryable=true]

INFO:   Emailed [id=P:cm:emailed]
[fileable=false] [queryable=true]

INFO:   Effectivity [id=P:cm:effectivity] [fileable=false]
[queryable=true]

INFO:   Attached [id=P:emailserver:attached] [fileable=false]
[queryable=true]

INFO:   EXIF [id=P:exif:exif] [fileable=false] [queryable=true]

...

INFO: Document [id=cmis:document] [fileable=true] [queryable=true]
[versionable=true] [content=ALLOWED]

INFO:   MyCompany Base Doc [id=D:myc:document] [fileable=true]
[queryable=true] [versionable=true] [content=ALLOWED]

INFO:    MyCompany IT Doc [id=D:myc:itDoc] [fileable=true]
[queryable=true] [versionable=true] [content=ALLOWED]

INFO:   Custom Document [id=D:cmiscustom:document]
[fileable=true] [queryable=true] [versionable=true] [content=ALLOWED]

INFO:   Transfer Record [id=D:trx:transferRecord] [fileable=true]
[queryable=true] [versionable=true] [content=ALLOWED]

......
```

Here we can see that all the aspects that are defined in the deployed content models
are defined as secondary types when CMIS 1.1 is supported by your Alfresco
server. If you are using a CMIS 1.0 server, the secondary types listed previously
representing Alfresco aspects will instead be exposed as policies as follows:

```
INFO: Policy [id=cmis:relationship] [fileable=false] [queryable=false]

...

INFO:   Google Editable [id=P:gd:googleEditable]
[fileable=false] [queryable=true]

INFO:   Subscribable [id=P:cm:subscribable]
[fileable=false] [queryable=true]

INFO:   Working Copy [id=P:cm:workingcopy]
```

```
[fileable=false] [queryable=true]
INFO:    Email Alias [id=P:emailserver:aliasable]
[fileable=false] [queryable=true]
INFO:    Author [id=P:cm:author] [fileable=false] [queryable=true]
```

Creating, updating, and deleting content

We now know how to list folder content and how to get the available content type hierarchy. It's time to look at how we can create objects.

Creating folders

Creating folders is easy, just get a `Folder` object for the parent folder in which you want to create a new folder and then use the `createFolder` method on the parent folder object as in the following code:

```java
public Folder createFolder(Session session) {
   String folderName = "OpenCMISTest";
   Folder parentFolder = session.getRootFolder();

   // Make sure the user is allowed to create a folder
   // under the root folder
     if (parentFolder.getAllowableActions().getAllowableActions().
       contains(Action.CAN_CREATE_FOLDER) == false) {
         throw new CmisUnauthorizedException(
           "Current user does not have permission to create a " +
           "sub-folder in " + parentFolder.getPath());
     }

   // Check if folder already exist, if not create it
   Folder newFolder = (Folder) getObject(
   session, parentFolder, folderName);
     if (newFolder == null) {
       Map<String, Object> newFolderProps =
       new HashMap<String, Object>();
       newFolderProps.put(
       PropertyIds.OBJECT_TYPE_ID, "cmis:folder");
       newFolderProps.put(PropertyIds.NAME, folderName);
       newFolder = parentFolder.createFolder(newFolderProps);

       logger.info("Created new folder: " + newFolder.getPath() +
         " [creator=" + newFolder.getCreatedBy() + "] [created=" +
         date2String(newFolder.getCreationDate().getTime()) + "]");
```

```
  } else {
    logger.info("Folder already exist: " + newFolder.getPath());
  }

  return newFolder;
}
```

Here we are creating the new folder under the root folder, which is represented by the / path, and is the same as /Company Home in Alfresco. Before we go ahead and create the folder, we first check if the current user is authorized to create a subfolder under the root folder. We can do this by getting the allowed actions on the root folder; if they contain the canCreateFolder action, we can go ahead and create the folder. If not, then we throw an unauthorized runtime exception that will stop execution. This is actually the same exception that will be thrown by the OpenCMIS library if we do not check anything before creating the folder with an unauthorized user.

When we know we are allowed to create a folder, we call a custom method named getObject, which we will define in a second. This method will return a Folder object if it can find it, or null if it can't. If the folder was not found, it will be created via the createFolder method.

The createFolder method takes a map of metadata that should be set for the new folder. The name and type of the folder are mandatory properties, so this is the minimum metadata we can use to create a folder. The createFolder method returns a new CMIS object that represents the newly created folder, which we can use in future methods to create documents in it and to log some information about the new folder.

Before we can run the code, we need to include the preceding method in the App class and also implement the getObject method as follows:

```
private CmisObject getObject(
Session session, Folder parentFolder, String objectName) {
  CmisObject object = null;

  try {
    String path2Object = parentFolder.getPath();
    if (!path2Object.endsWith("/")) {
      path2Object += "/";
    }
    path2Object += objectName;
    object = session.getObjectByPath(path2Object);
  } catch (CmisObjectNotFoundException nfe0) {
    // Nothing to do, object does not exist
  }

  return object;
}
```

The preceding method will use the `getObjectByPath` method on `session` to get the `Folder` object. If it cannot find an object at the specified path, then `null` is returned. The root folder is represented by `/`, so we need to check if we have this path separator or not before we add the object name to the path.

There is also the `date2String` method that we will use throughout this chapter; it is implemented as follows and used when logging date properties:

```
private String date2String(Date date) {
  return new SimpleDateFormat
  ("yyyy-MM-dd HH:mm:ss z").format(date);
}
```

Running the preceding code generates a log as follows:

INFO: Created new folder: /OpenCMISTest [creator=admin]
[created=2014-02-23 17:33:47 GMT]

If we run the code again, we should see a message saying the folder already exists.

The content model delivered with the book contains a custom `project` folder type defined as follows:

```
<type  name="myc:project" >
  <title>MyCompany Project</title>
  <parent>cm:folder</parent>
  <properties>
    <property name="myc:projectCode">
      <title>Project Code</title>
      <type>d:text</type>
    </property>
  </properties>
</type>
```

If we want to create a folder with the preceding custom type set, we can do that as follows by just specifying the type via the `OBJECT_TYPE_ID` property and making sure we prefix the type with `F:` (for folder):

```
public void createFolderWithCustomType(Session session) {
  String folderName = "OpenCMISTest2";
  Folder parentFolder = session.getRootFolder();

  // Check if folder already exist, if not create it
  Folder newFolder = (Folder)getObject(
  session, parentFolder, folderName);
  if (newFolder == null) {
    Map<String, Object> newFolderProps =
```

```
new HashMap<String, Object>();
newFolderProps.put(PropertyIds.OBJECT_TYPE_ID,
"F:myc:project");
newFolderProps.put(PropertyIds.NAME, folderName);
newFolderProps.put("myc:projectCode", "PROJ001");
newFolder = parentFolder.createFolder(newFolderProps);

logger.info("Created new folder: " + newFolder.getPath() +
" [creator=" + newFolder.getCreatedBy() + "] [created=" +
date2String(newFolder.getCreationDate().getTime()) + "]");
} else {
logger.info("Folder already exist: " + newFolder.getPath());
}
}
```

 If we are using a CMIS 1.0 Alfresco repository, the myc:projectCode
property on the custom project type has to be specified directly in the
type definition in the content model XML. It cannot be specified via an
aspect and then included in the type with the mandatory-aspects
syntax. Aspects were not supported by CMIS until Version 1.1 when they
were exposed as secondary types. We are coming to how aspects can be
used later on in this chapter, whether you are using Version 1.0 or 1.1.

Creating documents

After creating some folders, we probably want to create or upload documents into
them. Creating a document, or file if you like, is almost the same as creating a folder.
However, a document object can also contain content bytes in the form of a so-called
content stream that represents the physical bytes of the file.

So, to create a document object with content, we first create a content stream object
and then use that object when creating the document object as follows:

```
public Document createDocument(Session session, Folder
parentFolder)
throws IOException {
  String documentName = "OpenCMISTest.txt";

  // Make sure the user is allowed to create a document
  // in the passed in folder
  if (parentFolder.getAllowableActions().getAllowableActions().
  contains(Action.CAN_CREATE_DOCUMENT) == false) {
    throw new CmisUnauthorizedException("Current user does not "+
    "have permission to create a document in " +
```

```
      parentFolder.getPath());
  }

  // Check if document already exist, if not create it
  Document newDocument = (Document) getObject(
  session, parentFolder, documentName);
  if (newDocument == null) {
    // Setup document metadata
    Map<String, Object> newDocumentProps =
    new HashMap<String, Object>();
    newDocumentProps.put(PropertyIds.OBJECT_TYPE_ID,
    "cmis:document");
    newDocumentProps.put(PropertyIds.NAME, documentName);

    // Setup document content
    String mimetype = "text/plain; charset=UTF-8";
    String documentText = "This is a test document!";
    byte[] bytes = documentText.getBytes("UTF-8");
    ByteArrayInputStream input = new ByteArrayInputStream(bytes);
    ContentStream contentStream =
    session.getObjectFactory().createContentStream(
    documentName, bytes.length, mimetype, input);

    // Create versioned document object
    newDocument = parentFolder.createDocument(
    newDocumentProps, contentStream, VersioningState.MAJOR);

    logger.info("Created new document: " +
    getDocumentPath(newDocument) + " [version=" +
    newDocument.getVersionLabel() + "] [creator=" +
    newDocument.getCreatedBy() + "] [created=" +
    date2String(newDocument.getCreationDate().getTime())+"]");
  } else {
    logger.info("Document already exist: " +
    getDocumentPath(newDocument));
  }

  return newDocument;
}
```

The new document should be created in the OpenCMISTest folder that we just created in one of the previous examples. To do this, we feed the folder reference into the createDocument method as follows in the App class:

```
Folder folder = cmisClient.createFolder(session);
document = cmisClient.createDocument(session, folder);
```

So, as we can see, creating a document is similar to how folders are created. We start by checking if the user is allowed and then just specify a document type (that is, `cmis:document`) instead of a folder type, create the content stream with the document content, and use the `createDocument` method instead of the `createFolder` method on the parent `Folder` object.

There is also a difference between folders and documents when it comes to versioning. Folders cannot be versioned according to the CMIS specification, but documents can. If the document type is versionable, then using versioning is mandatory. So you cannot pass in `VersioningState.NONE` to the `createDocument` method in this case. You can extend the code to check the versioning state of the document type, as follows:

```
String typeId = "cmis:document";
VersioningState versioningState = VersioningState.NONE;
DocumentType docType =
(DocumentType)session.getTypeDefinition(typeId);
if (Boolean.TRUE.equals(docType.isVersionable())) {
  versioningState = VersioningState.MAJOR;
}
```

In the case of Alfresco, we cannot set versioning to NONE as the `cmis:document` type is always `versionable`. At first you might think that it's a bad idea to have versioning turned on for all content created in Alfresco. In reality this is not the case as by default autoversioning of content is turned off. More on this later when we talk about versioning with check out and check in.

In this example, the content stream is created from a `String` literal (that is, `documentText`) by passing the bytes of the string to the `createContentStream` method that is available on the session's object factory. We make sure to get the string bytes with UTF-8 encoding and setting UTF-8 encoding in the MIME type.

Running the preceding code generates the following log:

```
INFO: Created new document: /OpenCMISTest/OpenCMISTest.txt
[version=1.0] [creator=admin] [created=2014-02-23 17:33:47 GMT]
```

By using the MAJOR versioning state, we start the version label at 1.0. This example uses a custom method named `getDocumentPath` to find out the absolute repository path for a document. This method looks like the following:

```
private String getDocumentPath(Document document) {
  String path2Doc = getParentFolderPath(document);
  if (!path2Doc.endsWith("/")) {
```

```
        path2Doc += "/";
    }
    path2Doc += document.getName();
    return path2Doc;
}
```

What this method does is call another custom method named `getParentFolderPath` to get the path for the parent folder of the document object passed in. When it has this path, it checks if it ends in /;if not, it adds / (if it is the root folder, it will end in slash as it is represented by /). To complete the full path for the document, it then adds the name of the document to the parent folder path and returns the result.

The `getParentFolderPath` method is implemented as follows:

```
private String getParentFolderPath(Document document) {
    Folder parentFolder = getDocumentParentFolder(document);
    return parentFolder == null ?
    "Un-filed" : parentFolder.getPath();
}
```

The preceding code just calls another custom method named `getDocumentParentFolder` to get the parent `Folder` object for the passed in `Document` object. It then checks if it is null, which means that the document has not been filed/contained in any folder and is in a state called *unfiled*. If we have a parent folder object, we just return the absolute repository path for it.

The `getDocumentParentFolder` method is implemented as follows:

```
private Folder getDocumentParentFolder(Document document) {
    // Get all the parent folders (could be more than one
    // if multi-filed)
    List<Folder> parentFolders = document.getParents();

    // Grab the first parent folder
    if (parentFolders.size() > 0) {
        if (parentFolders.size() > 1) {
            logger.info("The " + document.getName() +
            " has more than one parent folder, it is multi-filed");
        }

        return parentFolders.get(0);
    } else {
        logger.info("Document " + document.getName() +
        " is un-filed and does not have a parent folder");
        return null;
    }
}
```

A document can have multiple folders as parents (that is, multifiled), so we start out by finding out what parents the document have by calling getParents on it. Then we grab the first parent in the list assuming that most document objects will only be filed/contained in one folder. If it is multifiled, we print out a message about that. If no parent folders could be found for the document, then it is unfiled and null is returned as the document does not have a parent folder. The preceding helper methods will be used throughout this chapter.

In the previous example, we did not upload a file from the disk. If we, for example, wanted to upload a PDF file from disk and set the document type to a custom type, such as the myc:itDoc type from the content model in the book, we could do the following:

```
public Document createDocumentFromFileWithCustomType(Session
session) {
  String documentName = "OpenCMISTest2.pdf";
  File file = new File("Some.pdf");
  Folder parentFolder = session.getRootFolder();

  // Check if document already exist, if not create it
  Document newDocument = (Document) getObject(
  session, parentFolder, documentName);
  if (newDocument == null) {
    // Setup document metadata
    Map<String, Object> newDocumentProps =
    new HashMap<String, Object>();
    newDocumentProps.put(
    PropertyIds.OBJECT_TYPE_ID, "D:myc:itDoc");
    newDocumentProps.put(PropertyIds.NAME, documentName);

    InputStream is = null;
    try {
      // Setup document content
      is = new FileInputStream(file);
      String mimetype = "application/pdf";
      ContentStream contentStream =
      session.getObjectFactory().createContentStream(
      documentName, file.length(), mimetype, is);

      // Create versioned document object
      newDocument = parentFolder.createDocument(
      newDocumentProps, contentStream, VersioningState.MAJOR);
      logger.info("Created new document: " +
      getDocumentPath(newDocument) + " [version=" +
```

```
              newDocument.getVersionLabel() + "][creator=" +
              newDocument.getCreatedBy() + "][created=" +
              date2String(newDocument.getCreationDate().getTime()) + "]");

              // Close the stream to handle any IO Exception
              is.close();
          } catch (IOException ioe) {
              ioe.printStackTrace();
          } finally {
              IOUtils.closeQuietly(is);
          }
      } else {
          logger.info("Document already exist: " +
              getDocumentPath(newDocument));
      }


      return newDocument;
  }
```

The difference in the previous example is that here we are uploading a PDF document named `Some.pdf`, which exists in the same directory that we are running the application from. We create a new file input stream and hand it over to the `createContentStream` method, which extracts the bytes from the file and writes them as file content in the repository. We make sure to close the input stream afterwards so that we don't lose OS file descriptors. The document type is set to the custom type `myc:itDoc`, prefixed with `D:` to indicate that it is a document type.

When creating folders or documents, it is not possible to set the `CREATED_BY`, `CREATION_DATE`, `LAST_MODIFIED_BY`, or `LAST_MODIFICATION_DATE` properties, as they are controlled by Alfresco. They belong to an Alfresco aspect named `cm:auditable`, which is managed completely by the system. So doing something like the following will not have any effect:

```
// Setup document metadata
Map<String, Object> newDocumentProps =
new HashMap<String, Object>();
newDocumentProps.put(PropertyIds.OBJECT_TYPE_ID, "cmis:document");
newDocumentProps.put(PropertyIds.NAME, documentName);
newDocumentProps.put(PropertyIds.CREATED_BY, "mjackson");
Calendar createdDate = Calendar.getInstance();
createdDate.set(Calendar.YEAR, 2011);
newDocumentProps.put(PropertyIds.CREATION_DATE,
createdDate.getTime());
newDocumentProps.put(PropertyIds.LAST_MODIFIED_BY, "mjackson");
newDocumentProps.put(PropertyIds.LAST_MODIFICATION_DATE,
createdDate.getTime());
```

The Alfresco system will still create the document with the user that was used to create the OpenCMIS session, and the current date and time. The code will run but it will not do anything.

It is also possible to create a document without specifying the parent folder that it should be contained in. This is then called an unfiled object. To do this, we have to use the `createDocument` method on the `session` object instead and pass in `null` as the folder reference. However, this will only work if the repository supports this. Check the `unfilingSupported` capability and make sure it is set to `true`. In an upcoming section in this chapter, the `deleteFolderTree` method shows how to check if this capability is set. The Alfresco 4.2 version that I use does not support it.

It is also possible that the requirement to create a document without a content stream may come up in a project, which basically means creating a metadata entry for the document in the repository. Then maybe some content bytes can be added for it in the future. This is possible in some repositories such as Alfresco; others, such as Microsoft SharePoint, require a content stream at all times. To figure out if your repository requires it, check the `contentStreamAllowed` attribute on the `cmis:document` object type. See the `logTypes` method previously described in this chapter for an example of how to check this. If it has the value `allowed`, the document may have a content stream, but may not need to. Other values are `required` and `notallowed`.

Updating folders and documents

To update the properties (that is, metadata) for a folder, we call the `updateProperties` method on it as follows:

```
public Folder updateFolder(Folder folder) {
  String newFolderName = "OpenCMISTest_Updated";
  Folder updatedFolder = null;

  // If we got a folder update the name of it
  if (folder != null) {
    // Make sure the user is allowed to update folder properties
    if (folder.getAllowableActions().getAllowableActions().
    contains(Action.CAN_UPDATE_PROPERTIES) == false) {
      throw new CmisUnauthorizedException(
      "Current user does not have permission to update " + "folder
      properties for " + folder.getPath());
    }

    // Update the folder with a new name
    String oldName = folder.getName();
```

```
        Map<String, Object> newFolderProps =
        new HashMap<String, Object>();
        newFolderProps.put(PropertyIds.NAME, newFolderName);
        updatedFolder = (Folder)
        folder.updateProperties(newFolderProps);

        logger.info("Updated " + oldName + " with new name: " +
        updatedFolder.getPath() + " [creator=" +
        updatedFolder.getCreatedBy() + "][created=" +
        date2String(updatedFolder.getCreationDate().getTime()) +
        "][modifier=" + updatedFolder.getLastModifiedBy() + "]
        [modified="+date2String(updatedFolder.
        getLastModificationDate().getTime()) + "]");
    } else {
        logger.error("Folder to update is null!");
    }

    return updatedFolder;
}
```

Here we are renaming a folder by updating its NAME property (that is, cmis:name). The updateProperties method returns a new Folder object with the latest properties set. Before we do the actual update, we check if the current user has permission to do an update of the object's properties; the canUpdateProperties action needs to be set to true for the object. After the update, we will have a new last modified date set as can be seen in the following log output produced by running the code:

```
INFO: Updated OpenCMISTest with new name: /OpenCMISTest_Updated [
creator=admin][created=2014-02-23 17:33:47
GMT][modifier=admin][modified=2014-02-23 17:33:48 GMT]
```

The process for updating a document is very similar; in fact, it is the same if we just want to update the properties for it. But we probably want to update the content for the document, and this can be done by updating the content stream for the document object with the setContentStream method. First, we need to make sure that the content can be updated without being checked out first. It is not mandatory for a repository to support this. We check this by looking at the contentStreamUpdatesCapability property and making sure that it is set to ANYTIME, as follows:

```
    public Document updateDocument(Session session, Document document)
    throws IOException {
        RepositoryInfo repoInfo = session.getRepositoryInfo();
        if (!repoInfo.getCapabilities().
        getContentStreamUpdatesCapability()
        .equals(CapabilityContentStreamUpdates.ANYTIME)) {
```

```
        logger.warn("Updating content stream without a checkout is" +
        " not supported by this repository [repoName=" +
        repoInfo.getProductName() + "][repoVersion=" +
        repoInfo.getProductVersion() + "]");
        return document;
    }

    // Make sure we got a document, then update it
    Document updatedDocument = null;
    if (document != null) {
      // Make sure the user is allowed to update the content
      // for this document
      if (document.getAllowableActions().getAllowableActions().
      contains(Action.CAN_SET_CONTENT_STREAM) == false) {
        throw new CmisUnauthorizedException("Current user does not"
        + " have permission to set/update content stream for " +
        getDocumentPath(document));
      }

      // Setup new document content
      String newDocumentText = "This is a test document that has " +
      "been updated with new content!";
      String mimetype = "text/plain; charset=UTF-8";
      byte[] bytes = newDocumentText.getBytes("UTF-8");
      ByteArrayInputStream input = new ByteArrayInputStream(bytes);
      ContentStream contentStream =
      session.getObjectFactory().createContentStream(
      document.getName(), bytes.length, mimetype, input);
      boolean overwriteContent = true;
      updatedDocument = document.setContentStream(
      contentStream, overwriteContent);
      if (updatedDocument == null) {
        logger.info("No new version was created when " +
        "content stream was updated for " +
        getDocumentPath(document));
        updatedDocument = document;
      }

      logger.info("Updated content for document: " +
      getDocumentPath(updatedDocument) +
      " [version=" + updatedDocument.getVersionLabel() + "]
      [modifier=" + updatedDocument.getLastModifiedBy() +
      "][modified=" + date2String(updatedDocument.
      getLastModificationDate().getTime()) + "]");
```

```
      } else {
        logger.info("Document is null, cannot update it!");
      }


      return updatedDocument;
    }
```

If we run the preceding code, we will get the following output, where we can see that a new version has not been created:

INFO: **No new version was created when content stream was updated for /OpenCMISTest_Updated/OpenCMISTest.txt**

INFO: **Updated content for document: /OpenCMISTest_Updated/OpenCMISTest.txt [version=1.0] [modifier=admin] [modified=2014-02-23 17:33:48 GMT]**

To update the content and create a new version, we have to check it out first, which we will cover later in this chapter.

Deleting a document, folder, or folder tree

Any CMIS object can be deleted with the `delete` method. We are going to start looking at how to delete one of the documents we created earlier:

```
    public void deleteDocument(Document document) {
      // If we got a document try and delete it
      if (document != null) {
        // Make sure the user is allowed to delete the document
        if (document.getAllowableActions().getAllowableActions().
        contains(Action.CAN_DELETE_OBJECT) == false) {
          throw new CmisUnauthorizedException("Current user does " +
          "not have permission to delete document " +
          document.getName()+" with Object ID "+document.getId());
        }

        String docPath = getDocumentPath(document);
        boolean deleteAllVersions = true;
        document.delete(deleteAllVersions);
        logger.info("Deleted document: " + docPath);
      } else {
        logger.info("Cannot delete document as it is null!");
      }
    }
```

When a document is deleted, we have the option to delete the document and all its previous versions or only the latest version. This is specified by passing an extra parameter to the `delete` method. If this parameter is set to `true`, all versions will be deleted like in a normal delete operation in Alfresco. If this parameter is set to `false` and versioning has been turned on for the document, only the latest version will be deleted. If there is only one version, the complete document will be deleted. After the document is deleted, we cannot use the `document` object anymore to, for example, get the path to the document. That's why we store the path in a separate `docPath` variable before deleting the object. Before we delete the object, we also make sure that the user has the permission to delete the object by checking whether the `canDeleteObject` action is allowed.

Now, we will also delete the folder that contained the document we just deleted:

```
public void deleteFolder(Folder folder) {
  // If we got a folder then delete
  if (folder != null) {
    // Make sure the user is allowed to delete the folder
    if (folder.getAllowableActions().getAllowableActions().
    contains(Action.CAN_DELETE_OBJECT) == false) {
      throw new CmisUnauthorizedException("Current user does "+
      "not have permission to delete folder " + folder.getPath());
    }

    String folderPath = folder.getPath();
    folder.delete();
    logger.info("Deleted folder: " + folderPath);
  } else {
    logger.info("Cannot delete folder that is null");
  }
}
```

The `folder` object that we want to delete is passed in to the method, and the first thing we check is whether the user has permission to delete it. Then we store the path to the folder as the `folder` object will not be usable after we delete the folder. Next, we execute the `delete` method on the `folder` object. Note that the folder has to be empty; it cannot contain subfolders or documents. If it contains any content, an exception will be thrown. If we have a folder with content, the `deleteTree` method needs to be used instead as shown in the following example:

```
public void deleteFolderTree(Session session) {
  UnfileObject unfileMode = UnfileObject.UNFILE;
  RepositoryInfo repoInfo = session.getRepositoryInfo();
  if (!repoInfo.getCapabilities().isUnfilingSupported()) {
```

```java
    logger.warn("The repository does not support unfiling" +
    " a document from a folder, documents will " +
    "be deleted completely from all associated folders " +
    "[repoName=" + repoInfo.getProductName() + "] [repoVersion=" +
    repoInfo.getProductVersion() + "]");
    unfileMode = UnfileObject.DELETE;
}


String folderName = "OpenCMISTestWithContent";
Folder parentFolder = session.getRootFolder();

// Check if folder exist, if not don't try and delete it
Folder someFolder = (Folder) getObject(
session, parentFolder, folderName);
if (someFolder != null) {
  // Make sure the user is allowed to delete the folder
  if (someFolder.getAllowableActions().getAllowableActions().
  contains(Action.CAN_DELETE_TREE) == false) {
    throw new CmisUnauthorizedException("Current user does" +
    " not have permission to delete folder tree" +
    parentFolder.getPath());
  }

  boolean deleteAllVersions = true;
  boolean continueOnFailure = true;
  List<String> failedObjectIds =
  someFolder.deleteTree(
  deleteAllVersions, unfileMode, continueOnFailure);
  logger.info("Deleted folder and all its content: " +
  someFolder.getName());
  if (failedObjectIds != null && failedObjectIds.size() > 1) {
    for (String failedObjectId : failedObjectIds) {
      logger.info("Could not delete Alfresco node with " +
      "Node Ref: " + failedObjectId);
    }
  }
} else {
  logger.info("Did not delete folder as it does not exist: " +
  parentFolder.getPath() + folderName);
}
}
```

Before running this code, we first need to create a folder named
OpenCMISTestWithContent with a subfolder and some documents in it. When this code
is executed, it uses the deleteTree method and takes the following three parameters:

- `deleteAllVersions`: If this parameter is set to `true`, all versions for all the documents will be deleted. This is not relevant to Alfresco because if you delete a folder, all the content is going to be deleted, including all versions, and moved to the archive store.

- `unfileMode`: This parameter can be set to `DELETE`, which means that the document should be completely deleted and unfiled from any folder referencing it. If set to `UNFILE`, this means that the document will be unfiled from the folder that is being deleted, and if set to `DELETESINGLEFILED`, the document will be deleted if it is only filed under the folder that is being deleted. This parameter is dependent on the value of the `isUnfilingSupported` capability, which for Alfresco 4.2 is set to `false`, so we cannot unfile documents.

- `continueOnFailure`: With this parameter set to `true`, folders and documents are deleted individually. If a document or folder cannot be deleted, the method moves to the next document or folder in the list. When the method completes, it returns a list of the document IDs and the folder IDs that were not deleted. With this parameter set to `false`, all the folders and documents can be deleted in a single batch, which depending on the repository design, may improve performance. If a document or folder cannot be deleted, an exception is raised.

Running the preceding code produces the following log:

```
WARNING: The repository does not support unfiling a document from a
folder, documents will be deleted completely from all associated
folders [repoName=Alfresco Enterprise] [repoVersion=4.2.0 (r57217-
b28)]
INFO: Deleted folder and all its content: OpenCMISTestWithContent
```

Now, let's create the `OpenCMISTestWithContent` folder again but with one of the documents checked out. This should lock the document, and it should not be possible to delete it. The following log is then produced:

```
INFO: Deleted folder and all its content: OpenCMISTestWithContent

INFO: Could not delete Alfresco node with Node Ref:
workspace://SpacesStore/c979a3e4-a9ea-498b-96aa-d17e6f29a832

INFO: Could not delete Alfresco node with Node Ref:
workspace://SpacesStore/5e0a1c1f-e279-403b-a04d-2ad164a7105a;1.0

INFO: Could not delete Alfresco node with Node Ref:
workspace://SpacesStore/c67e8807-5056-491e-afab-bc8d58eec85d;1.0

INFO: Could not delete Alfresco node with Node Ref:
workspace://SpacesStore/5e0a1c1f-e279-403b-a04d-2ad164a7105a;pwc
```

Here we can see that the `continueOnFailure` feature does not really work with Alfresco 4.2, and all documents and folders remain and cannot be deleted when one of them is locked. Also, note the log for the working copy (that is, ...;pwc), generated when the document was checked out.

Getting the content for a document

So far in this chapter, we have created the content in Alfresco based on in-memory text or from a file stored locally. Now, we will see how the content in the repository can be extracted and stored locally in a file. We will use an existing Alfresco e-mail template to demonstrate this. So if you are not running an Alfresco server, the path to the document will have to be changed in the following example.

To get the content of a document, we first have to get the Document object via path and then get the content stream. In this example, we want to get the content for the `invite-email.html.ftl` file located in the `/Company Home/Data Dictionary/ Email Templates/invite` folder in Alfresco. Then write the content of this file to a new local file with the same name. It will be written to the local directory from which we are running the application.

The following is the code:

```
public void getContentForDocumentAndStoreInFile(Session session) {
  // This is one of the out-of-the-box email templates in Alfresco
  String documentPath =
  "/Data Dictionary/Email Templates/invite/invite-email.html.ftl";

  // Get the document object by path so we can
  // get to the content stream
  Document templateDocument = (Document)
  session.getObjectByPath(documentPath);
  if (templateDocument != null) {
    // Make sure the user is allowed to get the
    // content stream (bytes) for the document
    if (templateDocument.getAllowableActions().
    getAllowableActions().contains(Action.CAN_GET_CONTENT_STREAM)
    == false) {
      throw new CmisUnauthorizedException(
      "Current user does not have permission to get the" +
      " content stream for " + documentPath);
    }

    File file = null;
    InputStream input = null;
    OutputStream output = null;
```

```
try {
  // Create the file on the local drive without any content
  file = new File(templateDocument.getName());
  if (!file.exists()) {
    file.createNewFile();
  }

  // Get the object content stream and write to
  // the new local file
  input = templateDocument.getContentStream().getStream();
  output = new FileOutputStream(file);
  IOUtils.copy(input, output);

  // Close streams and handle exceptions
  input.close();
  output.close();
} catch (IOException ioe) {
  ioe.printStackTrace();
} finally {
  IOUtils.closeQuietly(output);
  IOUtils.closeQuietly(input);
}

logger.info("Created a new file " + file.getAbsolutePath() +
" with content from document: " + documentPath);
} else {
  logger.error("Template document could not be found: " +
  documentPath);
  }
}
```

So we start off by getting the `Document` object for the template file by using the `getObjectByPath` method. We then use this object to check if the user has permission to get the content stream for it. After this, we create an empty `invite-email.html.ftl` file on disk that we can use to stream the document content to. The `getContentStream().getStream()` methods are then called to get directly to an `InputStream`, which we can use to read the bytes representing the template file. The Apache Commons IO library is used to copy the bytes from the input stream to the output stream. Note that we need to close all the streams so we don't keep file descriptors open. Also, it is not enough to just call `closeQuietly` on each stream; we have to first call `close`.

Running the preceding code produces the following log:

```
INFO: Created a new file /home/mbergljung/my-app/invite-
email.html.ftl with content from document: /Data Dictionary/Email
Templates/invite/invite-email.html.ftl
```

The Apache Commons IO library is included in the Maven project as follows:

```
<dependency>
    <groupId>commons-io</groupId>
    <artifactId>commons-io</artifactId>
    <version>2.4</version>
</dependency>
```

Copying and moving folders and documents

A document can be copied to a different folder with the Document object's copy method. The copy will be an independent document and it will be of the same type as the original document with the same properties and relationships.

The following code shows how to copy the previously uploaded OpenCMISTest2. pdf document to the /Company Home/Guest Home folder in Alfresco:

```
public void copyDocument(Session session, Document document) {
  Folder parentFolder = session.getRootFolder();
  String destinationFolderName = "Guest Home";
  Folder destinationFolder = (Folder)
  getObject(session, parentFolder, destinationFolderName);

  if (destinationFolder == null) {
    logger.error("Cannot copy " + document.getName() +
    ", could not find folder with the name " +
    destinationFolderName + ", are you using Alfresco?");
    return;
  }

  // Check that we got the document, then copy
  if (document != null) {
    try {
      document.copy(destinationFolder);
      logger.info("Copied document " + document.getName() +
      " from folder " + parentFolder.getPath() +
      " to folder " + destinationFolder.getPath());
```

```
      } catch (CmisContentAlreadyExistsException e) {
        logger.error("Cannot copy document " + document.getName() +
        ", already exist in to folder " +
        destinationFolder.getPath());
      }
    } else {
      logger.error("Document is null, cannot copy to " +
      destinationFolder.getPath());
    }
  }
```

So to copy the passed in document object, we first get the destination Folder object by path using the getObject custom method. This is all that is needed and we can then use the copy method and pass in the Folder object of Guest Home folder. Running the preceding code produces the following log:

INFO: Copied document OpenCMISTest2.pdf from folder / to folder /Guest Home

If we wanted to copy the document but not keep all the original properties, there is another variant of the copy method that takes a number of parameters with properties to be set and so on, which looks as follows:

```
copy(ObjectId targetFolderId, Map<String,?> properties,
VersioningState versioningState, List<Policy> policies,
List<Ace> addACEs, List<Ace> removeACEs, OperationContext context)
```

So if we wanted to copy the document but not the custom type, we could do something as follows:

```
Map<String, Object> documentProperties =
new HashMap<String, Object>(2);
documentProperties.put(PropertyIds.NAME, pdfDocument.getName());
documentProperties.put(PropertyIds.OBJECT_TYPE_ID, pdfDocument.
getBaseTypeId().value());
pdfDocument.copy(destinationFolder, documentProperties ,
null, null, null, null, null);
```

Folders cannot be copied via OpenCMIS. To copy a folder, first create the same folder manually via the createFolder method at the destination, copy the documents from the source folder, and manually create the subfolders recursively. You would do something as follows:

```
public void copyFolder(Folder destinationFolder,
Folder toCopyFolder) {
  Map<String, Object> folderProperties =
  new HashMap<String, Object>();
```

```
      folderProperties.put(PropertyIds.NAME, toCopyFolder.getName());
      folderProperties.put(PropertyIds.OBJECT_TYPE_ID,
      toCopyFolder.getBaseTypeId().value());
      Folder newFolder =
      destinationFolder.createFolder(folderProperties);
      copyChildren(newFolder, toCopyFolder);
    }

    public void copyChildren(
    Folder destinationFolder, Folder toCopyFolder) {
      ItemIterable<CmisObject> immediateChildren =
      toCopyFolder.getChildren();
      for (CmisObject child : immediateChildren) {
        if (child instanceof Document) {
          ((Document) child).copy(destinationFolder);
        } else if (child instanceof Folder) {
          copyFolder(destinationFolder, (Folder) child);
        }
      }
    }
  }
```

The first method named `copyFolder` copies the folder by manually creating a folder under the destination folder. Then the `copyChildren` method is called that copies each document child and calls the `copyFolder` method recursively for each folder child.

Both documents and folders can be moved with the move method that takes a source folder object and a target folder object as input. To move a document, the following code can be used:

```
    public void moveDocument(Session session, Document document) {
      Folder parentFolder = session.getRootFolder();
      Folder sourceFolder = getDocumentParentFolder(document);
      String destinationFolderName = "User Homes";
      Folder destinationFolder = (Folder) getObject(
      session, parentFolder, destinationFolderName);

      // Check that we got the document, then move
      if (document != null) {
        // Make sure the user is allowed to move the document
        // to a new folder
        if (document.getAllowableActions().getAllowableActions().
        contains(Action.CAN_MOVE_OBJECT) == false) {
          throw new CmisUnauthorizedException("Current user does" +
          " not have permission to move " +
          getDocumentPath(document) + document.getName());
```

```
    }

    String pathBeforeMove = getDocumentPath(document);
    try {
      document.move(sourceFolder, destinationFolder);
      logger.info("Moved document " + pathBeforeMove +
      " to folder " + destinationFolder.getPath());
    } catch (CmisRuntimeException e) {
      logger.error("Cannot move document to folder " +
      destinationFolder.getPath() + ": " + e.getMessage());
    }
  } else {
    logger.error("Document is null, cannot move!");
  }
}
```

The source folder's object is really only needed when the document has been multifiled in several folders, then the source folder's object specifies from which folder the document should be unfiled and moved from. In the preceding code, I could have, for example, changed the move method call to the following:

```
pdfDocument.move(pdfDocument.getParents().get(0),
destinationFolder);
```

And that would have also worked as the document only has one parent folder. Also note that we make sure the user has permission to move the document by checking that the canMoveObject action is allowed.

Working with Alfresco aspects

Alfresco has two types of classes that can be used to classify content, types and aspects. A node in Alfresco (that is, a CMIS object) can have one and only one type set but zero or more aspects applied. We have seen in a number of examples how we can set the basic CMIS types and custom types for a document or folder object. To manage the aspects for an object in Alfresco, we can use CMIS secondary types, as Alfresco exposes any aspects that are set on an object as secondary types. This will work if you are running Alfresco 4.2.e Community, Alfresco 4.2.0 Enterprise, or newer versions. With earlier versions, you have to use a special Alfresco OpenCMIS extension to manage aspects. We will look at both.

Using secondary types to manage aspects

When we want to manage aspects via secondary types, we will just use standard OpenCMIS library functions like we have done so far to manage properties. Secondary object types are managed in a specific multivalued property named `cmis:secondaryObjectTypeIds`. Using the following code, we will define it globally so that we can use it in subsequent methods:

```
private static final String SECONDARY_OBJECT_TYPE_IDS_PROP_NAME =
"cmis:secondaryObjectTypeIds";
```

Adding aspects when creating an object

To demonstrate how to add an aspect when we are creating an object, we will add one of the out-of-the-box Alfresco aspects called Titled (`cm:titled`) when we create a folder. This aspect, or the CMIS secondary type, requires two extra properties to be filled in, title and description:

```
public void createFolderWithTitledAspect(Session session) {
   String folderName = "OpenCMISTestTitled";
   Folder parentFolder = session.getRootFolder();

   // Check if folder already exist, if not create it
   Folder newFolder = (Folder) getObject(
   session, parentFolder, folderName);
   if (newFolder == null) {
     List<Object> aspects = new ArrayList<Object>();
     aspects.add("P:cm:titled");
     Map<String, Object> newFolderProps =
     new HashMap<String, Object>();
     newFolderProps.put(PropertyIds.OBJECT_TYPE_ID, "cmis:folder");
     newFolderProps.put(PropertyIds.NAME, folderName);
     newFolderProps.put(
     SECONDARY_OBJECT_TYPE_IDS_PROP_NAME, aspects);
     newFolderProps.put("cm:title", "Folder Title");
     newFolderProps.put("cm:description", "Folder Description");
     newFolder = parentFolder.createFolder(newFolderProps);

     logger.info("Created new folder with Titled aspect: " +
     newFolder.getPath() + " [creator=" + newFolder.getCreatedBy()
     + "] [created=" +
     date2String(newFolder.getCreationDate().getTime()) + "]");
   } else {
     logger.info("Cannot create folder, it already exist: " +
     newFolder.getPath());
   }
}
```

Here we first check whether the folder we intend to create already exists. If it doesn't, we go ahead and create a list of aspects that we want to set for the folder object. In this case, it is just the one aspect called `P:cm:titled` (P stands for policy; it is the way Alfresco traditionally exposes aspects, and you still have to use this prefix), but the `secondaryObjectTypeids` property is a multivalued property, so we need to keep the aspect name in a list. Then the standard properties map is created where one of the properties is the `secondaryObjectTypeIds` property, keeping the list of `aspects`. The folder is then created with this map of properties, and the aspect is set for us and exposed as a secondary type via CMIS.

Adding aspects to an existing object

If we already have an object and want to add an aspect to it, we can also use the `cmis:secondaryObjectTypeIds` property and update it via the `updateProperties` operation. We are going to use another of Alfresco's out-of-the-box aspects called Effectivity (`cm:effectivity`). It can be used to set a `from` date and a `to` date for an object, representing some form of time period when the object is effective. To do this for a document object, do as follows:

```
public void addAspectToExistingDocument(Document document) {
  String aspectName = "P:cm:effectivity";
  // Make sure we got a document, and then add the aspect to it
  if (document != null) {
    // Check that document don't already got the aspect applied
    List<Object> aspects = document.getProperty(
    SECONDARY_OBJECT_TYPE_IDS_PROP_NAME).getValues();
    if (!aspects.contains(aspectName)) {
      aspects.add(aspectName);
      Map<String, Object> properties =
      new HashMap<String, Object>();
      properties.put(
      SECONDARY_OBJECT_TYPE_IDS_PROP_NAME, aspects);
      properties.put("cm:from", new Date());
      Calendar toDate = Calendar.getInstance();
      toDate.add(Calendar.MONTH, 2);
      properties.put("cm:to", toDate.getTime());
      Document updatedDocument =
      (Document) document.updateProperties(properties);
      logger.info("Added aspect " + aspectName + " to " +
      getDocumentPath(updatedDocument));
    } else {
      logger.info("Aspect " + aspectName +
      " is already applied to " + getDocumentPath(document));
    }
```

```
    } else {
      logger.error("Document is null, cannot add aspect to it!");
    }
  }
}
```

The document object that we want to apply the aspect to is passed to the method. We start by getting currently set aspects, so we can see if the cm:effectivity aspect is already set. We also need to keep a list of aspects that are already set as we need to add them to the aspect list together with the new aspect. If we don't include the aspects that are already set, we will basically unset them when we update the properties.

Reading aspects

To read aspects that have been applied to an object, we just need to get the values of the multivalued cmis:secondaryObjectTypeIds property. For a document, this can be done as follows:

```
public void readAspectsForExistingDocument(Document document) {
  // Make sure we got a document, then list aspects
  if (document != null) {
    List<SecondaryType> aspects = document.getSecondaryTypes();
    logger.info("Aspects for: " + getDocumentPath(document));
    for (SecondaryType aspect : aspects) {
      logger.info("    " + aspect.getDisplayName() +
      " (" + aspect.getId() + ")");
    }
  } else {
    logger.error("Document is null, cannot list aspects for it!");
  }
}
```

The getSecondaryTypes method on a document object will respond with a list of the SecondaryType objects that we can list and print the display name for. Running this code produces the following log:

```
INFO: Aspects for: /User Homes/OpenCMISTest2.pdf
INFO:      Titled (P:cm:titled)
INFO:      Document Data (P:myc:documentData)
INFO:      Author (P:cm:author)
INFO:      Translation (P:sys:localized)
INFO:      Effectivity (P:cm:effectivity)
```

The Alfresco OpenCMIS extension to manage aspects

Now, if are not using an Alfresco version that exposes aspects as CMIS secondary types, we can still manage them with the Alfresco OpenCMIS extension (http:// code.google.com/a/apache-extras.org/p/alfresco-opencmis-extension/). To use it, we need to do two things. First, we need to add a dependency to the library in Maven POM as follows:

```
<dependency>
  <groupId>org.alfresco.cmis.client</groupId>
  <artifactId>alfresco-opencmis-extension</artifactId>
  <version>0.4</version>
  <exclusions>
    <exclusion>
      <groupId>org.apache.chemistry.opencmis</groupId>
      <artifactId>chemistry-opencmis-client-impl</artifactId>
    </exclusion>
  </exclusions>
</dependency>
```

The Alfresco OpenCMIS extension actually has a dependency on the OpenCMIS library, so we exclude it. This way, we don't end up with two different versions of the OpenCMIS library in, for example, WEB-INF/lib if we are building a WAR artifact.

Next, we need to update the object factory that OpenCMIS uses so that it creates Alfresco CMIS objects instead of CMIS objects. We do this by setting the OBJECT_FACTORY_CLASS session property to org.alfresco.cmis.client.impl. AlfrescoObjectFactoryImpl. In the getSession method that we created in the beginning, add the property as follows:

```
parameters.put(SessionParameter.OBJECT_FACTORY_CLASS,
"org.alfresco.cmis.client.impl.AlfrescoObjectFactoryImpl");
```

Adding aspects when creating an object

To apply the cm:titled aspect with the Alfresco OpenCMIS extension, we use the following code:

```
public void createFolderWithTitledAspectWithAlfrescoExtension (
Session session) {
  String folderName = "OpenCMISTestTitled";
  Folder parentFolder = session.getRootFolder();
```

```
// Check if folder already exist, if not create it
Folder newFolder = (Folder) getObject(
session, parentFolder, folderName);
if (newFolder == null) {
  Map<String, Object> newFolderProps =
  new HashMap<String, Object>();
  newFolderProps.put(
  PropertyIds.OBJECT_TYPE_ID, "cmis:folder,P:cm:titled");
  newFolderProps.put(PropertyIds.NAME, folderName);
  newFolderProps.put("cm:title", "Folder Title");
  newFolderProps.put("cm:description", "Folder Description");
  newFolder = parentFolder.createFolder(newFolderProps);

  logger.info("Created new folder with Titled aspect: " +
  newFolder.getPath() + " [creator=" +
  newFolder.getCreatedBy() + "][created=" +
  date2String(newFolder.getCreationDate().getTime()) +"]");
} else {
  logger.info("Folder already exist: " + newFolder.getPath());
}
}
```

The important thing here is to include the name of the aspect (or aspects) in the OBJECT_TYPE_ID property value. The fully qualified Alfresco aspect name, such as cm:titled, should be prefixed with P as aspects are handled as policy objects.

Then we can just add the custom properties belonging to the aspects to the properties map, and they will be applied to the object when it is created.

Adding aspects to an existing object

If we already have an object and want to add an aspect to it, we can use the addAspect method on the Alfresco object. To do this for a document object, do as follows:

```
public void addAspectToExistingDocumentWithAlfrescoExtension(
Session session) {
  String documentName = "OpenCMISTest2.pdf";
  String aspectName = "P:cm:effectivity";
  Folder parentFolder = session.getRootFolder();

  // Make sure document exists and get the object for it,
  // if not don't try and add the aspect
  AlfrescoDocument someDocument = (AlfrescoDocument)
  getObject(session, parentFolder, documentName);
  if (someDocument != null) {
```

```
    // Check that document don't already got the aspect applied
    if (!someDocument.hasAspect(aspectName)) {
      Map<String, Object> aspectProperties =
      new HashMap<String, Object>();
      aspectProperties.put("cm:from", new Date());
      Calendar toDate = Calendar.getInstance();
      toDate.add(Calendar.MONTH, 2);
      aspectProperties.put("cm:to", toDate.getTime());
      someDocument.addAspect(aspectName, aspectProperties);

      logger.info("Added aspect " + aspectName + " to " +
      getDocumentPath(someDocument));
    } else {
      logger.info("Aspect " + aspectName+" is already applied to "
      + getDocumentPath(someDocument));
    }
  } else {
    logger.info("Document does not exist, cannot add aspect to
    it:"
    + parentFolder.getPath() + documentName);
  }
}
```

Here we get a document object by path and then cast it to an `AlfrescoDocument`
object. This is possible as we are using the Alfresco object factory, which is provided
by the Alfresco OpenCMIS extension. If the `AlfrescoDocument` object is not `null`,
we check whether it already has the aspect applied with the `hasAspect` method. If
the aspect is not applied to the object, we set up a map with the two aspect properties
and then pass it, together with the aspect name, to the `addAspect` method.

Reading aspects

To read aspects that have been applied to an object, we first get an object via an ID
or path and then cast it to an Alfresco object. We can then use the `getAspects`
method to get a collection of the applied aspects, as shown in the following code:

```
public void readAspectsForExistingDocumentWithAlfrescoExtension (
Session session) {
  String documentName = "OpenCMISTest2.pdf";
  Folder parentFolder = session.getRootFolder();

  // Make sure document exists and get the object for it,
  // if not don't try and list aspects
  AlfrescoDocument someDocument = (AlfrescoDocument) getObject(
  session, parentFolder, documentName);
```

```
    if (someDocument != null) {
      Collection<ObjectType> aspects = someDocument.getAspects();
      logger.info("Aspects for: " +someDocument.getPaths().get(0));
      for (ObjectType aspect : aspects) {
        logger.info("     " + aspect.getDisplayName() + " (" +
        aspect.getId()+ ")");
      }
    } else {
      ogger.info("Document does not exist, cannot list aspects for
      it: " + parentFolder.getPath() + documentName);
    }
}
```

The getAspect method returns a collection of the ObjectType policy. Alfresco aspects are managed as policies. We can then get the aspect name with the getDisplayPath method and the aspect's fully qualified name with the getId method, according to how the aspect has been defined in the Alfresco content model.

Version management with check out and check in

As mentioned before, only document objects can be versioned. When a document is created via CMIS, it always has versioning enabled even if the check-out and check-in features have not been used. So when we created, for example, the OpenCMISTest.txt file with the createDocument method, Alfresco automatically applied the cm:versionable aspect and set its properties as follows:

- cm:autoVersionOnUpdateProps: This property is set to true, which means that a new version will be created every time a property is updated

- cm:versionLabel: This property is set to 1.0

- cm:autoVersion: This property is set to false, so a new version will not be created if content is updated for the document

- cm:initialVersion: This property is set to false, so an initial version will not be created in the version history when document is first created

Because the cm:autoVersion property is set to false, a new version will not be created if the document is updated . However, as the cm:autoVersionOnUpdateProps is set to true a new version will be created if any metadata/properties are updated for the document. To turn on automatic versioning of content, we have to use the checkOut method, which creates a **Private Working Copy (PWC)** that we later check in, which creates a new version.

For more information on the CMIS version service, refer to *Chapter 3, Advanced CMIS Operations*, and *Chapter 4, Alfresco and CMIS*.

Checking out a document

A document can be checked out using the `checkOut` method on the object:

```
public Document checkOutDocument(
Session session, Document document) {
// Check that we got the document before we try and do a check-out
  Document workingCopy = null;
  if (document != null) {
    // If it is already checked out cancel that checkout
    if (document.isVersionSeriesCheckedOut()) {
      document.cancelCheckOut();
      logger.info("Document was already checked out, "+
      "cancelled check out for document: " +
      getDocumentPath(document));
    }

    ObjectId workingCopyId = document.checkOut();
    workingCopy = (Document) session.getObject(workingCopyId);

    logger.info("Checked Out document:
    "+getDocumentPath(document)+
    " [version=" + document.getVersionLabel() + "] [pwcName=" +
    workingCopy.getName() + "]");
  } else {
    logger.error("Document is null, cannot check-out!");
  }

  return workingCopy;
}
```

Before the `OpenCMISTest2.pdf` document is checked out, we check if it has already been checked out with the `isVersionSeriesCheckedOut` method. If it has been checked out, we cancel that check out so that we can do a new check out. When a document is checked out, the PWC of the document is created. We can use this PWC to update the content of the document and then check in as a new version. The document is also locked, so other users cannot update it. Running the code produces the following log:

```
INFO: Checked Out document: /User Homes/OpenCMISTest2.pdf
[version=1.0] [pwcName=OpenCMISTest2 (Working Copy).pdf]
```

Updating the content of the checked-out document and then checking it in

When we have checked out the document and have a working copy, we can update the content by updating the content stream for the working copy. In the following example, we will update the content from an existing PDF file with the name `UpdatedContent.pdf` that needs to exist in the directory from where we are running the example:

```
public void updateContentAndCheckInDocument(
Session session, Document pwc) {
   String documentName = "OpenCMISTest2.pdf";
   File file = new File("UpdatedContent.pdf");

   InputStream is = null;
   ObjectId newObjectId = null;
   try {
     // Setup updated document content
     is = new FileInputStream(file);
     String mimetype = "application/pdf";
     ContentStream contentStream =
     session.getObjectFactory().createContentStream(
     documentName, file.length(), mimetype, is);

     // Check in the Private Working Copy (pwc) with new content
     boolean majorVersion = false;
     Map<String, Object> props = null;
     String checkInComment = "This is just a minor update";
     newObjectId = pwc.checkIn(
     majorVersion, props, contentStream, checkInComment);

     // Close stream and handle exceptions
     is.close();
   } catch (IOException ioe) {
     ioe.printStackTrace();
   } finally {
     IOUtils.closeQuietly(is);
   }

   // Get the document so we can check the new version
   Document updatedDocument = (Document)
   session.getObject(newObjectId);
   logger.info("Checked In document: " +
   getDocumentPath(updatedDocument) + " [newVersion=" +
```

```
    updatedDocument.getVersionLabel() + "][checkInComment=" +
    updatedDocument.getCheckinComment() + "]");
}
```

The content stream that points to the updated PDF is used to check in the private working copy. The `majorVersion` property is set to `false`, so we will update the version label in minor steps such as 1.0, 1.1, and so on. In this case, we are not updating any of the document's properties, so the property map is `null`. The last parameter sent to the `checkIn` method is the comment that we want to make about what was updated in the content.

We can now get the document object again and check the version label to see what it has been updated to. The check-in comment can also be retrieved from the document object. Running this code produces a log as follows:

```
INFO: Checked In document: /User Homes/OpenCMISTest2.pdf
[newVersion=1.1][checkInComment=This is just a minor update]
```

Managing permissions for documents and folders

ACLs are used to manage permissions for folders and documents. Each ACL contains one or more **Access Control Entries (ACE)**. Each ACE contains a principal, permission(s), and propagation direction. To add a new permission for an object such as a folder, we use the `addAcl` method on the object. To be able to use this method, we have to first check if the repository supports managing permissions, as follows:

```
public void addPermissionToFolder(Session session, Folder folder) {
  // Check if the repo supports ACLs
  RepositoryInfo repoInfo = session.getRepositoryInfo();
  if (!repoInfo.getCapabilities().getAclCapability().equals(
  CapabilityAcl.MANAGE)) {
    logger.warn("Repository does not allow ACL management" +
    " [repoName=" + repoInfo.getProductName() +
    "][repoVersion=" + repoInfo.getProductVersion() + "]");
  } else {
    // Check that we got the folder, if not don't
    // assign new permission to it
    if (folder != null) {
      List<String> permissions = new ArrayList<String>();
      permissions.add(
      "{http://www.alfresco.org/model/content/1.0}folder.
      Collaborator");
      String principal = "GROUP_MARKETING";
```

```
Ace aceIn = session.getObjectFactory().
createAce(principal, permissions);
List<Ace> aceListIn = new ArrayList<Ace>();
aceListIn.add(aceIn);
folder.addAcl(
aceListIn, AclPropagation.REPOSITORYDETERMINED);

logger.info("ACL for " + folder.getPath() +
" after adding an ACE:");
OperationContextImpl operationContext =
new OperationContextImpl();
operationContext.setIncludeAcls(true);
folder = (Folder) session.getObject(
folder, operationContext);
for (Ace ace : folder.getAcl().getAces()) {
  logger.info("     " + ace.getPrincipalId() +
  " " + ace.toString());
}
} else {
  logger.error("Folder is null, cannot add permission!");
}
}
}
}
```

When we have discovered that the repository supports permission management, by verifying that the ACL capability is set to MANAGE, we can create an ACL, which in itself is represented as a list of Ace objects. We can create each new ACE object that we need via the createAce method on the object factory. This method takes a principal, which is a user or group; one or more CMIS permissions (that is, cmis:read, cmis:write, and cmis:all); and/or repository-specific permissions (for example, {http://www.alfresco.org/model/content/1.0}folder.Collaborator).

In this example, we set up the MARKETING group to have the Collaboration role on the folder. When working with Alfresco groups, we have to prefix them with GROUP_ to distinguish them from, for example, roles that are prefixed with ROLE_. When we call the addAcl method on the folder and pass in the ACE list, we also specify how the ACL change should be propagated in the repository. In this case, when it is set to REPOSITORYDETERMINED, Alfresco will manage the ACL change as it normally manages changes to permissions.

After we have added the new permission to the folder, we will also want to list all the permissions for the folder after this. To do this, we have to get the folder object again and specify that we also want the access control list for the object returned. We do this with the getObject method and pass in an operational context that has includeAcls set to true. As the object ID, we pass in the Folder object as it extends the ObjectId class. Running the preceding code will print the following log:

```
INFO: ACL for /OpenCMISTest2 after adding an ACE:

    GROUP_MARKETING Access Control Entry [principal=Access Control
Principal [principalId=GROUP_MARKETING] [extensions=null],
permissions=[cmis:read, cmis:write,
{http://www.alfresco.org/model/content/1.0}cmobject.Collaborator], is
direct=true] [extensions=null]

    GROUP_EVERYONE Access Control Entry [principal=Access Control
Principal [principalId=GROUP_EVERYONE] [extensions=null],
permissions=[cmis:read,
{http://www.alfresco.org/model/content/1.0}cmobject.Consumer], is
direct=false] [extensions=null]
```

If we wanted to add a permission related to performing a specific operation, such as a check out, we can first ask the repository info object for the permissions needed to do this operation and then add those permissions to the principal. For example, to add check-out permissions for the OpenCMISTest2.pdf document to a user named mjackson, do as follows:

```
public void addCheckOutPermissionsToUser(
Session session, Document document) {
  String principal = "mjackson";
  Folder parentFolder = session.getRootFolder();

  // Make sure we got a document, if not don't
  // try and add permission
  if (document != null) {
    RepositoryInfo repositoryInfo = session.getRepositoryInfo();
    AclCapabilities aclCapabilities =
    repositoryInfo.getAclCapabilities();
    Map<String, PermissionMapping> permissionMappings =
    aclCapabilities.getPermissionMapping();
    PermissionMapping permissionMapping =
    permissionMappings.get(
    PermissionMapping.CAN_CHECKOUT_DOCUMENT);
    List<String> permissions = permissionMapping.getPermissions();
    Ace addAce = session.getObjectFactory().createAce(
    principal, permissions);
    List<Ace> addAces = new LinkedList<Ace>();
```

```
    addAces.add(addAce);
    document.addAcl(addAces, AclPropagation.REPOSITORYDETERMINED);

    logger.info("Added check-out permissions for user " +
    principal + " to " + getDocumentPath(document));
} else {
    logger.error("Document is null, cannot add permission!");
}
}
```

Here, we utilize the possibility to get the permission mapping for the check-out document operation directly from the repository. When we have the permission mapping for CAN_CHECKOUT_DOCUMENT, we can just ask for the permissions and then pass them in the addAcl method.

Managing relationships between objects

CMIS supports relationships, which is the same thing as an association in Alfresco. To set up a relationship between two objects with OpenCMIS, we first have to get the objects and then we can use the createRelationship method on the session object. In Alfresco, there are many associations defined and available out of the box. One of these associations is Copied From, and it is defined as follows in the Alfresco content model:

```
<aspect name="cm:copiedfrom">
    <title>Copied From</title>
    <associations>
        <association name="cm:original">
            <source>
                <mandatory>false</mandatory>
                <many>true</many>
            </source>
            <target>
                <class>cm:cmobject</class>
                <mandatory>false</mandatory>
                <many>false</many>
            </target>
        </association>
    </associations>
</aspect>
```

Note that the actual association is contained in an aspect, and we should not use the aspect name when we refer to the association but instead use the association name, which in this case is cm:original. In the following example, we are going to set up this association between two folders where one folder has been copied from the other.

The following code will first check whether the `cmis:relationship` base object type is supported by the repository as it is not a mandatory base type. Then we check whether the custom Alfresco association is available.

```
public void setupRelationshipBetween2Folders(Session session) {
    // First check that relationship types are supported and
    // that the custom Alfresco relationship/assocation is supported
    String cmisRelationshipTypeName = "cmis:relationship";
    String customCopiedFromAssociation = "R:cm:original";

    try {
        session.getTypeDefinition(cmisRelationshipTypeName);
    } catch (CmisObjectNotFoundException e) {
        logger.warn("Repository does not support " +
        cmisRelationshipTypeName + "objects");
    }

    try {
        session.getTypeDefinition(customCopiedFromAssociation);
    } catch (CmisObjectNotFoundException e) {
        logger.warn("Repository does not support " +
        customCopiedFromAssociation + " objects");
        return;
    }

    String oldFolderBeingReplacedName = "OpenCMISTest2";
    String newFolderName = "OpenCMISTestTitled";
    Folder parentFolder = session.getRootFolder();

    // Get the folder objects and check that the folders exists
    Folder sourceFolder = (Folder) getObject(
    session, parentFolder, newFolderName);
    Folder targetFolder = (Folder) getObject(
    session, parentFolder, oldFolderBeingReplacedName);
    if (sourceFolder == null || targetFolder == null) {
        logger.warn("Cannot setup relationship as at least one
        of the folders does not exist");
    }

    // Check that relationship does not already exist
    OperationContextImpl operationContext =
    new OperationContextImpl();
    operationContext.setIncludeRelationships(
    IncludeRelationships.SOURCE);
```

```
sourceFolder = (Folder) session.getObject(
sourceFolder, operationContext);
List<Relationship> existingRelationships =
sourceFolder.getRelationships();
for (Relationship existingRelationship : existingRelationships)
{
  logger.warn("Relationship: " +
  existingRelationship.toString());
  if (existingRelationship.getType().getId().
  equalsIgnoreCase(customCopiedFromAssociation)) {
    logger.warn("Folders are already setup with relationship:
    "+customCopiedFromAssociation);
  }
  return;
}

// Setup copiedFrom relationship between folders
Map<String, String> relationshipProperties =
new HashMap<String, String>();
relationshipProperties.put(
"cmis:objectTypeId", customCopiedFromAssociation);
relationshipProperties.put(
"cmis:sourceId", sourceFolder.getId());
relationshipProperties.put(
"cmis:targetId", targetFolder.getId());
session.createRelationship(
relationshipProperties, null, null, null);

logger.info("Setup " + customCopiedFromAssociation +
" relationship between folder " + sourceFolder.getPath() +
" and folder " + targetFolder.getPath());
}
```

After we have checked that the association is available, we get the Folder objects for the two folders between which we want to set up the relationship. When we have them, they will act as the source and target in the relationship.

Before we go ahead and set up the relationship, we need to check if it has already been set up. To do this, we need to get the source folder again with an operational context that is set up to include relationships. If the relationship already exists, we abort the operation as you cannot add the relationship if it is already there—you will get an exception.

When we specify the object type ID for the relationship/association, we must prefix it with `R:` when using Alfresco. The relationship is created with the `createRelationship` method on the `session`; in this case, we pass in `null` for policies and access control lists and keep the default one.

Searching

To be able to search for content is one of the main requirements you would have on a CMS system library such as OpenCMIS. And, it supports both searching in metadata and a full-text search in content. Before doing any searches, we first need to see which search features are supported by the repository. We want it to support both a metadata search and FTS:

```
public void searchMetadataAndFTS(Session session) {
  // Check if the repo supports Metadata search and
  // Full Text Search (FTS)
  RepositoryInfo repoInfo = session.getRepositoryInfo();
  if (repoInfo.getCapabilities().getQueryCapability().equals(
  CapabilityQuery.METADATAONLY)) {
    logger.warn("Repository does not support FTS [repoName=" +
    repoInfo.getProductName() + "] [repoVersion=" +
    repoInfo.getProductVersion() + "]");
  } else {
    String query = "SELECT * FROM cmis:document WHERE "+
    "cmis:name LIKE 'OpenCMIS%'";
    ItemIterable<QueryResult> searchResult =
    session.query(query, false);
    logSearchResult(query, searchResult);

    query = "SELECT * FROM cmis:document WHERE "+
    "cmis:name LIKE 'OpenCMIS%' AND CONTAINS('testing')";
    searchResult = session.query(query, false);
    logSearchResult(query, searchResult);
  }
}
private void logSearchResult(
String query, ItemIterable<QueryResult> searchResult) {
  logger.info("Results from query " + query);
  int i = 1;
  for (QueryResult resultRow : searchResult) {
    logger.info("----------------------------------------------\n" +
    i + " , " + resultRow.getPropertyByQueryName("cmis:objectId").
```

```
        getFirstValue() + " , " +
        resultRow.getPropertyByQueryName("cmis:objectTypeId").
        getFirstValue() + " , " + resultRow.getPropertyByQueryName
        ("cmis:name").getFirstValue());
        i++;
    }
}
```

When we know that the repository supports more than just a metadata search and the `CapabilityQuery` property is not set to `METADATAONLY`, we do the first search in metadata by looking for all the documents that have a name starting with `OpenCMIS%`. Then we do another search in both metadata and content by also looking for the word `testing` in the documents that matched the name `OpenCMIS%`. Running the preceding code produces a search result as follows:

```
INFO: Results from query SELECT * FROM cmis:document WHERE cmis:name
LIKE 'OpenCMIS%'

1 , D:myc:itDoc , OpenCMISTest2.pdf

2 , cmis:document , OpenCMISTest5.txt

INFO: Results from query SELECT * FROM cmis:document WHERE cmis:name
LIKE 'OpenCMIS%' AND CONTAINS('testing')

1 , cmis:document , OpenCMIS part 1 - DevCon 2010.pptx

2 , D:myc:itDoc , OpenCMISTest2.pdf
```

Note that the result will be different depending on what content you have in your repository. For more information on the CMIS Query language search syntax and examples, refer to *Chapter 3, Advanced CMIS Operations*.

Summary

In this chapter, we looked at the Apache Chemistry project and the OpenCMIS Java library and saw how much more efficient it is than using the AtomPub or Browser binding protocols directly. We have gone through most of the operations that one might want to perform against a repository, and we have also looked at how to use the Alfresco OpenCMIS extension for handling aspects when using an earlier Alfresco version.

In the next chapter, we will look at how you can access a CMIS-compatible repository using a scripting language such as JavaScript or Groovy.

6
Accessing a CMIS Server Using Scripting Languages

So far we have seen how we can access a CMIS server via basic protocol bindings and from an OpenCMIS Java abstraction layer. Sometimes it is also useful to be able to abstract the CMIS interface even further and access the CMIS server using a scripting language such as JavaScript or Groovy.

So why would we want to do that? Well, when working on web application development, it is often very useful to be able to make AJAX calls directly from JavaScript code to CMS servers and get back JSON with repository data.

Scripting languages also make the coding operation a lot quicker in many cases; they abstract the application programming interface even further, making it easier to work with the interface.

In this chapter, we learn how to do the following:

- Access a CMS server directly from the JavaScript code in the browser, and also see how that works if it is in a different domain
- Use jQuery to make the AJAX calls to the CMS server more efficient
- Populate JavaScript widgets directly with JSON from CMIS service calls
- Use Groovy to make CMIS service calls
- Use CMIS from the Spring Surf development framework

Using CMIS in JavaScript and web application pages

We have already seen how the Browser binding can be used to manage folders and documents directly from HTML forms. However, we did not go into how we can use JavaScript to call a CMIS service via the Browser binding and then process the JSON response.

Now let's see how easy it is to use the Browser binding and JSON to navigate through the repository and populate data trees and data lists. First thing first though, we need to get hold of the Alfresco repository ID so that we can use it in our service calls. If you remember, the Browser binding-based URL for Alfresco Version 4 is `http://localhost:8080/alfresco/cmisbrowser`, and it will return information about the repository, such as the ID.

 If you are using Alfresco Version 4.2.d Community, 4.2.0 Enterprise, or newer, then the correct CMIS browser binding URL is `http://localhost:8080/alfresco/api/-default-/cmis/versions/1.1/browser`.

Let's set up a web page that makes a service call to this URL, and then parse the JSON response to get to the repository ID.

Create a file called `testCMISfromJS.html` with the following initial content:

```
<!DOCTYPE html>
<html>
<head>
  <title>Testing CMIS from JavaScript</title>
  <meta charset="UTF-8">
  <meta http-equiv="Content-Type" content="text/html;
    charset=UTF-8">
  <script src="testCMISfromJS.js" type="text/javascript"></script>
</head>
<body>
<p>Get the Repository ID from the Alfresco server: </p>
<input type="button" value="Get Repository ID"
  onClick="getRepoId()">
<div id="repo_id"></div>
</body>
</html>
```

This HTML page will display a button and when we click on it, the `getRepoId` JavaScript function is called. This function is defined in the `testCMISfromJS.js` file that is loaded in the `head` section. Create this file and code the function as follows:

```
function getRepoId() {
  callCmisServer(
    "http://localhost:8080/alfresco/cmisbrowser",
    function (cmisServiceResponseJSON) {
      for (repositoryId in cmisServiceResponseJSON) {
        var repository = cmisServiceResponseJSON[repositoryId];
        document.getElementById('repo_id').innerHTML =
          "Repository found [id=" + repository.repositoryId +"]
          [name="+ repository.vendorName + "[version=" +
          repository.productVersion + "]";
      }
    }
  );
}
```

What this function does is call another function, `callCmisServer`, which is also
a custom function that we will define in a bit. It will make an AJAX call to the CMIS
server with the URL passed in. The server will respond with a result formatted as
JSON. You may remember from *Chapter 2, Basic CMIS Operations*, the JSON response
from the `http://localhost:8080/alfresco/cmisbrowser` call looks similar to
the following:

```
{
  f0ebcfb4-ca9f-4991-bda8-9465f4f11527: {
    principalIdAnyone: "GROUP_EVERYONE",
      principalIdAnonymous: "guest",
      repositoryDescription: "Main Repository",
      vendorName: "Alfresco",
      aclCapabilities: {
        permissionMapping: [...
      cmisVersionSupported: "1.0",
      productVersion: "4.2.0 (4480)",
      repositoryId: "f0ebcfb4-ca9f-4991-bda8-9465f4f11527",
  ...
}
```

The JSON response will be passed in as an argument to the anonymous function that
is passed in as the second argument to the `callCmisServer` function. The anonymous
function will loop through the JSON response as it can contain information for more
than one repository. For each repository ID it finds, it will get the value for it, which is
an object representing the repository information. It then prints a couple of properties
for the repository, such as `vendorName`. Running this program produces the following
output in `div` with the `repo_id` ID:

Get the Repository ID from the Alfresco server:

[Get Repository Id]

```
Repository found [id=f0ebcfb4-ca9f-4991-bda8-9465f4f11527]
[name=Alfresco[version=4.2.0 (4480)]
```

The `callCmisServer` function looks as follows:

```
function callCmisServer(cmisServiceUrl, callback) {
  var httpRequest = new XMLHttpRequest();
  var asynchronousRequest = true;
  var alfrescoUsername = "admin";
  var alfrescoPwd = "admin";
  httpRequest.callback = callback;
  httpRequest.open("GET", cmisServiceUrl, asynchronousRequest,
    alfrescoUsername, alfrescoPwd);
  httpRequest.onreadystatechange = handleCmisServiceCallResponse;
  httpRequest.send(null);
}
```

This program uses the `XMLHttpRequest` class to make an AJAX call to the CMIS server. The call is made to the URL that is passed in as the `cmisServiceUrl` parameter. The call will be asynchronous, and the function that should handle the response once it is complete is called `handleCmisServiceCallResponse`; we will define this function in a bit. We also set up the HTTP request object with a reference to the `callback` function, so we can access it from the handler function.

A CMIS call requires authentication, so we supply the username and password to the administrator in Alfresco. The last thing that is done is call the `send` function on the HTTP request object, and this executes the HTTP GET method and makes the CMIS service call.

The response handler function looks as follows:

```
function handleCmisServiceCallResponse() {
  var responseContentFinishedLoading = 4;
  var responseStatusCodeOk = 200;
  if (this.readyState == responseContentFinishedLoading &&
    this.status == responseStatusCodeOk) {
    var cmisServiceResponseJSON = JSON.parse(this.responseText);
    this.callback(cmisServiceResponseJSON);
  }
}
```

The function will take the JSON string that is returned by the server and parse it into a JSON object. This JSON object is then passed back into the callback function (that is, the anonymous function passed in as the second parameter to the `callCmisServer` function).

Now, if we just double-click on the `testCMISfromJS.html` file and open the page in a browser, it will not work to run the example. This is because of the **same origin** problem. The Alfresco CMIS server that we are accessing is running in the `http://localhost:8080/alfresco` domain, and the HTML page will have a path in the browser that looks like `file:///home/mbergljung/Documents/Alfresco%20CMIS/chapters/chapter%206/code/testCMISfromJS.html`. For security reasons, the browser will not allow the web page to make a call to a different domain.

To get around this, we can put the HTML file and the JS file in the `alfresco` directory under `<alfrescoinstalldir>/tomcat/webapps` and restart Tomcat. Then, we can access the web page with the `http://localhost:8080/alfresco/testCMISfromJS.html` URL, which would make both the web application and the CMS server reside in the same domain, and the call would work. However, this is not really a solution for a production web application that might call out to many different servers for information.

To get around this, we can use a technique that involves wrapping the response from the service call in a function, which can then be called to get the JSON object.

Solving the same origin policy problem

The technique that we will use to solve the problem of calling several different domains from a web application is sometimes referred to as JSONP, which stands for JSON with padding. This means that you wrap/pad the JSON response inside a JavaScript `function`, as in the following example:

```
getResponse(
{
  f0ebcfb4-ca9f-4991-bda8-9465f4f11527: {
    principalIdAnyone: "GROUP_EVERYONE",
    principalIdAnonymous: "guest",
    repositoryDescription: "Main Repository",
    vendorName: "Alfresco",
    aclCapabilities: {
      permissionMapping: [...
    cmisVersionSupported: "1.0",
    productVersion: "4.2.0 (4480)",
    repositoryId: "f0ebcfb4-ca9f-4991-bda8-9465f4f11527",
  ...
}
)
```

The CMIS service call will be made via a `script` tag directly in the page `body` instead of via the `XMLHttpRequest` class. When `script` is loaded, the function is defined and called.

Obviously, for this to work in our scenario, the CMIS server must support JSONP. The CMIS specification states that any CMIS-compliant server needs to support an optional URL parameter named `callback`. So, to get the above JSONP response, we would make the following call to the Alfresco server: `http://localhost:8080/alfresco/cmisbrowser?callback=getResponse`.

The following changes to the code are necessary to support JSONP and cross-domain calls. First make a copy of the HTML file we created earlier called `testCMISfromJS.html` and give it a new name, `testCMISfromJS-JSONP.html`. Update it to load a different JS file as follows:

```html
<!DOCTYPE html>
<html>
<head>
  <title>Testing CMIS from JavaScript (JSONP)</title>
  <meta charset="UTF-8">
  <meta http-equiv="Content-Type" content="text/html;
    charset=UTF-8">
  <script src="testCMISfromJS-JSONP.js"
    type="text/javascript"></script>
</head>
<body>
<p>Get the Repository ID from the Alfresco server (JSONP): </p>
<input type="button" value="Get Repository ID"
  onClick="getRepoId()">
<div id="repo_id"></div>
</body>
</html>
```

Then, starting with the `getRepoId` function, create the new `testCMISfromJS-JSONP.js` file as follows:

```javascript
function getRepoId() {
  var serviceCallUrl =
    "http://localhost:8080/alfresco/cmisbrowser?
    callback=listRepoInfo";
  var listRepoInfoScript = document.createElement('script');
  listRepoInfoScript.setAttribute('src', serviceCallUrl);
  listRepoInfoScript.setAttribute('type', 'text/javascript');
  document.body.appendChild(listRepoInfoScript);
}
```

In the preceding code, we can see that the service call URL has been appended with the name of the callback function that should wrap the returned JSON. Then, a `script` tag is created that will automatically call the CMIS service. The `listRepoInfo` callback function looks as follows:

```
function listRepoInfo(cmisServiceResponseJSON) {
    for (repositoryId in cmisServiceResponseJSON) {
        var repository = cmisServiceResponseJSON[repositoryId];
        document.getElementById('repo_id').innerHTML =
            "Repository found [id=" + repository.repositoryId +
            "] [name="+ repository.vendorName + "[version=" +
            repository.productVersion + "]";
    }
}
```

If we debug the preceding function, we will see the following HTML page after the button has been clicked on. Note the extra `script` tag in the `body` section of the page with the function call.

It will now work to just double-click on the `testCMISfromJS-JSONP.html` file and then click on the **Get Repository Id** button. So, this does not look that complicated. However, it's not the whole story. If we are building a real web application, we are going to need a lot more callback functions. What you normally do then is add an `id` parameter to the script, so it can be removed later on. This script ID needs to be modified for each request, and this requires a bit more logic and code to implement. Luckily, there are JavaScript libraries that provide this functionality, so we don't have to write it from scratch.

Using jQuery

One JavaScript library that provides JSONP functionality is jQuery. This library is also good to use in general as it covers a lot of the shortcomings of various other browsers. To rewrite our example with the jQuery library, we must first include its JS file in our HTML page. Copy the previous HTML file we created earlier and give it the name `testCMISfromJS-JQuery.html`. Then, update the file with an extra `script` tag, so it looks like the following:

```html
<!DOCTYPE html>
<html>
<head>
  <title>Testing CMIS from JavaScript (JQuery)</title>
  <meta charset="UTF-8">
  <meta http-equiv="Content-Type" content="text/html;
    charset=UTF-8">
  <script src="jquery-1.9.0.js" type="text/javascript"></script>
  <script src="testCMISfromJS-JQuery.js"
    type="text/javascript"></script>
</head>
<body>
<p>Get the Repository ID from the Alfresco server (JQuery): </p>
<input type="button" value="Get Repository ID"
  onClick="getRepoId()">
<div id="repo_id"></div>
</body>
</html>
```

In the preceding code, the jQuery library script is included and we have also changed the name of our custom JS file that will use the jQuery library. Note that you will have to download the jQuery library (http://jquery.com/) and put it in the same directory as the HTML file. Now, create a new JS file called `testCMISfromJS-JQuery.js` and implement the `getRepoId` function as follows:

```javascript
function getRepoId() {
  var useJSONP = true;
  $.ajax(
  {
    url: "http://localhost:8080/alfresco/cmisbrowser",
      data: null,
      dataType: (useJSONP ? "jsonp" : "json"),
      type: "GET",
      username: "admin",
      password: "admin",
      success: listRepoInfo,
      error: errorHandler,
```

```
        timeout: 5000
    }
    );
}
```

Now when we use the jQuery library, we can take advantage of the `ajax` function
to make the CMIS service call. It takes the service call URL as a parameter; note that
it does not need the callback function parameter. It also takes a parameter called
`dataType` that specifies if we want to use the JSONP functionality or not. We also
pass in the username and password for the Alfresco server. And finally, we specify
what function should be called if successful (`listRepoInfo`) and what function
should be called if an error occurs (`errorHandler`).

So we can see that it is much easier to make AJAX calls cross domains when using a
library such as jQuery, and it also gives us a chance to take care of service call errors.
In the following code, the `listRepoInfo` function looks the same as above, the error
function is new:

```
function listRepoInfo(cmisServiceResponseJSON) {
    for (repositoryId in cmisServiceResponseJSON) {
        var repository = cmisServiceResponseJSON[repositoryId];
        $('#repo_id').html("Repository found [id=" +
            repository.repositoryId + "]
            [name="+ repository.vendorName + "[version=" +
            repository.productVersion + "]");
    }
}


function errorHandler(event, jqXHR, settings, exception) {
    alert("CMIS Service call was aborted:" + jqXHR + " : " +
        event.statusText);
}
```

Now that we got the main structure of how to make CMIS calls from JavaScript,
it is easy to extend the example with other calls. Let's say that we also want to list
children of the top folder when clicking on the **Get Repository Info** button. We can
do that in a lot of different ways. A good and efficient way is to look for a widget that
can take a JSON response as data and load itself automatically. There are loads of
widgets that can do this with JavaScript libraries such as jQuery, **Yahoo UI Library
(YUI)**, and extJS.

In this example, we will use a table widget plugin for jQuery that is called **DataTables** (http://www.datatables.net). Follow the URL and download a file called something like jquery.dataTables-1.9.4.min.js. The DataTables plugin can use a JSON object downloaded from the server side in order to populate an HTML table. We will also use a theme called UI Darkness from the jQuery UI ThemeRoller to get a neater UI (you can download it from http://jqueryui.com/). jQuery UI consists of a JavaScript file called something like jquery-ui-1.10.0.custom.js, and a stylesheet called something like jquery-ui-1.10.0.custom.css.

For this example, we create a new HTML file called testCMISfromJS-JQuery-DataTable.html and include the extra JavaScript libraries and the jQuery UI stylesheet with an HTML table to populate, as follows:

```html
<!DOCTYPE html>
<html>
<head>
  <title>Testing CMIS from JavaScript (JQuery)</title>
  <meta charset="UTF-8">
  <meta http-equiv="Content-Type" content="text/html;
    charset=UTF-8">
  <script src="jquery-1.9.0.js" type="text/javascript"></script>
  <script src="jquery-ui-1.10.0.custom.js"
    type="text/javascript"></script>
  <script src="jquery.dataTables-1.9.4.min.js"
    type="text/javascript"></script>
  <script src="testCMISfromJS-JQuery-DataTable.js"
    type="text/javascript"></script>
  <link rel="stylesheet" href="jquery-ui-1.10.0.custom.css">
</head>
<body>
<p>Get the Repository ID from the Alfresco server (JQuery): </p>
<input type="button" value="Get Repository ID"
  onClick="getRepoId()">
<div id="repo_id"></div>
<br/>
<table id="folderContentDataTable" cellpadding="0" cellspacing="0"
  border="0">
  <thead>
  <tr>
    <th align="left">Name</th>
    <th align="left">Type</th>
    <th align="left">NodeRef</th>
  </tr>
  </thead>
  <tbody>
```

```
   <tr>
     <td>Row 1 Data 1</td>
     <td>Row 1 Data 2</td>
     <td>etc</td>
   </tr>
   <tr>
     <td>Row 2 Data 1</td>
     <td>Row 2 Data 2</td>
     <td>etc</td>
   </tr>
   </tbody>
  </table>
 </body>
 </html>
```

The HTML table is constructed with the number of columns that we want and their headers. There also need to be some dummy rows with data. The table identifier folderContentDataTable will be used later to hook up the JavaScript code with this table.

The new JavaScript file called testCMISfromJS-JQuery-DataTable.js contains a new function call listTopFolderChildren in the listRepoInfo function as follows:

```
function getRepoId() {
  var useJSONP = true;
  $.ajax(
  {
    url: "http://localhost:8080/alfresco/cmisbrowser",
      data: null,
      dataType: (useJSONP ? "jsonp" : "json"),
      type: "GET",
      username: "admin",
      password: "admin",
      success: listRepoInfo,
      error: errorHandler,
      timeout: 5000
  }
  );
}

function listRepoInfo(cmisServiceResponseJSON) {
  for (repositoryId in cmisServiceResponseJSON) {
    var repository = cmisServiceResponseJSON[repositoryId];
    $('#repo_id').html("Repository found [id=" +
      repository.repositoryId + "]
```

```
    [name="+ repository.vendorName + "[version=" +
    repository.productVersion + "]");
  listTopFolderChildren(repository.repositoryId);
  }
}
```

When the `listTopFolderChildren` function is called with the repository identifier, it will populate the new HTML table that we just added with the folders and documents in the `/Company Home` top folder in Alfresco as follows:

```
function listTopFolderChildren(repositoryId) {
  var listTopFolderChildrenUrl =
    "http://localhost:8080/alfresco/cmisbrowser/" +
      repositoryId + "/root";
  $("#folderContentDataTable").dataTable(
  {
    "bJQueryUI": true,
    "sAjaxSource": listTopFolderChildrenUrl,
    "sAjaxDataProp": "objects",
    "aoColumns": [
      { "mData": "object.properties.cmis:name.value" },
      { "mData": "object.properties.cmis:objectTypeId.value" },
      { "mData": "object.properties.cmis:objectId.value" }
    ],
    "fnServerData": function ( sSource, aoData, fnCallback ) {
      $.ajax( {
        url: sSource,
        data: aoData,
        dataType: "jsonp",
        type: "GET",
        username: "admin",
        password: "admin",
        success: fnCallback,
        error: errorHandler,
        timeout: 5000
      } );
    }
  }
  );
}
```

The first thing we do in this function is construct the URL that will list the children of the root folder; it has the following template `http://<host>:<port>/alfresco/cmisbrowser/<repositoryId>/root`. Getting this URL will return JSON as in the following example:

```
{
"hasMoreItems" : false,
  "objects" :
  [
    {
      "object" :
      {
        "properties" :
        {
          "cmis:objectTypeId" :
          {
            "id" : "cmis:objectTypeId",
            "localName" : "objectTypeId",
            "queryName" : "cmis:objectTypeId",
            "value" : "cmis:folder",
            "type" : "id",
            "displayName" : "Object Type Id",
            "cardinality" : "single"
          },
          "cmis:objectId" : { …
```

Next, we use the new DataTable widget that we downloaded by calling `$("#folderContentDataTable").dataTable`. This connects the JavaScript widget with the HTML table. Then, we initialize the DataTable widget to run in the AJAX source mode; for this you need to set the URL for the CMIS service call that will return JSON in the `sAjaxSource` parameter. The `bJQueryUI` Boolean property is set to `true`, so we can use the Darkness theme from the jQuery UI stuff that we included. The `sAjaxDataProp` and `aoColumns` properties tell the DataTable widget how it will be able to get to the name, type, and node reference for the folder or document retrieved via the CMIS AJAX call, compared to the getChildren JSON response previously discussed.

Then, because we are calling a CMS server located in a different domain, we again need to make a JSONP call. The standard AJAX call functionality in the DataTable widget does not support this, so we override the server-calling functionality by specifying the `fnServerData` property and setting it to use a normal jQuery AJAX call that uses the JSONP mechanism.

Running this example produces the output shown in the following screenshot:

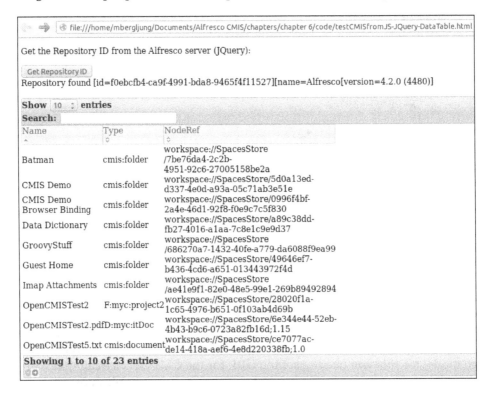

So, by using a couple of JavaScript libraries and some available stylesheets, we can produce a web page with a lot of functionality. It supports paging, sorting, searching, and setting number of items per page. And we got that for free. This also handled all the JSON processing and injecting that into the table.

Using CMIS in Groovy scripts

Using OpenCMIS to talk to a CMIS server via Java is quite easy compared to using basic protocol bindings such as the AtomPub binding. But by using the OpenCMIS API via the Groovy scripting language, we can also do the following:

- Get less code, making the application more readable
- Run the code without the need to compile it, making a round trip from code change to test quicker
- Script content updates so we can easily run checks or updates, such as `cron` jobs
- Use any Java library as Groovy runs on the JVM

Install Groovy using the following command:

```
$ sudo apt-get install groovy
```

If you are not familiar with Groovy, I recommend that you spend 1 to 2 hours reading a tutorial about it before coding anything in this section at http://groovy. codehaus.org/Beginners+Tutorial.

So to get started, create a file named testCMIS.groovy and add the following code to it to import the OpenCMIS classes that we need:

```
@Grab(group='org.apache.chemistry.opencmis', module='chemistry-
opencmis-client-impl', version='0.10.0')
import org.apache.chemistry.opencmis.commons.enums.BindingType
import org.apache.chemistry.opencmis.client.runtime.SessionFactoryImpl
import org.apache.chemistry.opencmis.client.api.Document
import org.apache.chemistry.opencmis.commons.exceptions.
CmisObjectNotFoundException
```

These classes live in some libraries that we need to resolve, and this is done with the help of the Groovy dependency resolution using Grape with Grab annotations. Now, add the following code to connect to the repository and set up a session:

```
// Setup session parameters to connect with
  def props = ['org.apache.chemistry.opencmis.user' : 'admin',
  'org.apache.chemistry.opencmis.password': "admin",
  'org.apache.chemistry.opencmis.binding.atompub.url' :
  "http://localhost:8080/alfresco/cmisatom",
  'org.apache.chemistry.opencmis.binding.spi.type' :
  BindingType.ATOMPUB.value(),
  'org.apache.chemistry.opencmis.binding.compression' : "true",
  'org.apache.chemistry.opencmis.cache.objects.ttl' : "0"]

// Get all repositories from the server and then use the first one
  def repositories =
  SessionFactoryImpl.newInstance().getRepositories(props)
  def alfrescoRepository = repositories.get(0)

// List info for all repos, if there would be more
// than one we would see it now
  repositories.eachWithIndex { repo, i ->
  println "Info about Alfresco repo # ${i}
  [ID=${repo.id}] [name=${repo.name}] [CMIS ver
  supported=${repo.cmisVersionSupported}]"
}

// Create a new session with the Alfresco repository
  def session = alfrescoRepository.createSession()
```

Running this code from the command line produces the following output:

```
$ groovy testCMIS.groovy
Info about Alfresco repo # 0 [ID=615c7c4c-05ff-4f73-b261-5a19b7c5bc34]
[name=Main Repository][CMIS ver supported=1.0]
```

Listing the top folders in the repository is easy; add the following code to the Groovy file:

```
def root = session.rootFolder
def contentItems = root.children
contentItems.each { contentItem ->
  if (contentItem instanceof Document) {
    def docContent = contentItem.contentStream
    println "${contentItem.name}
      [size=${docContent.length}][Mimetype=${docContent.mimeType}]
      [type=${contentItem.type.displayName}]"
  } else {
    println "${contentItem.name}
      [type=${contentItem.type.displayName}]"
  }
}
```

Running this code produces a log that looks as follows:

```
Data Dictionary [type=Folder]
Guest Home [type=Folder]
User Homes [type=Folder]
Imap Attachments [type=Folder]
Sites [type=Sites]
CMIS Demo [type=Folder]
CMIS Demo Browser Binding [type=Folder]
Simple (from Browser binding).txt [size=-1][Mimetype=text/plain]
[type=Document]
simple.txt [size=-1][Mimetype=text/plain][type=Document]
simple2.txt [size=-1][Mimetype=text/plain][type=Document]
SimpleBrowser.txt [size=-1][Mimetype=text/plain][type=Document]
SimpleBrowser2.txt [size=-1][Mimetype=text/plain][type=Document]
Some it doc.txt [size=-1][Mimetype=text/plain][type=MyCompany IT Doc]
OpenCMISTest_Updated [type=Folder]
OpenCMISTest2 [type=MyCompany Project]
OpenCMISTest2.pdf [size=-1][Mimetype=application/pdf][type=MyCompany IT
Doc]
OpenCMISTestTitled [type=Folder]
```

To create a folder, add the following code to the Groovy file:

```
def folderName = "GroovyStuff"
def someFolder = null

try {
  someFolder = session.getObjectByPath("/" + folderName)
} catch (CmisObjectNotFoundException nfe) {
  // Nothing to do, object does not exist
}

if (someFolder == null) {
  props = ['cmis:objectTypeId': 'cmis:folder',
    'cmis:name': 'GroovyStuff']
  someFolder = root.createFolder(props)

  println "Created new folder: " + someFolder.name + "
    [creator=" + someFolder.createdBy + "][created=" +
    someFolder.creationDate.time + "]"
} else {
  println "Folder already exist: " + folderName
}
```

The preceding code assumes that we already have the other Groovy code before this one, where the root folder has already been acquired and where the props variable has been defined. Running this code produces the following output:

Created new folder: GroovyStuff [creator=admin] [created=Fri Jan 11 13:14:18 GMT 2013]

When using Groovy, we can make use of a class named CMIS, which is available in the Apache Chemistry project in the CMIS.groovy file. If you cannot find it, try to Google it. Save this file in a directory named scripts, which should be a subdirectory to the directory where you have the testCMIS.groovy file.

The CMIS class contains a lot of helper methods, such as an easy method for creating a document. If you remember from the previous chapter, it requires creating a content stream, setting up properties, specifying a mime type, and so on. To create a document from a file on a disk with the CMIS helper class, use the following code:

```
// Load the CMIS Helper class
def cmis = new scripts.CMIS(session)

// Create doc
def groovyFolder = session.getObjectByPath '/GroovyStuff'
def file = new File('test.pdf')
def testDoc = cmis.createDocumentFromFile groovyFolder, file,
  "cmis:document", null
```

Here, I am expecting the `test.pdf` file to be in the same directory as the Groovy script. The `createDocumentFromFile` method in the `CMIS` class takes care of creating the content stream, figuring out the mime type, and setting up the necessary properties. The only property we pass in is the type of the document.

The `CMIS` class has loads of useful methods such as the following:

```
cmis.printProperties testDoc
cmis.download(testDoc, "/some/path/test.pdf")
cmis.delete testDoc.id
```

Have a look in the file for more useful methods.

By now we have seen that we get a lot less code using Groovy than when Java is used, and it's quicker to go from a code change to a test. We have also seen that if you get an example in Java on how to use OpenCMIS to perform a certain operation, it is then easy to convert the example to a Groovy code. So, refer to the previous chapter for information about how to do more with OpenCMIS in Groovy.

Using CMIS in Spring Surf Web Scripts

Many of Alfresco's user interfaces are built with a development framework called **Spring Surf**. The Spring Surf framework was originally developed by Alfresco and later on donated to the Spring Source foundation (http://www.springsource. org/extensions/se-surf). It is based on the Spring MVC framework and provides a way of breaking an HTML page into reusable component parts. This is also the framework that underpins the Alfresco Share application (the main user interface for Alfresco). One of the subprojects of Spring Surf is Spring Surf Web Scripts.

A Web Script is built up in the same way as a REST-based request and response model; the predominant web service design model. It is accessed via HTTP at a specific URL and when invoked, it responds with, for example, JSON. The Web Script implementation that produces the JSON response can use CMIS to talk to a CMS server to fetch data that should go into the JSON.

A Web Script is built up of a descriptor that specifies the URL it should be bound to, a controller that implements the logic that builds a data model (usually coded in JavaScript), and a template that produces the response, such as JSON, based on the data model.

Setting up a build project for Spring Surf with CMIS

Before we start creating Web Scripts that uses CMIS to talk to Alfresco, we need to have a look at how to set up a build project for Spring Surf. We also need to know how Web Scripts come into the picture when using the Spring Surf web development framework.

There is a great starting point available in the form of a Maven artifact for a Spring Surf project. To create a project based on it, run the following command:

```
$ mvn archetype:generate -DarchetypeCatalog=https://artifacts.alfresco.
com/nexus/content/groups/public-snapshots/archetype-catalog.xml
```

This brings up a list of available Alfresco artifacts, and last time I checked, number 10 in the list is the one you want. The resulting project structure looks like what is shown in the following screenshot:

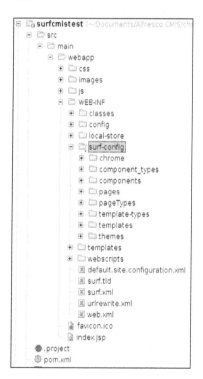

All the configuration for web pages built with Spring Surf reside in the `surf-config` directory under `WEB-INF`. This book is not about Spring Surf development, so we will not go too much into this. However, a quick run through of how it all goes together is necessary.

A Spring Surf web page is defined in the pages directory under surf-config as an XML file, and it uses a template instance that is defined in the templates directory under surf-config as an XML file. The template instance in turn points to a FreeMarker template located in the templates directory under WEB-INF.

A FreeMarker template defines regions that are implemented as components, and they are defined in the components directory under surf-config. Each one of the components is implemented with a Web Script defined in the webscripts directory under WEB-INF. As said before, a Web Script is made up of a descriptor, controller, and a template. CMIS can be used in the controller to talk to any CMIS repository.

Confused yet? Coding with Spring Surf means creating lots of files, but it also means that the web application framework is very flexible and allows web page components to be reused.

If we build and package the generated web application and put the resulting WAR into the webapps directory under alfresco/tomcat (or in another Tomcat), then the home page of the web app can be accessed with the http://localhost:8080/ surfcmistest-1.0-SNAPSHOT/page/home URL. The following screenshot shows what the home page looks like:

Now, if we wanted to update the home page for it to use CMIS to connect to, for example, an Alfresco server, and then show its repository ID, we need to bring in some more libraries.

Updating the Spring Surf project so that CMIS can be used

We want to update the Spring Surf project so that we can make CMIS calls from the Spring Web Script controllers implemented in either Java or JavaScript. To do this, we have to add a few libraries to our Maven project as follows:

- First, we want to bring in OpenCMIS so that we can make use of a high-level API in our Java-based controllers.

- If we are using Alfresco, it is also good to be able to handle aspects. So, we will bring in the Alfresco OpenCMIS extension library.

- We also want to be able to use the OpenCMIS API from JavaScript controllers via a new root object called `cmis`.

Add the following libraries to the dependency section of the POM as follows:

```
<dependencies>
...
  <dependency>
    <groupId>org.apache.chemistry.opencmis</groupId>
    <artifactId>chemistry-opencmis-client-impl</artifactId>
    <version>0.10.0</version>
  </dependency>
  <dependency>
    <groupId>org.alfresco.cmis.client</groupId>
    <artifactId>alfresco-opencmis-extension</artifactId>
    <version>0.4</version>
    <exclusions>
      <exclusion>
        <groupId>org.apache.chemistry.opencmis</groupId>
        <artifactId>chemistry-opencmis-client-impl</artifactId>
      </exclusion>
    </exclusions>
  </dependency>
  <dependency>
    <groupId>org.springframework.extensions.surf</groupId>
    <artifactId>spring-cmis-framework</artifactId>
    version>1.2.0-SNAPSHOT</version>
    <exclusions>
      <exclusion>
        <groupId>org.apache.chemistry.opencmis</groupId>
        <artifactId>chemistry-opencmis-client-impl</artifactId>
      </exclusion>
    </exclusions>
  </dependency>
</dependencies>
```

First, we bring in the OpenCMIS Java library. When you are reading this, there might be a newer version than 0.10.0. After this, we bring in the Alfresco OpenCMIS extensions library to manage aspects. When we do this, we also exclude the dependency on OpenCMIS, so we do not end up with multiple versions of the OpenCMIS libraries in `WEB-INF/lib`. This can happen if, for example, the POM file for the Alfresco OpenCMIS extension library contains a dependency to a different version of the OpenCMIS library than 0.10.0.

The last library we bring in is the Spring Surf CMIS extension library that provides a `cmis` root object to use in JavaScript controllers, and also authentication and configuration functionality. We exclude the OpenCMIS library here too, so we don't end up with multiple versions of it in the WAR.

All the libraries that we need are now included in the project. But we also need to load some beans from the Spring Surf CMIS extension project to register, for example, the `cmis` JavaScript root object. Add the following `import` tag to the beginning of the `surf-config.xml` Spring context file as follows:

```xml
<?xml version="1.0" encoding="UTF-8"?>
<beans

  ...
<import
  resource="classpath*:org/springframework/extensions/
  cmis/*-context.xml" />
<import
  resource="classpath*:org/springframework/extensions/
  webscripts/*-context.xml" />
<import
  resource="classpath*:org/springframework/extensions/surf/*-
  context.xml" />
<bean id="handlerMappings" parent="webframeworkHandlerMappings">
  <property name="order" value="0" />
  <property name="defaultHandler">
  <bean
    class="org.springframework.web.servlet.mvc.
    UrlFilenameViewController" />
  </property>
</bean>
</beans>
```

The last thing we need to do before we can start using CMIS is configure the connection parameters. This is done in the `surf.xml` file under `surfcmistest/src/main/webapp/WEB-INF`; add the following section at the end with the OpenCMIS configuration parameters:

```
<alfresco-config>
  ...
  <!-- Open CMIS client configuration -->
  <plug-ins>
    <element-readers>
      <element-reader element-name="cmis-servers"
        class="org.springframework.extensions.cmis.
        CMISServersConfigElementReader"/>
    </element-readers>
  </plug-ins>

  <config evaluator="string-compare" condition="CMIS">
    <cmis-servers>
      <!-- Configure a locally running Alfresco Server -->
        <server>
          <parameter key="name" value="default"/>
          <parameter key="description"
            value="Local Alfresco Server"/>
          <parameter key="org.apache.chemistry.opencmis.user"
            value="admin"/>
          <parameter key="org.apache.chemistry.opencmis.password"
            value="admin"/>
          <parameter
            key="org.apache.chemistry.opencmis.binding.spi.type"
            value="atompub"/>
          <parameter
            key="org.apache.chemistry.opencmis.binding.atompub.
            url" value="http://localhost:8080/alfresco/cmisatom"/>
          <parameter
            key="org.apache.chemistry.opencmis.binding.
            compression" value="true"/>
          <parameter
            key="org.apache.chemistry.opencmis.cache.objects.ttl"
            value="0"/> <!-- no content caching is done -->
          <!-- Override Object Factory class when running with
            Alfresco CMIS extensions for Aspect support -->
          <parameter
            key="org.apache.chemistry.opencmis.objectfactory.
            classname" value="org.alfresco.cmis.client.impl.
            AlfrescoObjectFactoryImpl"/>
        </server>
    </cmis-servers>
  </config>
</alfresco-config>
```

We first define a plugin that can read the `<cmis-servers>` element with the entire OpenCMIS configuration, and then we define the connection and configuration parameters to talk to a local Alfresco server. We are now ready to use CMIS in our Surf Web Script controllers.

Updating the home page to display repository info via CMIS

To update a Spring Surf page, we have to first figure out what regions it has and which one our new content should go into. As mentioned previously, the regions are defined in the page's FreeMarker template. The template for the home page in our example application is located in the `package` directory under `surfcmistest/src/main/webapp/WEB-INF/templates/org/example` and is called `home.ftl`.

After opening this file, we will discover that it has three regions defined as follows:

```
<html>
  <head>
    <title>Example Surf Page</title>
    ...
  </head>
  <body>
    <div id="main">
      <@region id="header" scope="page"/>
      <@region id="body" scope="page"/>
    </div>
      <@region id="footer" scope="page"/>
  </body>
</html>
```

We will add our new repository information to the `body` region. This means that we have to add it to the controller for the body Web Script defined by the `body.get.desc.xml` descriptor under `surfcmistest/src/main/webapp/WEB-INF/webscripts/home`. In the `home` directory, we can see that there is no controller defined for this Web Script; it would have been in a file named `body.get.js`. There's just a template to display static content for the home page. So, we got to add a file called `body.get.js` to the `home` directory under `surfcmistest/src/main/webapp/WEB-INF/webscripts`. It will contain the following code:

```
var SERVER_NAME = "default";
var CONNECTION_ID = "my-webapp-" + SERVER_NAME;
var connection = cmis.getConnection(CONNECTION_ID);
if (connection == null) {
  var serverDefinition = cmis.getServerDefinition(SERVER_NAME);
```

```
    if (serverDefinition == null) {
      status.code = 400;
      status.message = "Could not find server definition for server
        name " + SERVER_NAME + " - see surf.xml!";
      status.redirect = true;
    }
    try {
      connection = cmis.createUserConnection(serverDefinition,
        CONNECTION_ID);
      logger.warn("Connected with connection id: " + CONNECTION_ID);
    } catch (e) {
      logger.warn((e.javaException == null ?
        e.rhinoException.message : e.javaException.message));
    }
  } else {
    logger.warn("Already connected with connection id: " +
      CONNECTION_ID);
  }
```

This code basically sets up an OpenCMIS connection to the CMIS repository that we configured in the <cmis-servers> section of the surf.xml file. This configuration section has the CMIS server name set to default; so we set up a variable named SERVER_NAME with this value. We then put together a connection identifier by using the server name and the client application name and keep this in the CONNECTION_ID variable. We then pass in the connection ID to the Spring Surf CMIS extension method getConnection, which will return a connection object if we already have a connection established for the connection ID passed in.

If there is no connection available, we use the connection ID to get the server configuration via the Spring Surf CMIS extension method named getServerDefinition. The server definition, together with the connection ID, is then used to create a connection via another Spring Surf CMIS extension method named createUserConnection.

We are now ready to use this connection and work with the OpenCMIS API as we normally do. To get the repository information, we use the following code:

```
var repoInfo = connection.session.getRepositoryInfo();

model.productName = repoInfo.getProductName();
model.productVersion = repoInfo.getProductVersion();
```

Here, we are setting up two new properties in the model that are passed between the controller and the template. The first property will contain the CMS server product name, and the second property will contain the version of the product. We also need to update the template file body.get.html.ftl under surfcmistest/src/main/webapp/WEB-INF/webscripts/home as follows, so it shows the product information:

```
<@link href="${url.context}/res/css/body.css" group="default"/>
<div class="body">
  <p>
    <strong>Connected to CMIS Repository</strong>: ${productName}
      ${productVersion}
  </p>
</div>
```

This is all that is necessary to display that extra repository information in the home web page.

Updating the home page to display text from a file in the repository

Now we can just keep building on this with other OpenCMIS calls. Let's say, for example, that we wanted to display the text from a file stored in the repository on the home page right under the repository information. Let's say that the file is called `Page.txt` and stored directly under `/Company Home` in Alfresco. We can do this by adding the following code to the JavaScript controller (that is, `body.get.js`):

```
var pageTextObject =
  connection.session.getObjectByPath("/Page.txt");
var contentStreamInfo = pageTextObject.getContentStream();
model.pageText =
  cmisUtil.inputStream2Text(contentStreamInfo.getStream());
```

The first thing we do here is get a `Document` object for the `Page.txt` file under `/Company Home`. Then, we get the content stream object with information such as mime-type, content length, and access to the input stream for the file. The last line uses a custom root object named `cmisUtil`, which we will define in a minute, to get the text contained in the file via a custom method that converts an input stream to text. The custom root object is defined in a Java class called `CmisUtils` as follows:

```
package com.mycompany.util.jscript;
import org.apache.commons.io.IOUtils;
import org.springframework.extensions.webscripts.processor.
  BaseProcessorExtension;
import java.io.InputStream;
import java.io.StringWriter;

public class CmisUtils extends BaseProcessorExtension {
  public String inputStream2Text(InputStream inputStream) throws
    java.io.IOException{
    StringWriter writer = new StringWriter();
    IOUtils.copy(inputStream, writer, "UTF-8");
```

```
        return writer.toString();
    }
}
```

We make use of the Apache commons IO Utils to make a safe copy of the input stream to a string writer (that is, the input stream will be closed). Then, we just return what was written to the string writer. This class needs to extend the Spring Web Scripts base process extension class to hook into the root object framework. Finally, we need to define a Spring bean for it and configure what root object name we want to use in the JavaScript when referring to this utility; add the following bean to `surf-config.xml`:

```xml
<bean id="cmisUtil" parent="baseScriptExtension"
  class="com.mycompany.util.jscript.CmisUtils">
    <property name="extensionName" value="cmisUtil" />
</bean>
```

The `body.get.js` controller also sets up a new property called `pageText` in the model, so we need to display it in the home web page by adding the following code to the `body.get.html.ftl` template:

```html
<@link href="${url.context}/res/css/body.css" group="default"/>
<div class="body">
  <p>
    <strong>Connected to CMIS Repository</strong>: ${productName}
      ${productVersion}
  </p>
  <p>
    ${pageText}
  </p>
</div>
```

Hopefully, this has given you some ideas on how you can use CMIS to talk to a CMS server from a web application developed with the Spring Surf UI Development framework.

Using CMIS calls in Alfresco Share extensions

The stuff that we just went through to set up the possibility of using OpenCMIS and the `cmis` root object in Spring Surf Web Scripts is not necessary if you are working with Spring Surf Web Scripts in the Alfresco Share web application. It has already been set up, so you have full access to the OpenCMIS Java API from Java-backed controllers, and access to the `cmis` root object from controllers written in JavaScript.

Summary

In this chapter, we have looked at how to access a CMS server directly from a JavaScript code in the browser. We also saw how the JSONP mechanism can be used to get around the same origin policy. The jQuery JavaScript library was used to make it more efficient to develop AJAX calls to the CMS server. We also saw how we can load JavaScript widgets such as a data table with JSON coming directly from a CMIS service call.

The Groovy scripting language was explored to demonstrate that you can use the OpenCMIS API directly from your scripting code. This makes your normal OpenCMIS Java code shorter and easier to grasp. It is also quick to make a change and test it immediately without the need to compile and build.

Then we had a look at how we can incorporate the OpenCMIS library to talk to CMS servers when building web applications with the Spring Surf development framework.

In the final chapter, we will look at different types of integrations that use CMIS, such as Drupal's integration with Alfresco through CMIS.

7
System Integration with CMIS

In this chapter, we will take a look at how to integrate different systems or applications with CMIS. First we will see how the Drupal **Web Content Management (WCM)** system can be integrated with a CMS server to fetch information about documents in the repository to keep the content in one place. Then we will look at **Enterprise Application Integration (EIA)** with Mule ESB and how it can talk to CMS servers. In the last part of this chapter, we will see how CMIS can be used to talk to Alfresco's Cloud offering.

In this chapter we learn how to:

- Display a file link in Drupal that references a document in a CMIS repository
- Display a table of files in Drupal that references documents in a folder in a CMIS repository
- Use an **Enterprise Service Bus (ESB)** to poll for files in a folder and store them in a CMS server
- Use an ESB to transfer documents between Alfresco and a filesystem folder
- Talk to the Alfresco Cloud service

Integrating Drupal with a CMS server

In this section, we will look at how you can integrate Drupal 7 with a CMIS server via a couple of Drupal modules. I have already installed a **LAMP** stack (`http://en.wikipedia.org/wiki/LAMP_%28software_bundle%29`) plus Drupal 7 on an Ubuntu 12.04 box.

Note that it is possible to integrate any PHP application with a CMIS repository by using the Apache Chemistry subproject PHP Client (`http://chemistry.apache.org/php/phpclient.html`). We can, for example, write our own Drupal module using this library. However, we are not going to do that now; we will look at some available modules instead.

The CMIS-related modules require Drupal to be configured to use clean URLs (`http://drupal.org/getting-started/clean-urls`), and for the Apache `mod_rewrite` module to be installed. The Drupal application should also be accessible directly as the root web application under /, for example, as `http://localhost/`. Drupal is probably installed in a directory such as `drupal` under `/var/www`. So within Apache, we would want to have a virtual host configuration for our site in, for example, `/etc/apache2/sites-enabled/000-default` as follows:

```
<VirtualHost 127.0.1.1:80>
    ...
            DocumentRoot  /var/www/drupal
```

The CMIS modules will assume that Drupal is the root web application and use URLs such as `http://localhost/cmis/browser`.

The CMIS API module

The CMIS API module (`http://drupal.org/project/cmis`) provides a generic API to integrate with CMIS-compliant repositories. The CMIS API module is made up of a number of submodules as follows:

- `cmis.module`: This is the CMIS client API

- `cmis_common.module`: This is the CMIS common-client library implementation

- `cmis_browser.module`: This is the CMIS repository tree browser

- `cmis_field.module`: This defines a new Drupal field type called **CMIS Field,** which can be used to attach one or more repository files to a Drupal content entity

- `cmis_query.module`: This provides the ability to run CMIS 1.0 queries against the current CMIS repository

- `cmis_sync.module`: This allows synchronization between Drupal nodes and CMIS objects

- `cmis_headerswing.module`: This is the demo module that demonstrates using `hook_cmis_invoke()` to access the CMIS repository via header-based authentication such as Basic Auth or NTLM

- `cmis_dev.module`: This provides CMIS repository information such as repo name, repo description, vendor name, product name, and product version

Installing the CMIS API module is easy; after downloading and extracting the package (`cmis-7.x-1.x-dev.tar.gz` from `https://drupal.org/node/1118770`), copy the `/cmis` folder into the Drupal `modules` directory under `/var/www/drupal/sites/all/` as follows:

```
/var/www/drupal/sites/all/modules$ sudo cp -r ~/Downloads/cmis .
/var/www/drupal/sites/all/modules$ sudo chown -R www-data:www-data cmis
```

Note that it is important to change the file permissions for the new module so that the Apache HTTP server can read the files; this is what we do with the recursive `chown` command. Now we need to enable the CMIS modules. So click on **Modules** in the top Drupal toolbar and scroll down to the CMIS section. Then, enable all the CMIS modules as a Drupal site administrator and click on **Save configuration**.

Before we do anything, we need to configure at least one CMIS repository. Open up the `settings.php` file located in the `default` directory under `/var/www/drupal/sites/`. Add the following CMIS repository configuration to the end of the file:

```
$conf['cmis_repositories'] = array(
   'default' => array(
     'user' => 'admin',
       'password' => 'admin',
       'url' => 'http://localhost:8080/alfresco/cmisatom'
   )
);
```

The `user` and `password` parameters is for an account that exists in Alfresco. The `url` parameter, in this case, is the CMIS URL for the AtomPub binding when using Alfresco Version 4.

 If you are using Alfresco Version 4.2.d Community, 4.2.0 Enterprise, or newer, the correct CMIS Atom binding URL is `http://localhost:8080/alfresco/api/-default-/cmis/versions/1.1/atom`.

We can now log in to our Drupal site via, for example, `http://brutor.com`, and we should see some new links on the home page, as shown in the following screenshot (my hostname is set to `brutor` in this case):

We can click on the **CMIS Information** link, and it will display information about the repository we are connected to, as shown in the following screenshot:

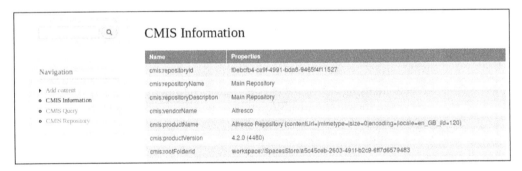

If you cannot see this page, maybe the URL in the configuration is not correct or you have specified an incorrect username or password.

 To find out whether there are any errors, click on the **Reports** main menu item in Drupal, then click on the **Recent log messages** menu item. On this page, you will see a list of logs. All error logs are displayed in red. You should also have a look at the Apache logs in `/var/log/apache2`.

The next link, **CMIS Query**, provides a page where we can try out CMIS queries, as in the following example:

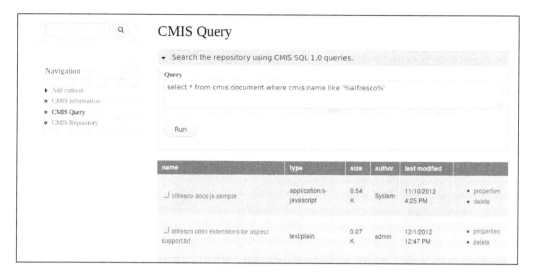

The last link, **CMIS Repository**, just gives you a folder view into the repository from the top-level folder, as shown in the following screenshot:

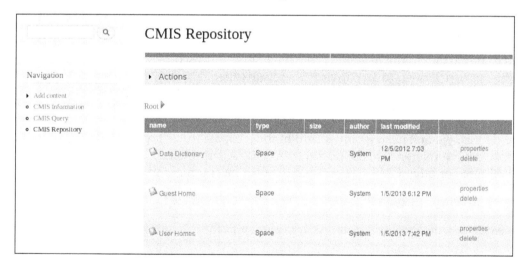

From this folder view, we can actually manipulate the folder hierarchy by clicking on **Actions** at the top, and then clicking on, for example, the **delete** link in each folder row.

Displaying a CMS repository file link on a Drupal page

In the following example, we will extend the out-of-the-box Drupal Article content type with an extra field that will contain a link to a file held within our CMS server repository. The new field will be called **More Info**, and if we write an article with some Alfresco information and a link to more information about Alfresco, it will look something like what is shown in the following screenshot:

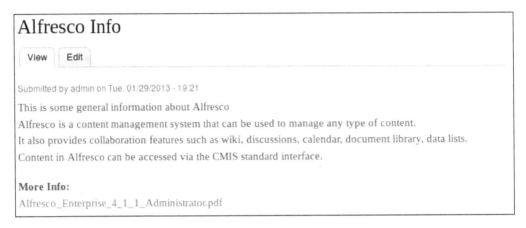

Clicking on the **More Info** link downloads the `Administrator Guide` PDF.

As example files in the repository, we have some Alfresco-related documents and white papers located in an Alfresco Share site called Alfresco Information (`/Company Home/Sites/alfresco-information`). We want to display one of these documents in an article about Alfresco Information as previously discussed.

To do this, we first need to add a field to the Drupal Article type, which will represent the reference to the document on the Alfresco Share site (or any document in Alfresco or other CMS systems that the user has permission to view).

Go to **Structure** | **Content Types** and then click on **manage fields** for the **Article** type.

Create a new field called `More Info`, as shown in the following screenshot:

After clicking on the **Save** button, accept the default settings for help text, field size, required, number of values, and so on, for the new field.

Now, add a new Article by going to **Add content | Article**. Call it, for example, `Alfresco Information` and fill in some text for the body. Then set up a link to a document in Alfresco by clicking on the **Browse** button after the field representing **More Info**. This brings up a CMIS browser where we can navigate to the desired document. Then, click on the **Choose** link at the end of the document row, as shown in the following screenshot:

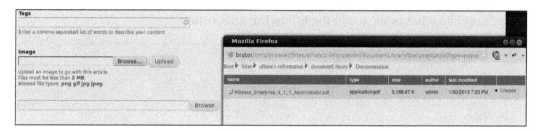

If we want the CMIS browser to start browsing further down in the folder hierarchy, we can set that up by going to **Structure | Content Types | Article | manage fields | More Info | edit**. Then, select a new root directory (that is, a new folder to start browsing from).

The CMIS Views module

The CMIS Views project (`http://drupal.org/project/cmis_views`) aims to build on the Drupal CMIS API by allowing Drupal developers to save a list of folder contents from a CMIS repository as a block or field, and then display this at runtime. This functionality is dynamic; so if the folder content in the CMIS repository changes, the Drupal display reflects this. A new Drupal field type called **CMIS Folder** is available for this.

In addition to creating blocks and fields based on the CMIS Folder type, it is also possible to write your own specific CMIS queries to pull content items back by their tags, title, or any other metadata that is exposed via CMIS.

Download the CMIS Views package (`cmis_views-7.x-1.x-dev.tar.gz`) and unzip it into the `modules` directory under `/var/www/drupal/sites/all/`. This module is dependent on the ctools module (`http://drupal.org/project/ctools`), so download and install this package too (`ctools-7.x-1.x-dev.tar.gz`).

We need to enable the new modules, so click on **Modules** in the toolbar at the top in Drupal and scroll down first to the Chaos Tool Suite and enable all modules, and then scroll to the CMIS Views section and enable the CMIS Views module. Then, click on **Save configuration**.

Displaying a CMS repository folder on a Drupal page

In the following example, we will extend the out-of-the-box Drupal Article content type with a field that can contain a reference to a folder in Alfresco with presentations. If we update our Alfresco information article with a presentations field of the type CMIS Folder and have it displayed in a table widget, it will look something like what is shown in the following screenshot:

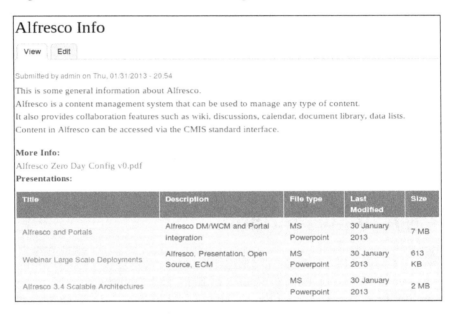

In this example, we have some Alfresco-related presentations located in the Alfresco Share site called Alfresco Information, which we used previously for the More Info field. To display these in a table at the end of the article on Alfresco Information, we first need to add another field to the Drupal Article type to hold the reference to the folder in the Alfresco Share site (or any folder in Alfresco or other CMS systems that the user has the permission to view).

Go to **Structure | Content Types** and then click on **manage fields** for the **Article** type.

Create a new field called `Presentations`, as shown in the following screenshot:

After clicking on the **Save** button, accept the default settings for the new field. Now update the Alfresco Information article we created earlier by clicking on **Find content**. Set up a link to a folder in Alfresco by clicking on the **Browse CMIS Repository** button after the field representing **Presentations**. This brings up a CMIS browser where we can navigate to the desired folder; click on the **Select This Folder** button, as shown in the following screenshot:

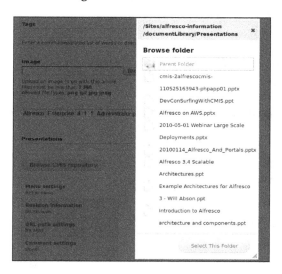

Finally, click on **Save** for the updated article and we should now have the table of presentations listed at the end of the Alfresco Information article. To get the table widget instead of a list, we have to change the display of the field. Go to **Structure | Content Types**. Click on **manage display** for the **Article** type and choose the **Table with file name, title, description, type, size and date** option from the **Format** list for the **Presentations** field, as shown in the following screenshot:

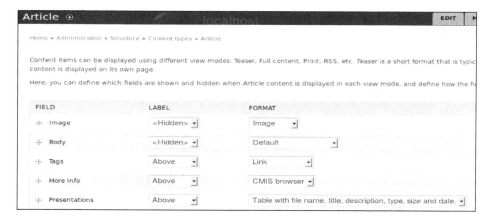

In the preceding screenshot, we can see that we switched to using a table instead of a bullet list.

 This switching only works with Alfresco by default. This is due to Alfresco using additional title and description metadata that is not part of the standard CMIS specification. And the standard file-path query performs a join to retrieve this extra data.

Displaying a result from a CMIS query on a Drupal page

So far we have displayed links to a single file or files from a folder on a Drupal page by adding a field to the Article type. We can also define a CMIS View block and have it represent the result of a CMIS query. This block can then be displayed in a region somewhere on the web page. Let's say we want to display all the files in the repository that have `alfresco` in their name in the footer of all pages, as in the following screenshot:

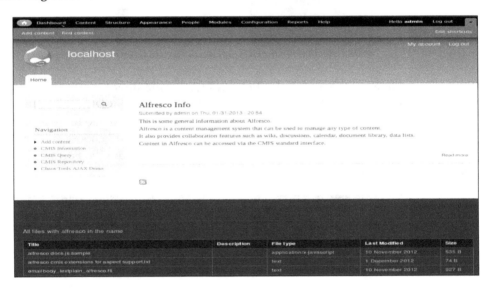

We can get the files with the following CMIS query:

```
SELECT * FROM cmis:document WHERE cmis:name LIKE '%alfresco%'
```

To do this, we start by defining a new CMIS View block by navigating to **Structure |
Blocks | Add a CMIS View**. Then, we give the view a name, click on the CMIS radio
button to make that a CMIS query, and specify the query, as shown in the
following screenshot:

In this example, we also change the display of the view to a table so that it looks better.

The only thing we still need to do is to select which region should contain the view.
Go to **Structure | Blocks** and then scroll down to the **disable** section where you will
find the new CMIS View block. In the **Region** combobox, select **Footer**.

Synchronizing the CMS content with Drupal content

The CMIS Sync feature pulls content from Alfresco and creates a copy in Drupal.
The module is intended for use with HTML or TEXT content, as that is what Drupal
understands in nodes. If you need to sync images, or for example, PDFs, use the
CMIS Field or CMIS Folder field type instead, as described in previous sections.
These field types store the file reference or folder reference in Drupal and the actual
content is not downloaded from Alfresco until the user requests it; the content is
never cached in Drupal.

When working with the CMIS Sync Module Version 7.x-1.x-dev, I had to manually update the code to get the content sync to work. The patch that was supposed to fix this, `syncfixes-1291988.patch`, has been applied to my build, but it is still not working; only metadata is synced. I had to update the code in `cmis_sync.cmis.inc` located in the `cmis_sync` directory under `sites/all/modules/cmis/` and around line 240, which is as follows:

```
try {

    // Strip of version number
    $cmis_object->id = substr($cmis_object->id, 0, -4);


    _cmis_sync_drupal_node_field_value($node,
        $sync_map_type['content_field'],
        cmisapi_getContentStream($repository->repositoryId,
        $cmis_object->id),
        $cmis_content_context);
```

The fix is to strip off the version information (that is, 1.0) from the end of the node reference.

So if we want to synchronize HTML files from Alfresco and then display them in Drupal as nodes, here is what we need to do. First find out where the HTML files that we want to sync are located in Alfresco. For this example, we have created a new folder in Alfresco called `/WebPageContent` directly under the root folder. I have added an HTML file to this folder, as shown in the following screenshot:

The file contains some styled text. We want any file in this folder synchronized over to Drupal as the Basic Page Drupal type (that is, `page`). To make this happen, we have to set up a sync configuration in `/var/www/drupal/sites/default/settings.php` as follows:

```
$conf['cmis_sync_map'] = array(
   'page' => array(
      'enabled' => TRUE,
```

```
        'cmis_repositoryId' => 'default',
        'cmis_type' => 'cmis:document',
        'cmis_folderPath' => '/WebPageContent',
        'content_field' => 'body',
        'fields' => array(
          'title' => 'cmis:name'),
          'full_sync_next_cron' => TRUE, // Grab only new items if
          FALSE, otherwise sync all items under cmis_folderPath ,
          deletes' => TRUE
    )
);
```

This will enable a synchronization process that will synchronize (that is, copy) Alfresco nodes of type `cmis:document` under the `/WebPageContent` folder into Drupal page nodes. The title of each Drupal page node will be set to `cmis:name`, and `body` of the page node will be set to the CMIS object's content stream.

A lot of the properties that have been specified are not strictly necessary as they have the same values by default (that is, `cmis_repositoryId`, `cmis_type`, `content_field`, `fields`, and `full_sync_next_cron`). But it's good to know what properties are available; you can check the module documentation for more information about the sync feature.

The actual sync process does not just happen by itself; something needs to kick it off. It is hooked up to Drupal's cron process. So if we go to **Configuration | Cron** and then click on **Run cron**, this will start the CMIS sync process. The result will look like what is shown in the following screenshot in Drupal:

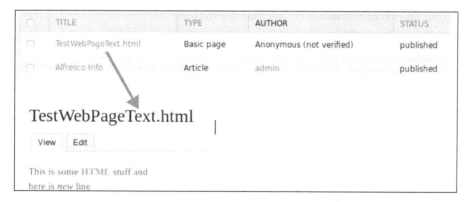

The synchronization also works in the opposite direction; create a basic page node in Drupal and it will show up in Alfresco. However, I could only get this to work if I did not use any HTML markup or new lines.

Enterprise integration with CMIS

If you are working on a larger enterprise integration project, some form of integration framework is probably used, such as an ESB. Sooner or later, you would want to use the ESB to fetch content from one system and maybe do some processing on it, and then inject it into a CMS server. There are several integration frameworks that you could use for this, some of which are as follows:

- **Apache Camel**: This is an open source Java framework that focuses on making integration easier (`http://camel.apache.org/`). It has a CMIS connector to talk to CMS servers.

- **Mule ESB**: This is an ESB and integration framework (`http://www.mulesoft.org/`). It has a CMIS connector to talk to CMS servers.

- **Spring Integration**: This is an open source Java framework for enterprise application integration (`http://www.springsource.org/spring-integration`).

In this section, we will use Mule ESB to demonstrate how to integrate CMS servers in a larger enterprise application scenario.

An ESB such as Mule can help out when CMS servers need to participate in an enterprise application integration scenario; Mule has a CMIS Cloud Connector (`http://www.mulesoft.org/extensions/cmis-cloud-connector`) that can be used for this. With the CMIS Connector module, we can do the following:

- Create documents and folders
- Retrieve documents and contents of a folder
- Manage document properties
- Query the repository
- Query the change log

For the examples in this section, we will use Mule Studio with which we can both graphically draw our message flow and run in an embedded Mule runtime. The Mule community edition includes Mule Studio and can be downloaded from `http://www.mulesoft.org/download-mule-esb-community-edition`.

Moving a file from a folder into a CMS server using Mule

A common use case is to have files dropped into a folder, then have the ESB pick them up for some processing, and finally store them in a CMS server. To implement this example, we will use Mule Studio and assume that we are importing PDF files.

Start up Mule Studio and create a new Mule project by navigating to **File | New | Mule Project**. Call the project `File Importer` and select to create a Maven `pom.xml` file. Now, in the Message Flow view/tab, draw the following message flow:

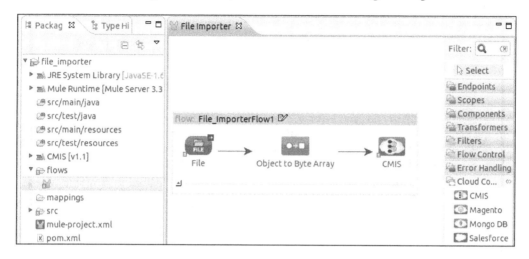

We now have to configure the components in the message flow. Start with the **File** inbound endpoint. We will pick up PDF files from a folder in our project workspace and poll this folder every 3 seconds for new files. When a new file is found, the ESB will grab it and feed it into the message pipeline after which the file will be deleted. To configure this, right-click on the inbound **File** component and select **Properties** from the pop-up menu; the resulting window is shown in the following screenshot:

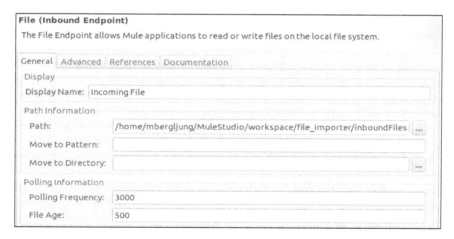

In the **Advanced** tab in the **Properties** dialog, we also select to scan only for the `application/pdf` MIME type.

The next component to configure is the object-to-byte-array transformer that loads the file in-memory (see the following information box for an alternative). The only configuration needed for it is to set the MIME type to `application/pdf`.

When implementing a more complex and bigger message pipeline, it might not make sense to pass around the complete content of a document as a message payload in memory. Out-of-memory errors will probably happen sooner or later because of resource exhaustion. Consider implementing the Claim Check EAI pattern instead (`http://eaipatterns.com/StoreInLibrary.html`) where you check-in the document content in a durable storage and get a claim check back, which you pass around between components. The claim check could be, for example, the CMIS object ID for the document (that is, Alfresco node reference). Each component could then decide whether it is interested in any of the content or metadata for the document and retrieve it via the Claim Check EAI pattern. This will make the system more performant, scalable, and easier to troubleshoot.

The last component will make the CMIS call and should be configured as follows. In the **Properties** dialog, start by configuring the **CMIS** configuration; it will keep information about how to connect to Alfresco. Click on the plus (**+**) sign after the **Config Reference** field:

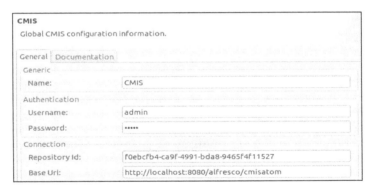

Here we are configuring the username and password for the Alfresco account that we want to connect with; in this case, we connect as admin. We then specify the **Base Url** as the AtomPub CMIS binding URL for Alfresco (this would be different for another CMS server). If we do an HTTP GET on this URL in a browser, we can also find out the **Repository Id** in the Service Document page that is returned. That's it for the connection configuration; click on **OK** to get back to the main **Properties** dialog.

Now we also need to configure what CMIS service call/operation we want to make. From the **Operation** drop-down list, select **Create document by path**; this displays the relevant configuration properties for this operation, as shown in the following screenshot:

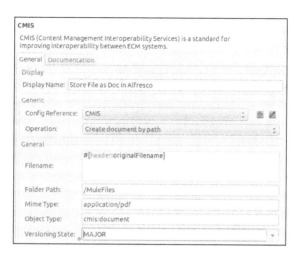

The first property we set up is the **Filename** for the new document that will be created in Alfresco. This is picked up from the Inbound File Transport component with the #[header:originalFilename] expression. I have created a folder in Alfresco named /Company Home/MuleFiles so that the **Folder Path** property is set to /MuleFiles. We are storing PDF files; so **Mime Type** is set accordingly. Then we have to decide what CMIS **Object Type** the new file should have in the CMIS repository; in this case, we are just using the base document type cmis:document. Finally, **Versioning State** is set to MAJOR as the document type cmis:document is versionable.

If we now switch to the **Configuration XML** tab in Mule Studio, we should see the XML configuration for this message flow looking something like the following code:

```xml
<?xml version="1.0" encoding="UTF-8"?>
<mule ...>
  <cmis:config name="CMIS" username="admin" password="admin"
    repositoryId="f0ebcfb4-ca9f-4991-bda8-9465f4f11527"
    baseUrl="http://localhost:8080/alfresco/cmisatom"
    doc:name="CMIS"/>
  <flow name="File_ImporterFlow1" doc:name="File_ImporterFlow1">
    <file:inbound-endpoint responseTimeout="10000"
      doc:name="Incoming File"
      path="/home/mbergljung/MuleStudio/workspace/file_importer/
      inboundFiles" pollingFrequency="3000"
      mimeType="application/pdf"/>
      <object-to-byte-array-transformer doc:name="Object to Byte
```

```
              Array" mimeType="application/pdf"/>
        <cmis:create-document-by-path config-ref="CMIS"
          doc:name="Store File as Doc in Alfresco"
          filename="#[header:originalFilename]"
          folderPath="/MuleFiles" mimeType="application/pdf"
          objectType="cmis:document" versioningState="MAJOR"/>
    </flow>
  </mule>
```

To try this out, we can kick off this message flow in the Mule Studio's embedded ESB runtime. In the **Package Explorer** pane, right-click on the `File Importer.mflow` file, then go to **Run As | 1. Mule Application**. Now all we have to do is to drag-and-drop a PDF file into the `inboundFiles` directory under `/home/mbergljung/MuleStudio/workspace/file_importer/`, and it should be picked up by Mule and stored in Alfresco in the `/Company Home/MuleFiles` folder. After an import, the file is removed from the `inboundFiles` directory.

If you wanted to save a copy of the file after it has been processed on the Mule server, a directory for processed files can be specified in the Inbound File's endpoint **Move to Directory** property. In a production environment, we would also want to handle any errors happening when processing the incoming files. There is plenty of Mule documentation about this at `http://blogs.mulesoft.org/error-handling-in-mule-3-3-catch-exception-strategy/` and `http://www.mulesoft.org/documentation/display/current/Error+Handling`.

Getting a document from a CMS server via Mule

What if we wanted to get a document from a CMS server and store it in a folder in the local filesystem? This can also be handled with the Mule ESB in the same way that we stored files in the CMS server. The use case is this: a one-way HTTP request comes into to Mule requesting a document from the CMS server to be stored in the filesystem in a specific folder. The document is identified via its Object ID (that is, the ID part of the Alfresco node reference).

Create a new project called `Get Document` and draw up the following message flow in Mule Studio:

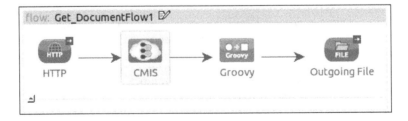

This flow starts with an inbound HTTP endpoint that will take care of our HTTP request. The CMIS Object ID for the document is then passed on to the CMIS component that will get the content stream for the document via CMIS. The content stream is then extracted via some Groovy code and written to a file via the File outbound endpoint.

Start configuring the HTTP inbound endpoint as shown in the following screenshot:

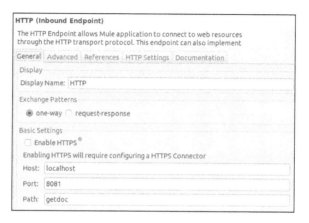

We are setting two properties for the HTTP endpoint. The first one is **Exchange Patterns**, which we set to **one-way**. We set it to **one-way** as we cannot read the content stream more than once (that is, we cannot send the content stream to both the browser and to a file). The second property we are setting is the URL **Path**, which we set to getdoc.

The next component to configure is the CMIS connector; start by configuring the CMIS connection properties in the same way we did when storing a file in Alfresco via Mule (see the previous section). Then, set the CMIS **Operation** to **Get content stream**, as shown in the following screenshot:

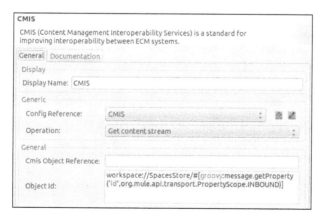

There are two ways of specifying what document we want to download the content stream for; the first one is to use an already fetched `Document` object (that is, metadata for a document file) and then pass that in as the **Cmis Object Reference** property. The other way is to specify a CMIS **Object Id** (Alfresco node reference). We will use the **Object Id** method as we have not previously fetched a `Document` object. We specify it as `workspace://SpacesStore/#[groovy:message.getProperty('id',org.mule.api.transport.PropertyScope.INBOUND)]`, which means that we will, with the help of some Groovy code, construct the CMIS Object ID. So, when we make the call from the browser, we would have to specify a URL parameter as follows: `?id=<UUID of the Alfresco Node Ref>`.

The next component to configure is the Groovy script component, as shown in the following screenshot:

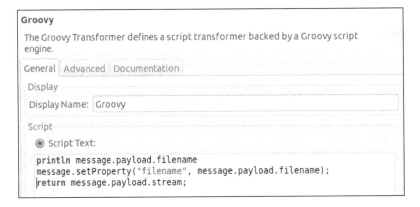

What we do here is just print the name of the file and then set up the name to be accessible via the filename property. Finally, we return the content stream for the file so that it can be written to the local filesystem in the File outbound endpoint. The final component to configure is the one that stores the file in the local filesystem, as shown in the following screenshot:

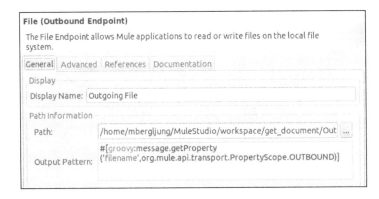

We store the file under an `Output` directory in the project workspace, specified by the `Path` property. The filename will be fetched from the `filename` property we set in the Groovy script component.

The XML for this message flow configuration will look as follows:

```xml
<?xml version="1.0" encoding="UTF-8"?>
<mule  ...>
  <cmis:config name="CMIS" username="admin" password="admin"
    repositoryId="f0ebcfb4-ca9f-4991-bda8-9465f4f11527"
    baseUrl="http://localhost:8080/alfresco/cmisatom"
    doc:name="CMIS"/>
  <flow name="Get_DocumentFlow1" doc:name="Get_DocumentFlow1">
    <http:inbound-endpoint exchange-pattern="one-way"
      host="localhost" port="8081" path="getdoc" doc:name="HTTP"/>
      <cmis:get-content-stream config-ref="CMIS"  doc:name="CMIS"
        objectId="workspace://SpacesStore/#[groovy:message.
        getProperty('id',org.mule.api.transport.PropertyScope.
        INBOUND)]"/>
    <scripting:transformer doc:name="Groovy">
      <scripting:script engine="Groovy">
        <scripting:text><![CDATA[println message.payload.filename
          message.setProperty("filename",
          message.payload.filename);
        return message.payload.stream;]]></scripting:text>
      </scripting:script>
    </scripting:transformer>
    <file:outbound-endpoint responseTimeout="10000"
      doc:name="Outgoing File"
      outputPattern="#[groovy:message.getProperty
      ('filename',org.mule.api.transport.PropertyScope.OUTBOUND)]"
      path="/home/mbergljung/MuleStudio/workspace/get_document/
      Output"/>
  </flow>
</mule>
```

We can try this now by first starting the Mule ESB via the **Package Explorer** pane; right-click on the `Get Document.mflow` file, and then go to **Run As | 1. Mule Application**. Now, all we have to do is request the following URL from a web browser: `http://localhost:8081/getdoc?id=794f7b2e-e6ee-4265-9ad7-e0193486c006`; where `id` in this case corresponds to the ID part of the Alfresco node reference for the file we previously stored in Alfresco via Mule.

> If we want to return the content output stream to the browser instead of writing it to a file, we can remove the File outbound endpoint and change `Exchange Patterns` for the HTTP endpoint to `request-response`.

Talking to Alfresco in the Cloud via CMIS

The Alfresco CMS server that we have been using throughout this book is also available as a Cloud service. It's free and it's easy to set up an account and get our own CMS service in the cloud. Besides using the normal Alfresco Share UI to manage content in the cloud, we can also use CMIS to talk to our Alfresco Cloud instance.

This section will go through how to use CMIS to talk to Alfresco in the cloud.

Setting up an account

The first thing we need to do is to create an account for the Alfresco Cloud service. This can be done from the `http://www.alfresco.com/products/cloud` page, which at the time of writing this book, offered a 10 GB free storage area in the cloud. However, this is if signing up with a company e-mail address (might work for private e-mails when this book is published). Fill in your company e-mail address and click on the **Get Started** button.

You will receive a welcome e-mail with an **Activate Account** button; click on it and it will take you to the `https://my.alfresco.com/share/` site, where you can complete your profile with your name and password. After completing the profile, you will see your personal dashboard and there will also be an Alfresco Share site created in your name. This site is private and cannot be seen by any other person. We will upload content via CMIS to this personal site that was created automatically for us.

Registering a client application

When we talk to Alfresco Cloud via CMIS, we have to authorize a client application for it to be granted access to talk to our personal site. Basically, we will tell Alfresco Cloud that we have a client application called, for example, MyEnterpriseApp, that wants to talk to it using the account that we just created.

To configure a new client application with access to Alfresco Cloud, we have to use the Alfresco Developer portal, which is accessible via the `https://developer.alfresco.com/` URL. On the main page in the portal, under the **In the cloud** section, click on the **Register as a developer** link to get going. Fill in your name, e-mail address, and password to create a developer account. A developer account activation e-mail is sent to your e-mail address. After clicking on the link in this activation e-mail, you can log in to the developer portal. You should see something like what is shown in the following screenshot:

To register a new application that wants to talk to Alfresco Cloud click on the **APPLICATIONS** menu item on the left-hand side. As this is your first application you will see an **Add Application** button; click on it.

Fill in the **Application Information** tab as follows:

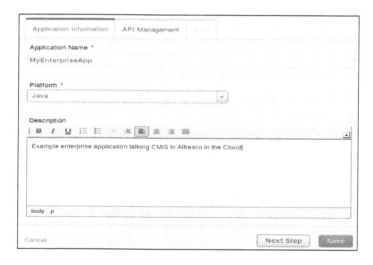

Choose the Java platform (used by Alfresco to see what the community is mostly using) as we will be talking to CMIS via the OpenCMIS Java library.

Alfresco Cloud services uses OAuth2 (`http://en.wikipedia.org/wiki/OAuth`) for authorization. OAuth2 provides a process for end users to authorize (allow) third-party access (that is, MyEnterpriseApp) to their server resources (that is, content in Alfresco) without sharing their credentials. This means that the username and password for the Alfresco Cloud account we just set up is never exposed to third-party applications.

The following diagram illustrates the OAuth2 authorization flow:

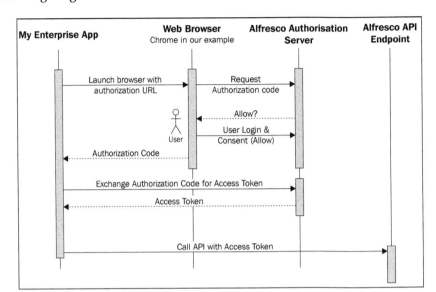

To specify the needed parameters for the OAuth2 authorization, click on the **API Management** tab; there is only one API, so select that from the drop-down box. Agree to the terms and conditions for the API. Then click on the last tab called **Auth**.

What we need to specify here is the callback URL that Alfresco will be invoking to notify MyEnterpriseApp about an authorization code. Set this URL to `http://localhost:8090/callback`. Once the application receives the authorization code, it can exchange the code for an access token and a refresh token.

When we register the MyEnterpriseApp client application, it is assigned an API key and a secret. We need to make a note of them as they will be used when we make the connection from our Java code. They are displayed in the **Auth** tab under **Key** and **Secret**, as shown in the following screenshot:

This is all that is required to enable a new application to talk to Alfresco in the cloud via CMIS.

Setting up a development project

We will be using Maven to build this solution as we can bring in all the needed libraries automatically. We will need the OpenCMIS Java library from the Apache Chemistry project to make CMIS calls, Google's OAuth2 client for Java for authorization, and Jetty Servlet engine for callbacks.

When this book is published, Version 0.11.0 of the OpenCMIS library may be released. It contains support for OAuth2, so it may be a more straightforward alternative to using Google OAuth2 libraries. See `http://svn.apache.org/repos/asf/ chemistry/opencmis/trunk/chemistry-opencmis-client/ chemistry-opencmis-client-bindings/src/main/java/ org/apache/chemistry/opencmis/client/bindings/ spi/OAuthAuthenticationProvider.java` (for the Jira issue at `https://issues.apache.org/jira/browse/CMIS-745`. Also have a look at the Alfresco extension OAuth2 at `https:// code.google.com/a/apache-extras.org/p/alfresco- opencmis-extension/source/browse/trunk/src/main/ java/org/alfresco/cmis/client/authentication/ OAuthCMISAuthenticationProvider.java?r=19`.

Start by creating a basic Java client project as follows by using the Maven Quick Start archetype:

```
$ mvn archetype:generate -DgroupId=com.mycompany.app -DartifactId=my-
enterprise-app -DarchetypeArtifactId=maven-archetype-quickstart
-DinteractiveMode=false
```

This command gives us a build project, a directory structure, and a Java file (App. java at com/mycompany/app) to put some code in. To bring in the necessary libraries, we need to first configure them in the POM's dependency section; open the generated pom.xml file and add the following contents:

```
<project ...
  <dependencies>
    <!-- Bring in the OpenCMIS library for talking to CMIS servers
      -->
    <dependency>
      <groupId>org.apache.chemistry.opencmis</groupId>
      <artifactId>chemistry-opencmis-client-impl</artifactId>
        <version>0.10.0</version>
    </dependency>
```

```xml
      <!-- Bring in the Google Auth library for Authorization with
         Alfresco Cloud -->
      <dependency>
        <groupId>com.google.oauth-client</groupId>
        <artifactId>google-oauth-client</artifactId>
          <version>1.13.1-beta</version>
      </dependency>
      <dependency>
        <groupId>com.google.http-client</groupId>
        <artifactId>google-http-client-jackson</artifactId>
          <version>1.13.1-beta</version>
      </dependency>

      <!-- Bring in the Servlet API and Jetty Servlet Engine so we
         can handle authorization callback -->
      <dependency>
        <groupId>javax.servlet</groupId>
        <artifactId>servlet-api</artifactId>
          <version>2.5</version>
            <scope>provided</scope>
      </dependency>
      <dependency>
        <groupId>org.mortbay.jetty</groupId>
          <artifactId>jetty</artifactId>
          <version>6.1.26</version>
      </dependency>

    <!-- Bring in commons logging library -->
      <dependency>
        <groupId>commons-logging</groupId>
        <artifactId>commons-logging</artifactId>
          <version>1.1.1</version>
      </dependency>
      <dependency>
        <groupId>junit</groupId>
        <artifactId>junit</artifactId>
          <version>3.8.1</version>
            <scope>test</scope>
      </dependency>
  </dependencies>
</project>
```

I added the Apache Commons Logging library so that we can do some logging from our examples. We will also add another Java class named `CmisClient` in the same package as the autogenerated `App` class; create it with your favorite editor so it looks like the following code:

```
public class CmisClient {
  private static Log logger =
    LogFactory.getLog(CmisClient.class);
  public CmisClient() {     }
}
```

This is all that is required; now we can start implementing the OAuth2 communication and CMIS calls to Alfresco Cloud.

Authorizing the client application

Before we start making any CMIS calls, some code is required to handle the OAuth2 communication. We will use classes from Google's client API to help out. We can base this on some existing sample code from Google and Alfresco.

In the `CmisClient` class, start by adding a number of constants with URLs to access Alfresco Cloud. Also, add the client app key and secret that we previously generated via the developer portal as follows:

```
public class CmisClient {
  private static Log logger =
    LogFactory.getLog(CmisClient.class);
  public static final String ALFRESCO_API_URL =
    "https://api.alfresco.com/";
  public static final String TOKEN_SERVER_URL = ALFRESCO_API_URL
    + "auth/oauth/versions/2/token";
  public static final String AUTHORIZATION_SERVER_URL =
    ALFRESCO_API_URL + "auth/oauth/versions/2/authorize";
  public static final String ATOMPUB_URL = ALFRESCO_API_URL +
    "cmis/versions/1.0/atom";
  public static final String SCOPE = "public_api";
  public static final String CLIENT_APP_ID =
    "l7xx5e11e85c4a764cc********************";
  public static final String CLIENT_APP_SECRET =
    "c7fa1952bfaf4cb7**********************";
  public static final HttpTransport HTTP_TRANSPORT =
    new NetHttpTransport();
  public static final JsonFactory JSON_FACTORY =
    new JacksonFactory();
```

We also define the URL for the CMIS AtomPub binding (that is, ATOMPUB_URL); note that it is not the standard Alfresco 4.0 URL that we have been using before (that is, http://<hostname>:<port>/alfresco/cmisatom), it looks more like the 4.2 URLs such as http://<hostname>:<port>/alfresco/api/-default-/cmis/versions/1.0/atom.

Then, define a new method called authorizeAndMakeCmisCalls, which will be our only public method with the main method doing most of the work by calling other private methods as follows:

```
public void authorizeAndMakeCmisCalls() throws Exception {
  VerificationCodeReceiver receiver = new
    LocalServerReceiver();
  try {
    // Authorize this client application
    String callbackURL = receiver.getRedirectUri();
    launchBrowserAndMakeTokenRequest(
      "google-chrome", callbackURL, CLIENT_APP_ID, SCOPE);
    final Credential credential =
      exchangeCodeForToken(receiver, callbackURL);
    HttpRequestFactory requestFactory =
      HTTP_TRANSPORT.createRequestFactory(
      new HttpRequestInitializer() {
        @Override
        public void initialize(HttpRequest request)
          throws IOException {
          credential.initialize(request);
          request.addParser(new JsonHttpParser(JSON_FACTORY));
          }
      });
    // Make some CMIS calls
    makeCmisCall(requestFactory, credential);
  } catch (Exception e) {
    e.printStackTrace();
  } finally {
    eceiver.stop();
  }
}
```

The previously discussed method starts by creating a new
`VerificationCodeReceiver` parameter, which will run a local Jetty server on port
8090 and wait for OAuth2 to redirect to it via the `http://localhost:8090/callback`
URL. This is the same URL that we entered under the **Auth** tab in the developer
portal when registering the client application. The redirection call will contain the
verification code. This class will not be displayed here, but you can download the
source code to see how it looks. When the Jetty server is started, we get the redirection
URL and then pass it on to a method called `launchBrowserAndMakeTokenRequest`,
which will open up the Google Chrome web browser and call the Alfresco Cloud
Authorization service. The URL will look something like `https://api.alfresco.`
`com/auth/oauth/versions/2/authorize?client_id=l7xx5e11e85c4a764cc9af`
`182c35e0711854&redirect_uri=http://localhost:8090/callback&response_`
`type=code&scope=public_api`.

When this happens, we will be prompted to enter the username and password for
the Alfresco Cloud user account that we set up in the beginning, as shown in the
following screenshot:

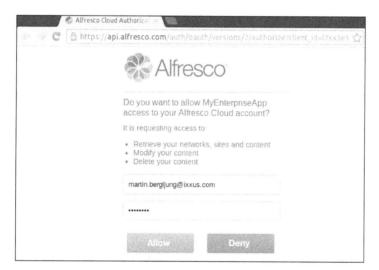

Clicking on **Allow** here means that I will grant access to my content in the Alfresco
Cloud for the client application via my user account. The Alfresco server will now
respond with an authorization code that we can use to get an access token; this is
what we do with the `exchangeCodeForToken` method. With the accesses token,
we can start calling the CMIS services; this is what we do with the `makeCmisCall`
method.

You can download the source code for the `launchBrowserAndMakeTokenRequest`
and `exchangeCodeForToken` methods from the book's website; the code is not
relevant to CMIS, so is beyond the scope of this book.

Making CMIS calls

The `makeCmisCall` method, however, is of interest and looks like the following code:

```
private void makeCmisCall(
  HttpRequestFactory requestFactory, Credential credential)
  throws IOException {
    String accessToken = credential.getAccessToken();
    Session cmisSession = getCmisSession(accessToken);

    // Get information about the repository we are connected to
    RepositoryInfo repositoryInfo =
      cmisSession.getRepositoryInfo();

    logger.info("   Name: " + repositoryInfo.getName());
    logger.info(" Vendor: " + repositoryInfo.getVendorName());
    logger.info(" Version: " +
      repositoryInfo.getProductVersion());
}
```

Passed into this method is a credential object that contains the access token that we need to make a CMIS call. We pass the token into the `getCmisSession` method, which will use it to create a new session that we can use for our CMIS service calls. When we get the session, we can start by getting information about the repository that we are connected to by using the `getRepositoryInfo` method. From now on, we can basically use the normal OpenCMIS Java API calls that we saw in *Chapter 5, Accessing a CMIS Server with a Java Client*.

The `getCmisSession` method has the following code to pass the access token to Alfresco Cloud:

```
public Session getCmisSession(String accessToken) {
    // default factory implementation
    SessionFactory factory = SessionFactoryImpl.newInstance();
    Map<String, String> parameter = new HashMap<String, String>();

    // connection settings
    parameter.put(SessionParameter.ATOMPUB_URL, ATOMPUB_URL);
    parameter.put(SessionParameter.BINDING_TYPE,
      BindingType.ATOMPUB.value());
    parameter.put(SessionParameter.AUTH_HTTP_BASIC, "false");
    parameter.put(SessionParameter.HEADER + ".0", "Authorization:
      Bearer " + accessToken);
      java.util.List<Repository> repositories =
        factory.getRepositories(parameter);
      return repositories.get(0).createSession();
}
```

So, as we can see, setting up a CMIS session with the OpenCMIS library is the same as before with the extra thing that we need to pass the access token in the Authorization header as a Bearer token (defined by the RFC6750 standard — `http://tools.ietf.org/html/rfc6750`).

If we run the preceding code we will get the following output:

```
my-enterprise-app$ mvn compile exec:java -Dexec.mainClass="com.mycompany.
app.App"
[INFO] Scanning for projects...
11-Feb-2013 16:57:48 com.mycompany.app.CmisClient
authorizeAndMakeCmisCalls
INFO: Access token:baf86fdd-bf6f-4f2f-bc95-88b5f34ffa67
INFO:     Name: ixxus.com
INFO:    Vendor: Alfresco
INFO:   Version: 4.0.2 (Cloud 351)
```

Summary

In this chapter, we have seen that CMIS is becoming a major part of many different environments that integrate CMS systems into enterprise solutions. Drupal is one of the major WCM systems used today. We looked at how easy it is to display documents, links, or folder listings from a CMS repository to a web page generated by Drupal. This is important as we don't want to store our content in more than one place.

Next, we enabled a CMS system to participate in ESB message flows, which is a commonplace scenario in many large enterprises.

Finally, we saw how we can use CMIS to talk to Alfresco in the cloud. This was based on the use of the OAuth2 authorization protocol and the OpenCMIS Java library to make CMIS service calls.

In this book, we have seen that the **Content Management Interoperability Services (CMIS)** standard is something to count on in the future. It is a comprehensive standard that has been adopted in many different places. Most CMS server providers support it, WCM systems support it, tools support it, Enterprise Integration products support it, and so on. It provides ways of working with content from many different platforms and from all kinds of languages.

Index

Symbols

#sudo apt-get install curl command 25

A

Abdera libraries 102
Access Control Entry. *See* ACE
Access Control List. *See* ACL
access controls
  concepts 81
ACE 16, 113, 136, 175
ACL
  about 16, 80, 113, 136
  capabilities 80
  service methods 18
ACL services 18
alfcmis:nodeRef property 35
Alfresco
  about 101
  URL, for installation file of Community
    version 24
AlfrescoCmisServiceImpl component 104
Alfresco CMIS stack 104
Alfresco content model mapping, to CMIS
    object model
  access control 113-115
  change log 115, 116
  object paths explanation 108-112
  property mappings 107, 108
  rendition support 116, 118
  repository capabilities 105, 106
  search capability 118, 119
  type mappings 106
  versioning 112, 113

Alfresco, in Cloud via CMIS
  account, setting up 232
  client application, authorizing 237-239
  client application, registering 232-234
  CMIS calls, making 240, 241
  development project, setting up 235, 237
Alfresco OpenCMIS extension
  aspects, adding to existing object 170, 171
  aspects, adding when creating object
    169, 170
  aspects, managing 169
  aspects, reading 171
Alfresco Records Management module 103
Alfresco server
  URL, for downloading 24
Alfresco Share extensions
  CMIS calls, using in 209
allowable actions 83, 114
Apache Camel
  about 224
  URL 224
Apache Chemistry
  about 128
  URL 127
Apache Maven
  URL 128
API (Application Programming Interface) 8
appendContentStream service call 59
append parameter 102
Application to Multiple Repositories
    (A2MR) 13
Application to Repository (A2R) 12
applyACL service call 80

aspects
adding, to existing object 167-170
adding, when creating object 166, 167
managing, secondary types used 166
overview 119-123
reading 168, 171
working with 165
Association for Information and Image Management (AIIM) 8
AtomPub binding
content, obtaining with 50-53
document, checking out with 74, 75
document check-out, cancelling with 75
document, creating with 63-65
document, deleting with 68
document, updating with 67
folder, creating with 59, 60
folder, deleting with 68
metadata, obtaining with 50-53
permissions, managing with 84-86
relationships, creating with 90, 91
relationships, reading with 90, 91
repository information, obtaining via 30, 31
subtypes, listing with 47, 48
types, listing with 47, 48
used, for document check-in 76
used, for listing children of root folder 36, 38
used, for searching 95-97
used, for updating physical content of checked-out document 75
version management 73
ATOMPUB_URL parameter 132
authentication
performing, with repository 25

B

BINDING_TYPE parameter 132
Browser binding
about 21
content, obtaining with 53-56
document check-out, cancelling with 78
document, creating with 66
document, deleting with 69
document, updating with 67
folder, creating with 61

folder, deleting with 69
metadata, obtaining with 53-56
permissions, managing with 87-89
physical content, updating of checked-out document 78
relationships, creating with 92
relationships, reading with 92
repository information, obtaining via 31, 32
REST-based approach, used 21
subtypes, listing with 49
types, listing with 49
used, for document check-in 79, 80
used, for document check-out 77, 78
used, for listing children of root folder 39-41
build environment
setting up 128, 129
build project
setting up, for Spring Surf with CMIS 201, 202
bulkUpdateProperties service 103
bulkUpdateProperties service call 59

C

CACHE_TTL_OBJECTS parameter 133
callCmisServer function 185
capabilities, access control list (ACL)
capabilityACL 80
propagation 80
capabilities, of searching
capabilityJoin 95
capabilityQuery 94
capabilities properties
capabilityChanges 28
capabilityCreatablePropertyTypes 29
capabilityMultifiling 28
capabilityNewTypeSettableAttributes 29
capabilityRenditions 28
capabilityUnfiling 28
capabilityVersionSpecificFiling 29
capabilityAllVersionsSearchable property 72
capabilityChanges property 27, 28
capabilityContentStreamUpdatability property

about 66, 72
values 72
capabilityCreatablePropertyTypes property 29
capabilityGetDescendants property 33
capabilityGetFolderTree property 33
capabilityJoin property 95
capabilityMultifiling property 28
capabilityNewTypeSettableAttributes 29
capabilityOrderBy property 33
capabilityPWCSearchable property 72
capabilityPWCUpdatable property 72, 76
capabilityQuery property 94
capabilityRenditions property 28
capabilityUnfiling property 28
capabilityVersionSpecificFiling property 29
categories
overview 124
change log 115, 116
changesIncomplete property 27
changesOnType property 27
checked-out document
physical content, updating with AtomPub binding 75
physical content, updating with Browser binding 78
checkIn service call 71
checkOut service call 173 71
children
listing, of root folder 32, 33, 136, 137
listing, of root folder with AtomPub binding 36, 38
listing, of root folder with Browser binding 39-41
listing, of top folder 136, 137
Claim Check EAI pattern 226
cm:autoVersion aspect 172
cm:initialVersion aspect 172
CMIS
about 7-10
build project, setting up for Spring Surf 201, 202
domain model 14-17
protocol bindings 20, 21
query examples 98
query language 18, 19
services 17, 18

supported permissions 82, 83
supporting companies 10, 11
supporting products 10, 11
use cases 12, 13
using, benefits 11, 12
using, in Groovy scripts 196-200
using, in JavaScript 184-187
using, in Spring Surf Web Scripts 200
using, in web application pages 184-187
CMIS 1.1 standard
features, not supported in Alfresco Version 4.2 103
cmis.alfresco.com
using 24
cmis:allowedChildObjectTypeIds property 34
CMIS API module
about 212
installing 213, 214
submodules 212
URL 212
cmis:baseTypeId property 35
CMIS benefits
bigger customer base applications 12
easy workflow integration 12
language neutral 11
one application to access them all 11
platform independence 11
standard and easy-to-learn query language 11
standard service API 11
cmis_browser.module 212
CMIS call
addDocumentToFolder 114
cancelCheckout 114
checkIn 114
checkOut 114
deleteAllVersions 114
deleteContentStream 114
deleteObject 114, 115
deleteTree 115
getAllVersions 114
getChildren 115
getContentStream 115
getDescendants 115
getDocumentParents 114
getFolderParent 115

getProperties 115
getRelationships 115
making 240
setContentStream 114
updateProperties 114, 115
using, in Alfresco Share extensions 209
cmis:changeToken property 34
CMIS Cloud Connector
functions 224
URL 224
cmis_common.module 212
CMISConnector 104
cmis:contentStreamFileName property 63
cmis:contentStreamId property 62
cmis:contentStreamLength property 62
cmis:contentStreamMimeType property 62
cmis:createdBy property 35
cmis:creationDate property 34
cmis_dev.module 212
CMIS Field 212
cmis_field.module 212
CMIS Folder 217
cmis_headerswing.module 212
CMIS, in Spring Surf Web Scripts
build project, setting up for Spring Surf
201, 202
home page, updating for repository info
display 206, 207
home page, updating for text display in
repository 208, 209
Spring Surf project, updating for CMIS
usage 203-206
cmis:item Object Type 103
cmis:lastModificationDate property 35
cmis:lastModifiedBy property 35
cmis.module 212
cmis:name property 34
cmis:objectId property 35
cmis:objectTypeId property 34
cmis:parentId property 35
cmis:path property 34
CMIS properties
allowedChildObjectTypeIds 34
baseTypeId 35
changeToken 34
contentStreamFileName 108
contentStreamLength 107

contentStreamMimeType 108
createdBy 35, 107
creationDate 34
isLatestVersion 107
isMajorVersion 107
lastModificationDate 35, 107
lastModifiedBy 35, 107
name 34, 107
nodeRef 35
objectId 35
objectTypeId 34
parentId 35
path 34, 108
versionLabel 107
CMIS Query Language (QL) 93, 118
cmis_query.module 212
CMIS server
installing 24
setting up 24
CMIS services
ACL services 18
Discovery services 17
Multifiling services 17
Navigation services 17
Object services 17
Policy services 18
Relationship services 18
Repository services 17
Versioning services 18
cmis_sync.module 212
CMIS usage
Spring Surf project, updating for 203-206
CMIS Version 1.1 standard
support 102
cmisVersionSupported property 26
CMIS Views module
about 217
URL 217
CMS content
synchronizing, with Drupal content
221-223
CMS repository file link
displaying, on Drupal page 216, 217
CMS repository folder
displaying, on Drupal page 218-220
CMS server
Drupal, integrating with 211, 212

cm:versionLabel aspect 172
COMPRESSION parameter 132
CONTAINS keyword 123
content, obtaining
   for document 160, 161
   with AtomPub binding 50-53
   with Browser binding 53-56
Content Management Interoperability
      Services. *See* CMIS
Content Management Systems (CMS) 7
continueOnFailure parameter 159
createDocumentFromSource service call 57
createDocument service call 57
createFolder service call 58, 145
createItem service call 58
createPolicy service call 58
createRelationship service call 58
CRUD (Create, Read, Update, and Delete)
      operations 17
cURL
   about 25
   URL, for downloading 25

D

DataTables
   about 192
   URL 192
deleteAllVersions parameter 159
deleteContentStream service call 59
delete method 157
deleteObject service call 59
deleteTree service call 59, 158
Digital Asset Management (DAM)
      system 116
document
   checking, in with AtomPub binding 76
   checking, in with Browser binding 79, 80
   checking out 173
   checking, out with AtomPub binding 74, 75
   content, obtaining for 160, 161
   copying 162-165
   creating 147-153
   creating, with AtomPub binding 63, 64
   creating, with Browser binding 66
   deleting 156-158
   deleting, with AtomPub binding 68

   deleting, with Browser binding 69
   obtaining, from CMS server 228-231
   moving 162-165
   permissions, managing for 80
   updating 153-156
   updating, with AtomPub binding 67
   updating, with Browser binding 67
document check-out
   cancelling, with AtomPub binding 75
   cancelling, with Browser binding 78
   with Browser binding 77, 78
Document Management (DM) 8
domain model
   about 14
   base types 15
   objects 14-17
   property types 15
domain model base types
   custom subtypes 15
   Document 15
   Folder 15
   Item 15
   Policy 15
   Relationship 15
Drupal
   integrating, with CMS server 211, 212
Drupal content
   CMS content, synchronizing with 221-223
Drupal page
   CMS repository file link, displaying on
      216, 217
   CMS repository folder, displaying on
      218-220
   result, displaying from CMIS query on
      220, 221

E

Enterprise Application Integration
      (EIA) 211
Enterprise Content Management (ECM) 8
Enterprise integration, with CMIS
   about 224
   Apache Camel 224
   Mule ESB 224
   Spring Integration 224
Enterprise Service Bus (ESB) 13, 211

extended features discovery 103
extJS 191

F

file
    moving, from folder into CMS server with
        Mule 224-228
folder
    copying 162-165
    creating 144-146
    creating, with AtomPub binding 59, 60
    creating, with Browser binding 61
    deleting 156-158
    deleting, with AtomPub binding 68
    deleting, with Browser binding 69
    moving 162-165
    permissions, managing for 80
    updating 153-156
folder tree
    deleting 156-158
FreeMarker template 202
Full-Text Search (FTS) 19, 93, 118

G

getACL service call 80, 84
getAllowableActions service call 58
getChildren service
    optional parameters 42
getChildren service, with AtomPub binding
    optional parameters 43, 44
getChildren service, with Browser binding
    optional parameters 45, 47
getCmisSession method 240
getContentStream service call 58
getDocumentParentFolder method 150
getObjectByPath service call 58
getObject service call 58, 145
getParentFolderPath method 150
getProperties service call 58
getRenditions service call 58
getRepoId function 184
getRepositoryInfo service call 26, 72, 240
getTypeChildren service 47
Groovy
    URL, for tutorial 197

Groovy scripts
    CMIS, using in 196-200

H

home page, updating
    for repository info display 206, 207
    for text display in repository 208, 209
HTTP 25

I

includedInSuperType property 19
installation, CMIS API module 213, 214
installation, CMIS server 24
isLatestMajorVersion property 73
isLatestVersion property 73

J

Java Community Process 9
Java Content Repository. See JCR
JavaScript
    CMIS, using in 184-187
JavaScript Object Notation (JSON) 21
Java Virtual Machine (JVM) 132
JCR 9
jQuery
    about 190
    URL 190
    used, for making AJAX calls 190-195
jQuery UI
    URL 192
JSONP functionality 190

L

LAMP stack 211
latest version 73

M

major version 73
makeCmisCall method 240
Message Transmission Optimization
    Mechanism (MTOM) 21

metadata, obtaining
  with AtomPub binding 50-53
  with Browser binding 53-56
moveObject service call 59
Mule
  document, obtaining from CMS server
    228-231
  used, for moving file from folder into
    CMS server 224-228
Mule ESB
  about 224
  URL 224
multifiling services 17

N

Navigation services 17

O

OASIS 7
OAuth2
  URL 233
object
  aspects, adding to 167, 168
  relationships, managing between 90,
    178-181
object model. *See* domain model
object paths 108-112
object service 17, 90
OpenCMIS library 128
  adoptions benefits, for Alfresco 104, 105
OpenCMIS Service Provider Interface
    (SPI) 104
OperationContext class 138
optional parameters, for getChildren
    service
  about 138-140
  hasMoreItems 42
  maxItems 42
  numItems 42
  skipCount 42
Organization for the Advancement of
    Structured Information Standards. *See*
    OASIS

P

parameters, deleteTree method
  continueOnFailure 159
  deleteAllVersions 159
  unfileMode 159
PASSWORD parameter 132
PathSegments
  path 109
permission mapping 84
permissions, managing
  for documents 80, 175-178
  for folders 80, 175-178
  with AtomPub binding 84-86
  with Browser binding 87-89
permissions, by CMIS
  all 83
  read 83
  write 83
physical contents
  updating, of checked-out document with
    AtomPub binding 75
  updating, of checked-out document with
    Browser binding 78
policy services 18
principalAnonymous property 27
Private Working Copy (PWC) 72, 172
properties, versioning
  isLatestMajorVersion 73
  isLatestVersion 73
  versionLabel 73
  versionSeriesId 73
property mappings 107, 108
protocol bindings
  about 20
  Browser (CMIS 1.1) 21
  RESTful AtomPub 20, 21
  Web Service 21

Q

queryable property 18
query language
  properties 18
  using 18, 19
query method 18
queryName property 19

R

relationships
  creating, with AtomPub binding 90, 91
  creating, with Browser binding 92
  managing, between objects 90, 178-181
  reading, with AtomPub binding 90, 91
  reading, with Browser binding 92
relationship services 18, 90
renditions support 116, 118
repository
  connecting to, by ID 134
  used, for performing authentication 25
repository capabilities 105, 106
repositoryId property 26
repository information, obtaining
  about 26-29, 134, 135
  via AtomPub binding 30, 31
  via Browser binding 31, 32
Repository services 17
Repository to Repository (R2R) 12
REST binding
  about 20
  service collections 20
result, from CMIS query
  displaying, on Drupal page 220, 221
Retention and Hold support feature 103
root folder
  children, listing of 32, 33

S

same origin policy problem
  about 187
  solving 187-189
searching
  about 93, 181, 182
  with AtomPub binding 95, 96
  with Browser binding 96, 97
secondary types
  used, for managing aspects 166
service collections
  Bulk Update collection 20
  Checked-Out collection 20
  Query collection 20
  Root collection 20
  Type Children collection 20
  Unfiled collection 20

service document 20, 30
session
  connecting to 129-134
  setting up, with repository 129-134
Session Factory interface 129
setContentStream service call 59
Spring Integration
  about 224
  URL 224
Spring Source foundation
  URL 200
Spring Surf project
  updating, for CMIS usage 203-206
Spring Surf Web Scripts
  CMIS, using in 200
submodules, CMIS API module
  cmis_browser.module 212
  cmis_common.module 212
  cmis_dev.module 212
  cmis_field.module 212
  cmis_headerswing.module 212
  cmis.module 212
  cmis_query.module 212
  cmis_sync.module 212
subtypes, listing
  about 141-143
  with AtomPub binding 47, 48
  with Browser binding 49
succinct representation 55
support, CMIS Version 1.1 standard
  browser binding 102
  content, appending 102
  secondary types 102
supportedPermissions property 82
support, for Alfresco-specific features
  aspects 119-123
  categories 124
  tags 123

T

tags
  overview 123
ThemeRoller 192
timeline
  overview 101, 102
Time To Live (TTL) 133

tool setup
  for making HTTP requests 25
transactions 99
type mappings 106
type mutability feature 103
types, listing
  about 141-143
  with AtomPub binding 47, 48
  with Browser binding 49

U

UI Darkness theme 192
unfileMode parameter 159
universally unique identifier (UUID) 131
updateProperties service call 59
use cases, example
  A2MR 13
  A2R 12
  R2R 12
USER parameter 132

V

values, capabilityContentStream
      Updatability property
  anytime 72
  none 72
  pwconly 72
versioning 112, 113
versioning capabilities
  capabilityAllVersionsSearchable 72
  capabilityPWCSearchable 72
  capabilityPWCUpdatable 72
versioning services 18, 71
versionLabel property 73
version management
  content of checked-out document,
      updating 174, 175
  document, checking in 174, 175
  document, checking out 173
  with AtomPub binding 73
  with Browser binding 77
  with checkIn service call 71, 172
  with checkOut service call 71, 172
version series 72
versionSeriesId property 73

W

web application pages
  CMIS, using in 184-187
Web Content Management (WCM)
      system 116, 211
Web Distributed Authoring and Versioning
      (WebDAV) 9
Web Service binding 21

X

xmlstarlet command-line tool 30
XPath 30

Y

Yahoo UI Library (YUI) 191

Thank you for buying
Alfresco CMIS

About Packt Publishing

Packt, pronounced 'packed', published its first book "*Mastering phpMyAdmin for Effective MySQL Management*" in April 2004 and subsequently continued to specialize in publishing highly focused books on specific technologies and solutions.

Our books and publications share the experiences of your fellow IT professionals in adapting and customizing today's systems, applications, and frameworks. Our solution based books give you the knowledge and power to customize the software and technologies you're using to get the job done. Packt books are more specific and less general than the IT books you have seen in the past. Our unique business model allows us to bring you more focused information, giving you more of what you need to know, and less of what you don't.

Packt is a modern, yet unique publishing company, which focuses on producing quality, cutting-edge books for communities of developers, administrators, and newbies alike. For more information, please visit our website: www.packtpub.com.

About Packt Open Source

In 2010, Packt launched two new brands, Packt Open Source and Packt Enterprise, in order to continue its focus on specialization. This book is part of the Packt Open Source brand, home to books published on software built around Open Source licences, and offering information to anybody from advanced developers to budding web designers. The Open Source brand also runs Packt's Open Source Royalty Scheme, by which Packt gives a royalty to each Open Source project about whose software a book is sold.

Writing for Packt

We welcome all inquiries from people who are interested in authoring. Book proposals should be sent to author@packtpub.com. If your book idea is still at an early stage and you would like to discuss it first before writing a formal book proposal, contact us; one of our commissioning editors will get in touch with you.

We're not just looking for published authors; if you have strong technical skills but no writing experience, our experienced editors can help you develop a writing career, or simply get some additional reward for your expertise.

www.ingramcontent.com/pod-product-compliance
Lightning Source LLC
Chambersburg PA
CBHW060531060326
40690CB00017B/3450